THIS IS THE
PEKINGESE

ROSE MARIE KATZ

Published by T.F.H. Publications, Inc., T.F.H. Building, 245 Cornelison Avenue, Jersey City 2, N. J., USA. Distributed in the British Isles by T.F.H. Publications (London), Ltd., 59 Station Road, Redhill, Surrey, England. In Canada by Canadian Aquaria Supply Co. Ltd. & Viobin, 1125 Talbot Street, St. Thomas, Ontario, Canada. In Australia by Exotic Aquarium & Pet Supplies Pty., 248-252 High Street, Northcote, Melbourne, Australia.

Distributed to the Book Trade by Sterling Publishing Co., Inc., New York 16, N. Y.

© 1962 by T.F.H. Publications, Inc.

ACKNOWLEDGMENTS

It would be impossible for me to list by name all the Pekingese lovers who helped me put this book together. I received photos from hundreds of ardent dog-lovers and could only use a fraction of what I received. Add to this my serious illness and the editorial help I had from my dear husband and the staff of TFH and I truly am indebted to many people...some of whom I've never met.

Really sincere thanks are due to Dr. Leon Whitney, Ernest Hart and Dr. Herbert R. Axelrod for their writing chapters II, V, VI, VII, IX, X, XI and XII.

My husband also helped by writing the last chapter "Eye Diseases of Pekingese". This is the only Peke book that has such a chapter.

Contents

I   A FEARLESS COMPANION OF HONORABLE ANCESTRY 5
A Fearless Companion ... Ancient and Honorable Ancestry ... The Imperial Pekingese ... Captured by the English ... Additions to the Pedigree ... The Pekingese Comes to America

II   YOUR DOG'S HEREDITY 19
Germ Plasm ... Old Ideas ... Mutations ... Inbreeding ... Twins ... Mental Aptitudes ... Coat Characteristics

III   PEKINGESE STANDARD INTERPRETED 41
Standard of the Pekingese ... Scale of Points for Judging Pekingese ... Interpretation of the Standard ... Head ... Eyes ... Nose ... Muzzle and Mouth ... Ears ... Body and Legs ... Coat ... Size ... Action ... The Perfect Pekingese

IV   HOW TO PURCHASE A PEKINGESE 58
Reliable Breeders vs. Petshops ... A Peke for Pet, Breeding, or Show ... For a Pet ... For Breeding ... Age to Buy ... Purchasing a Bitch ... Purchasing a Male ... For Exhibiting ... Selecting the Best Puppy

V   REPRODUCTION IN THE BITCH 73

VI   REPRODUCTION IN THE MALE 84

VII   REARING PUPPIES 89
Dewclaws ... Worming ... Weaning ... Hernia ... Teeth

VIII   CARE OF THE NEW PEKINGESE 100
New Quarters ... Feeding ... Puppy Schedule ... Adult Schedule ... Vitamins ... Papers and Requisite Information ... Care ... Toys ... Daily Care ... Cold Weather ... Hot Weather ... Protection from Pests ... Exercise ... Teeth ... Nails ... Watch your Peke ... Training of a Tyrant ... House Manners ... Lead Training ... Obedience Training

IX   DISEASES 130
Navel Infection ... Eye Infections ... Diarrhea in Very Young Puppies ... Diarrhea in Older Puppies ... Poisoning ... Parasitic Infections ... Coccidiosis ... Virus Diseases ... Carre Distemper ... Methods of Successful Carre Distemper Immunization ... Infectious Hepatitis ... Pharyngo-Laryngo-Tracheitis ... Influenza ... Bacterial Diseases ... Deficiency Diseases ... Fits ... Skin Diseases

X PARASITES 177
   Roundworms ... Hookworms ... Whipworms ... Tapeworms ...
   How the Presence of Worms is Detected ... The Louse ... Fleas
   Ticks ... Mange ... Misinformation Concerning Worms ...
   Deworming ... Deworming small Puppies

XI EARLY TRAINING 189
    Training your Dog ... Basic Principles for Training ... Training
    the House Dog ... Positive Training ... Negative Training

XII PENS AND BEDDING 207
     Material for Runs ... Wire Bottom Pens ... Construction of Wire
     Bottom Pens

XIII EXERCISING AND GROOMING 215
      Combing and Brushing ... Nail Care ... Care of the Ears ...
      Anal Glands ... Teething and Tooth Care ... Bathing

XIV GROOMING THE PEKINGESE COAT 219
     Coat Care of the Average Pekingese ... No Baths ... Instead of a
     Bath ... Grooming for the Show

XV EYE DISEASES OF PEKINGESE 241
    Medications ... Essential Anatomy ... Eye Diseases ... Conjunc-
    tivitis ... Diseases of the Lids ... Diseases of the Cornea ...
    Chronic Ulcers ... Pigmentary Degeneration of the Cornea ...
    Glaucoma ... Cataract ... Proptosis of the Eyeball

Index

Index

Acquired characters,
  inheritance of, 20, 24
  non-inheritance of, 20
Action, 57
Additions to the pedigree, 15
Advertising to sell puppies, 98
Alfalfa leaf meal, 167
Anal glands, 121
  emptying, 121
Ancestry of the Pekingese, 9
Anemia from hookworm infection, 178
Anesthetics to facilitate grooming, 34
Animal protein factor, 166
Anorchidism, 85
Art of grooming, 223
Autointoxication as a cause of fits, 172
Avianized virus in immunization, 150

Bacterial diseases, 156
Basic principles in training, 193
Bathing, 220
  methods of, 220
  soaps, 220
B-Complex Vitamins,
  functions and sources, 165
Bedding materials, 207
Behavior patterns in dogs, 28
Birth, assisting with, 90
  behavior of the dam before, 89
  preparing the bitch before, 89
Bitch's milk, as a guide to nutrition, 96
  like light cream, 96
Bitch, reproduction in the, 73
Bleeding of puppies dangerous, 91
Body shape influenced by
  early mating, 82
Breed, purity established through
  line breeding, 27
Breeding, careless, and
  effect on the breed, 27
  early, 82
  frequency to insure conception, 83

Calcium: functions and sources, 167
  and phosphorus and Vitamin D, 167
Cavicola fever, 156
Capture of Pekingese by English, 13

Carotene, provitamin A, 164
  as source of Vitamin A, 164
Carre's Disease, and diarrhea, 145
Carre Distemper, 145
  symptoms, 146
  treatment, 147
  prevention, 149
  immunization methods, 152
  maternal immunity to,
  in puppies, 146
  effect on puppies, 146
  use of serum in treatment and
    prevention, 152
  Green method of immunization, 151
  Laidlow Dunkin method of
    immunization, 150
Carrying, love of, 36
Cellar, raising pups in, 211
Characteristics, fixed by inbreeding, 26
Children learning by watching canine
  reproduction, 73
Chromosomes, 19
Cinders, use of in runs, 209
Combing and brushing, 219
Coat, coarseness of, 40
  inheritance of, 40
  characteristics, 38
  thin, inherited, 38
  color, fading, 54
  color, inheritance of, 21
  color, symbols for genes, 21
  wooly, 53
  length of, inheritance of, 40
  unthrifty, as a result of Vitamin A
    deficiency, 160
Cobalt, in growth, 143
Coccidiosis, no cure for, 144
  treatment of, 144
  types found in puppies, 143
Cod liver oil, 163
Cold, dog's ability to withstand, 113
Conception, eggs nesting in uterus, 79
  failure of, 79
Concrete, cleaning problems of, 209
  floors and navel infection, 131
  use in runs, 209
Copper, functions and sources, 168

i

Coprophagy, dung eating, 36
Copulation in dogs, 75
Coughing in puppies
  due to roundworms, 177
Cryptorchidism, 85

Day length, changing and
  coming into heat, 76
Defecation in puppies,
  encouraged by dam's lapping, 90
Deficiency diseases, 159
Deformities: hernias, 97
  cryptorchidism, 85
Degeneration from inbreeding, 25
Dewclaws, removal of, 91
  valuable in hunting breeds, 91
Deworming, 187
  early, 95
  little puppies, 187
  without adequate diagnosis, 186
Dextrose (glucose),
  in treatment of hepatitis, 153
Diarrhea,
  symptom of many ailments, 136
  in young puppies, 136
  in older puppies, 138
  and diet, 139
Diet and diarrhea, 139
Diseases, 130
Distemper, 145
  and convulsions, 147
  a complex of diseases, 145
Dog biscuits for dogs, 106
Dominance of characters, 20
Dudley nose, 46
Dung eating, a cure for, 36
D-Vitamins, functions and sources, 162

Ears, 49
  care of, 121
Early training, 189
Eczema, 172
Eggs, ova, ripening of, 76
Electric clipper, reaction to, 34
Embryo, development of, 76
  in early stage likened to
    hollow ball, 79
Emetic, hydrogen peroxide as, 142

Encephalitis, 170
  following housedog disease, 171
  in puppies, 171
Epsom salts, as antidote, 124
Epsom salts (magnesium sulphate), 142
Exercise, amount necessary, 215
  and grooming, 215
  retrieving golf balls, 217
Extruded foods, 91
E-Vitamin, functions and sources, 167
Eye infections of puppies, 134, 241
Eye, nictitating membrane of,
  inverted, 134
  treatment, 134
Eyes, 45, 241
  daily care, 111

Fallopian tubes, 75
Fasting, need for,
  prior to deworming, 187
Fertilization, how accomplished, 75
Fetal envelopes,
  removing from puppy, 90
Fish liver oils,
  as source of Vitamin A, 163
  value of, 163
Fits, convulsions, 170
Fleas, 181
  life history of, 182
  control of, 182
Follicular hormone, 77
Follicles of ovaries, 77
Foods, extruded, 91
Food poisoning in dogs, 141
  for puppies, simple feeding best, 104
  requirements of dogs, 105
Foreign bodies in stomach as a cause of
  fits, 172
Formula for puppies, 104
Fungus diseases of skin, 172

Garlic not a deworming drug, 184
Genes, 19
  doubled by inbreeding, 25
  for coat color, 38
Germ plasm, 19
  in ovaries, 19
Gestation, 80
Globulin, use in disease control, 149

Glucose, in treatment of hepatitis, 153
Grass runs, 210
Green method in immunization, 151
Grooming, 219
  equipment, 219
Ground bone, as a source of calcium and phosphorus, 162
Growth stunted as a result of Vitamin A deficiency, 160
Gun shyness, inheritance in, 34

Hair, length of, inherited, 38
Head, 44
Heat, dog's ability to withstand, 14
  periods, at which to mate dogs, 76
Hepatitis, infectious, 153
  in mature dogs, 153
  in puppies, 153
  symptoms of, 153
Heredity, principles of, 19
Hernias, in puppies, repair of, strangulation, 97
Hookworms, 178
  life history, 178
  coughing due to, 178
Hormone APL to cause descent of retained testicles, 85
Hormones, to bring bitch into heat, 83
Housebreaking, 122
Housedog disease, 154
How to Breed Dogs, book, 28
Hydrogen peroxide as emetic, 142
Hypodermic syringe,
  reaction of puppies to, 32

Inbreeding, effects of, 25
Incoordinated movements as a result of Vitamin A deficiency, 161
Incubation of worm eggs, 177
Infertility, as a result of Vitamin A deficiency, 160
Influenza, 156
Inheritance of behavior patterns, 29
Instruction of children,
  using dogs as examples, 73
Intussusceptions, 169
  diagnosis of, 170
Inverted nictitating membrane of eye, 134

Iodine, functions and sources, 169
Iodized salt, 169
Iron, in diet, 168
  functions and sources, 168

Kayquinone, 167
Kibbled biscuits for dogs, 106
Kibbled dog food, as cause of fits, 171
  with agene as a cause of fits, 171
  too rough for puppies' stomachs, 171
K-Vitamin, functions and sources, 167

Laidlaw-Dunkin method for immunization, 150
Legs, 50
Leptospirosis, 156
  how contracted, 157
  diagnosis of, 157
  in puppies, 157
  symptoms, 157
Loss of weight, as a result of Vitamin A deficiency, 160
Lice, 181
  infestation, symptoms of, 181
Line breeding, definition, 27
Litter registration, 108
Location, changing from north to south and effect on mating cycle, 76
Louse, life history of, 181

Magnesium, 168
  functions and sources, 168
Mange, demodectic or red, 183
  symptoms of, 183
  treatment for, 183
Mange, ear, 183
  symptoms, 183
Mange mites, life history of, 183
Mange, sarcoptic, 182
  symptoms of, 183
  treatment of, 183
Material for runs, 209
Mating cycle of bitch, 76
  using daylight to change, 76
Meat in diets, 104
  rich in Vitamin B, 165
Menstruation in human compared with mating cycle of dogs, 76
Mental aptitudes in dogs, 28

Mental heredity, 28
Mental suffering from noise, 34
Milk, differences in composition, 96
Milk of bitch, like light cream, 96
Mineral deficiencies, 167
Minerals for dogs, 168
   functions and sources, 168
Mismating does not ruin bitches, 23
Monorchidism, 85
Mother-love, hormone, prolactin, 82
Mouth, 48
Mutation, changes in heredity, 24
Mute trailers, 29
Muzzle, 48

Nail care, 119
Nails, filing, 119
   trimming of to prevent
      eye injury, 136
Navel infection in puppies, 131
N-butylchloride as deworming drug, 185
Negative training, 203
Night blindness as a result of
      Vitamin A deficiency, 160
Nipples, cleaning before birth, 89
Noise shyness, 34
Norwegian elkhounds, coats of, 38
Nose, 46
Nose color, 46
Nutritional requirements of dogs, 103

Old wive's tales, 23
Outbreeding, definition, 27
Ova, 20
   eggs, fertilization, 77
   eggs, movement of, 77
Ovaries of bitch, 75
Ovulation, 76
   indicated by softening of vulva, 78

Paint poisoning, 142
Palpation to determine pregnancy, 80
Parasites, 177
Parasitic diseases, 143
Parasitic infestation, as a cause of
      convulsions, 171
Parti-colored Pekingese, 43
Pekingese comes to America, 15
Penis, 87

Pens and bedding, 101, 207
Percomorph oil, 163
Perfect Pekingese, 57
Pests, protection from, 115
Phantom pregnancy normal, 80
Pharyngo-Laryngo-Tracheitis
   (P-L-T), 154
Phosphorus, functions and sources, 167
Piddling, hereditary, 34
Pin worms not found in dogs, 180
Piperazine as deworming drug, 188
Pitocin as adjunct to whelping, 90
Placenta, consuming of by bitch, 90
   removal of, 90
P-L-T, 154
   as cause of convulsions, 155
   symptoms contrasted with
      Carre's distemper, 154
Poisoning, diagnosis of, 141
   in dogs, 141
   symptoms of, 141
   treatment for, 142
Positive training, 199
Pregnancy and luteal bodies, 78
Pregnant mare serum to produce
      ovulation, 83
Protein foods, 85
Pseudo pregnancy, 80
Punishment in training, 123
Puppies, first natural food of, 96
   food for weaning, 103
   rearing, 96
   sale of, 98
   value of vaccination against
      hepatitis in, 153
   weaning of, 95
Puppy diseases, 130
Puppy shots, a vague term, 150
Purchasing a Pekingese, 58
   for breeding, 66
   for exhibiting, 69
   for pet, breeding or show, 60

Rabies, 176
   vaccination as preventative, 176
Recessiveness of character, 20
Registration, recommendation for
      accuracy of, 108
Retrieving, 35

Rewards, use in training, 123
Reproduction in the bitch, 73
　in the male, 84
Rickets in Vitamin D deficiency, 161
Roundworms, 177
　how contracted, 177
　life history, 177

Salmonella, cause of diarrhea, 139
Salt, 169
Sand, washed, in runs, 209
Scaling skin, as a result of Vitamin A deficiency, 160
Scrotum, 84
Serum, use in Carre distemper, 152
Shigella organisms, cause of diarrhea in puppies, 139
Show Standard and Point Score, 41
Sickness, its effect on teeth, 97
Sight hounds, hunting with, 30
Size, inheritance of, 56
　variation in, 56
Skin diseases, 172
　and parasites, 174
Sodium, functions and sources, 169
Spaniel behavior and poodles, 30
Sperm, 20, 86
　description, 84
　manufactured in testicles, 88
　migration of, 88
　passage to ovaries, 88
　swarm, need for, 77
Standards, interpretation, 43
Staphylococcus, infection in eyes, 134
Stonehenge, author of "On the Dog," 30
Straight hair, recessive, 40
Swimming, desire for, inheritance of, 38

Tail, 54
Tapeworms, 179
　from fleas, 179
　from rabbits, 180
　life history, 179
　segments mistaken for pinworms, 180
Teeth, pitting, causes of, 97
　canine, failure to fall out, 119
　cleaning of, 119
Teething and tooth care, 119
　as a cause of convulsions, 172

Temperament,
　effect of inbreeding on, 25
Temperature, high, as a cause of convulsions, 172
Testicles, descended at birth, 85
　descent of, 85
Tetrachlorethylene for deworming, 187
　for puppies, 187
Tetracycline in treatment of leptospirosis, 157
Thunder shyness, 34
Ticks, a mature dog parasite, 182
Toenail clipper and file in grooming, 119
Toys for dogs, 110
Trail barking, inheritance of, 29
Training the house dog, 122, 189, 198
Twins, ordinary and identical, 27
Tying, how accomplished, 87
　duration of, 87

Urination, by puppies, encouraged by dam's lapping, 90
Uterus of bitch, 75

Vaccination against 3 diseases, 154
　against hepatitis, 153
　against leptospirosis, 157
　against rabies, 176
Veterinarian to help with deworming, 185
Virus, diseases, 145
Vitamin A, deficiency of, 160
Vitamin B Complex, deficiency of, 164
　symptoms of deficiency, 164
Vitamin B_1, destruction of, 164
　foods rich in, 165
Vitamin B_{12}, 166
Vitamin C, 166
　deficiency of, 166
Vitamin deficiency, diagnosis of, 159
Vitamin D requirements, 161
　sources of, 162
　in summer, 162
Vitamin E, tocopheral, 167
Vitamin K, 167
Vitamins for dogs, 107
Vulva, softening of, as a proper time to permit mating, 79

Weaning, crucial time in puppies, 95
   how to start, 95
Wheat germ, 107
Whelping, assisting with, 90
Whipworms, 179
   life history of, 179
Wire bottom pens, 210
   construction of, 213
Worm eggs on nipples, 177
Worm eggs, size of, 177
Worming, how early to do it, 187
Worms, determining the
   presence of, 180
   how contracted, 94
   misinformation concerning, 184

THIS IS THE
PEKINGESE

I
A Fearless Companion of Honorable Ancestry

What has created your interest in this charming little dog? After all, why does one want a dog and why will the Pekingese fill these needs so completely?

A FEARLESS COMPANION

If you feel the need of a watchdog, do you really want a large ferocious creature who attacks every deliveryman as well as any intruder, bringing lawsuits and problems to his owner? Certainly any dog that sounds an alarm and puts on a show of fearlessness is adequate protection in this modern age, and what better burglar alarm than a Peke. Its fearless lion heart brings to mind the mythical legend of a marmoset and a lion who fell in love but because of the difference in size could not mate. The lion agreed to forego his size for the love of his lady fair. He was granted the tiny size although privileged to retain the heart and courage of the lion, hence he became a Pekingese.

Eng. Ch. Salote of Wanstrow, owned by Mrs. Donald Wilson.

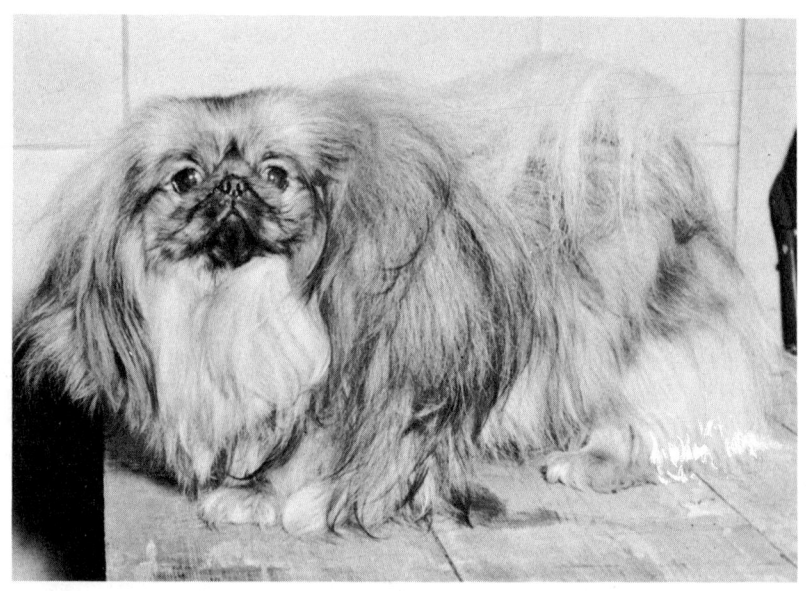

Ch. Copplestone Pu-Zee. Sire: I.K.C. Ch. Copplestone Ku-Zee of Loofoo; Dam: Shu-lo of Faygold.

Perhaps this story also accounts for the great love and affection this little dog has for his human companions. Legally you may own a Pekingese, but actually you are owned by him. You find yourself delightfully and most pleasurably enslaved by an animated furry charmer. He never tires of human love and companionship, preferring it to that of his own dog family and will exert himself to any degree for love and affection of those whom he considers are his. Perhaps no other dog or living creature is more companionable than a Pekingese. Food, so important to most other dogs, is secondary to affection for him. He is sensitive to your individual moods. If you are busy, your Peke is content to lie quietly and await the first indication that you at last have time for him. He is adaptive to the type of life you prefer whether it be apartment living in small quarters with little or no exercise or suburban life with long walks and capers. He is your devoted and willing companion. Because of his size he is easy to live with and to take travelling. He will occupy only a small space in your bed, which he always prefers to his own unless the weather is exceptionally torrid. Never noisy or yapping, he will sound an alarm if strangers are around, but he will quickly quiet down as soon as he realizes all is well. Once he has acquired his adult teeth, he never gnaws, scratches, or is at all destructive for he has a truly aristocratic dignity which we can

Ch. El-Acre Sea-Foam, owned by Vivian H. Longacre. This is the only white American-bred male Champion in U.S.A.

better understand from a study of his background. Owning a Pekingese is the nearest thing to having a constant childlike companion, and he will never grow up to have friends of whom you disapprove or show the ingratitude that sometimes is the lot of well-meaning parents. You can dominate him with your love but never by command for the Peke is a stubborn little creature with all his oriental background and personality. Remember that for many generations Pekingese were considered to have great religious significance for the Chinese Buddhists. The dogs were, according to some, actually given human slaves and eunuchs to wait upon their every whim—some even owning their own palaces. Indeed one account mentions that they were actually nursed by human slaves whose unwanted girl children were taken from them. Pekingese for hundreds of years were never *even seen* by any but the most privileged persons of the royal court in China. Hence, today they accept your homage graciously. Try to force a Peke to do your bidding and you will definitely meet with cold, iron resistance; ask him and he obeys joyously because he is the biggest hearted and most loving little companion in the world.

Pekingese have always appealed to those people who appreciate the better things of life. Invariably we discover that Peke owners or admirers are interested in art, music, antique collections, and oriental rugs. Looking back into history, we find that at one time only royalty itself and royal favorites were permitted to own Pekingese.

Ku Kuan of Dah-Lyn, H. Louise Ruddell, owner. Sire: Ch. Bettina's Kow Kow; Dam: Ch. Canerack Lydia of Dah Lyn.

Ch. Roh Kai Genie's Ching Jen, Lloyd Stacy, owner. Sire: Ch. Roh Kai Ladin's Genie; Dam: Ch. Czarina of St. Aubrey and Roh Kai.

ANCIENT AND HONORABLE ANCESTRY

The breed originated in China very long ago and perhaps even the accounts of which we read are mixed up with other breeds. Historical accounts of an oriental people who spurned the "foreign devils" written in a foreign language are of course filled with more than the usual discrepancies. Probably the actual beginning of Chinese reverence for the Pekingese started with the conversion to Buddhism of the Emperor Ming Ti in the first century A.D. The symbol of the new religion was the lion, one of the most dreaded of wild beasts whom Buddha was said to have so subdued that he followed him like a dog as servant and faithful companion. The Chinese Emperor was regarded as the Son of Heaven and earthly symbol of Buddha. What an embarrassment to find that in all of China there were no lions! In all probability those lions that were sent to China were, after the long trip and change of climate, rather poor excuses for the king of beasts. Furthermore, they did not survive long. It is probable that some imaginative individual looking around for a substitute discovered that nothing resembled the lion so much as the Emperor's little Pekingese dog. It was also much safer and easier for the

Emperor to take with him wherever he went than a lion would be. One can understand how the Pekingese and the lion could become interchanged in the minds of the devout Chinese. As the dogs were bred selectively, they were probably bred more and more to resemble lions. Throughout this period Pekingese were bred in the palace under the direction of the emperors of China until the downfall of the Imperial rulers.

Of course under some dynasties the Pekingese fared better than under others. During the reign of the Empress Tzu Hsi, 1862-1908 (either as regent or as empress), the Pekingese dogs were bred in great numbers. Eunuchs were in charge of the Imperial kennels, and only the best dogs were kept; those which were defective or not to the pleasure of the Empress were banished, probably sold. According to written history, nobody seems to be able to find Pekingese outside of the Imperial Palace. It is true that some of the court ladies and favorites of the Empress owned these little dogs, but they were probably conferred as a mark of favoritism. Furthermore, such persons always lived in apartments within the Palace. At one time, according to Miss Dixey in *The Lion Dog of Pekin*, death by stoning or ten-thousand slices was the penalty for the person responsible for a dog's removal from the walls of the Palace. Elsewhere it was written that the eunuchs bred their own Pekingese, but perhaps this was done within the precincts of the Palace.

Ch. Mar-Pat Jade, Martha Bingham and Pat Miller, owners. Sire: Ch. Tiko of Pekeboro.

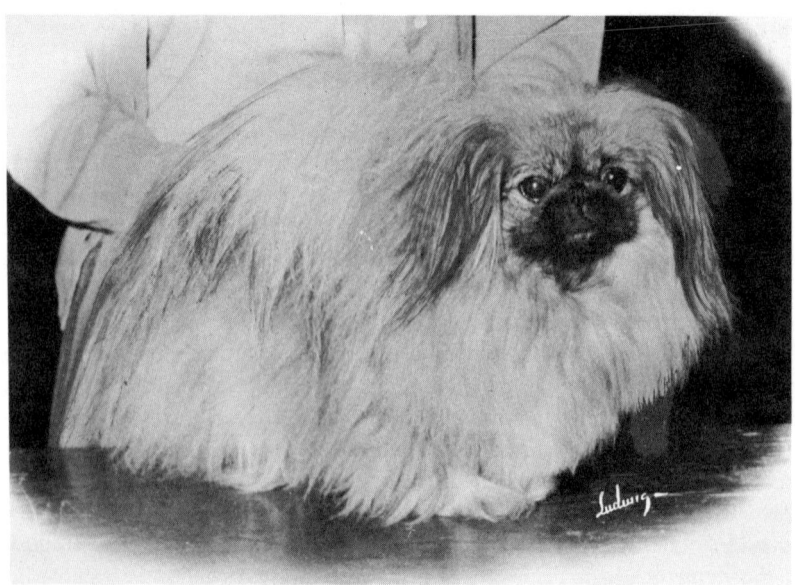

Ch. Chik Tsun of Tien Hia, Mrs. Murray Brooks, owner.

It is interesting to note that the Dowager Empress Tzu Hsi bred her Pekingese for color alone, preferring the brighter shades to go with all the imperial costumes. The only color that she did not like was the whites, because they represented the Chinese color of mourning. This may in some slight degree account for the poor development of quality in this color today. The Chinese Palace Pekingese were said to be of various sizes. The ladies preferred the smaller ones that could be carried in their tremendous sleeves. Elsewhere we find both sexes carrying the small ones in their sleeves. However, *The Pearls* of the Empress (attributed to her and written before she became Empress) indicates that she, too, considered other factors in breeding. *The Pearls* from which present-day Pekingese Standards have been derived is given here. However, her veterinary practices and diet are not recommended.

THE IMPERIAL PEKINGESE

Pearls dropped from the Lips of Her Imperial Majesty Tzu Hsi, Empress of the Flowery Land

Let the Lion Dog be small; let it wear the swelling cape of dignity around its neck; let it display the billowing standard of pomp above its back.

Let its face be black; let its forefront be shaggy; let its forehead be straight and low.

Let its eyes be large and luminous; let its ears be set like the sails of a war junk; let its nose be like that of the monkey god of the Hindus.

Let its forelegs be bent, so that it shall not desire to wander far, or leave the Imperial precincts.

Let its body be shaped like that of a hunting lion spying for its prey.

Let its feet be tufted with plentiful hair that its footfall may be soundless; and for its standard of pomp let it rival the whisk of the Tibetan's yak, which is flourished to protect the Imperial litter from flying insects.

Let it be lively that it may afford entertainment by its gambols; let it be timid that it may not involve itself in danger; let it be domestic in its habits that it may live in amity with the other beasts, fishes or birds that find protection in the Imperial Palace.

And for its color, let it be that of the lion—a golden sable, to be carried in the sleeve of a yellow robe; or the color of a red bear, or a black and white bear, or striped like a dragon, so that there may be dogs appropriate to every costume in the Imperial wardrobe.

Let it venerate its ancestors and deposit offerings in the canine cemetery of the Forbidden City on each new moon.

Let it comport itself with dignity; let it learn to bite the foreign devils instantly.

Let it be dainty in its food so that it shall be known as an Imperial dog by its fastidiousness; sharks' fins and curlews' livers and the breast of quails, on these may it be fed; and for drink give it the tea that is brewed from the spring buds of the shrub that groweth in the province of Hankow, or the milk of the antelopes that pasture in the Imperial parks.

Thus shall it preserve its integrity and self-respect; and for the day of sickness let it be anointed with the clarified fat of the leg of a sacred leopard, and give it to drink a throstle's egg shell full of the juice of the custard apple in which has been dissolved three pinches of shredded rhinoceros horn, and apply to it piebald leeches.

So shall it remain—but if it die, remember thou too art mortal.

CAPTURED BY THE ENGLISH

In 1860, as a reprisal for some Chinese atrocities, the English raided the Summer Palace from which the royalists had already fled. Apparently left behind, was the aunt of the Emperor who preferred suicide to becoming the prisoner of the foreigners. Surrounding her body were her five (some say six) little Pekingese. These were taken to England and became the foundation of our modern Pekingese. All were small dogs of sleeve or miniature proportions.

General Dunne gave the fawn and white parti-colored female to Queen Victoria, who called her "Looty." According to the best sources, Looty was never bred. Her picture was painted by either Landseer or his pupil E. Keye (there seems to be some disagreement here as to which one). She died in 1872.

Of the other four Admiral Lord John Hay retained the red brindle male Schlorff, who lived to an old age; a black and white bitch called "Hytien" was given by Lord Hay to his sister the Duchess of Wellington; Sir George Fitzroy presented the other two red females with black markings called "Guh" and "Meh" to his cousin the Duchess of Richmond and Gordon. It is these latter two that are behind most of the modern pedigrees. They started the Goodwin strain and were bred from far more than Schlorff and Hytien.

Ch. Bu-Ku of Kaytocli and Miralac, Mrs. Everett M. Clark, owner. Sire: Bu-Ti of Kaytocli; Dam: Minalphi Primula.

ADDITIONS TO THE PEDIGREE

In 1893 Captain Loftus-Allen brought to his wife, who also bred other dogs, a gray brindle dog called "Pekin Peter," which was reputed to come from the Chinese Palace. Pekin Peter was the first Pekingese ever to be exhibited in England. This was at the Chester show of 1894. In 1896 Pekin Prince and Pekin Princess, both blacks, were brought back by Captain Allen from another trip to China. In the same year the red dogs Ah Cum and Mimosa were secured by T. Douglas Murray. In 1898 the Chinese Minister Li Hung Chang presented Chang and Lady Li to Lt.-Colonel and Mrs. Heuston who used them to start the Greystone kennels in Ireland. Major Gwynne imported the last of the Palace dogs, Glenbrane Boxer and Quaema, in 1900. All of these dogs and a few others are the foundation of the Pekingese in England and America.

The first separate classes for Pekingese in English dog shows were started in 1898. Before that time Pekingese were shown in variety classes.

The first English Champion was Ch. Goodwood Lo. The second Champion was Goodwood Chum, a grandson of the gray brindle Pekin Peter. The first English female Champion was Ch. Gia Gia.

Ch. Toto Tonya Rose Pelal, Mrs. Elinor Scott, owner. Sire: Thomas' Ho Ting's Quong Kee; Dam: Seekey Toto.

Ch. Rosy Ridge Hai Charles, Merritt Olds and David Beuers, owners. Sire: Ch. Rosy Ridge Kai Chu.

Thus in a short time of breeding among these few dogs, we find a great popularity for this wonderful breed in England. Important stud forces were the litter brothers Ch. Chu Erh of Alderbourne and Sutherland Ave. Ouen Teu T'ang (never exhibited) as well as Ch. Broadoak Beetle, which sired the very great winner Ch. Kotzu of Burderop. In 1917 what is called the "Alderbourne split" occurred. This split formed the Tai Choo of Caversham line and the Yu Tuo of Alderbourne-Puff Ball of Chungking line. From the latter came most of the post-war champions including such notables as Ch. Yu Tong of Alderbourne and his son Ch. Tong Tuo of Alderbourne, also Ch. Ku Chi of Caversham and his son Ch. Caversham Ku Ku of Yam, which is perhaps England's greatest modern Pekingese from both a winning and reproducing standpoint.

THE PEKINGESE COMES TO AMERICA

The Empress Tzu Hsi seems to have favored Americans since she gave several Palace dogs to them as gifts. A black called "Chaou Ching Ur" was given to Dr. Mary H. Cotton. In 1908, she became the first United States Pekingese Champion female. Mr. J. Pierpont Morgan had two parti-colors from her Imperial Majesty. Miss Carl who painted the portrait of the

A father-son championship team. Left: Ch. Rikki of Calartha, the son.

Empress also received a Pekingese as did Mrs. Alice Roosevelt Longworth. The first Pekingese exhibited in America was Peking I, in 1901 at Philadelphia. The first United States Champion was Tsang of Downshire owned by Mrs. Morris Mandy.

The Pekingese Club of America was founded in 1909, and their first show was a great social success. By 1915 there were 155 entries at their specialty. Miss Margaret Van Buren Mason's Hop Ting of Downshire was the first American-bred Pekingese dog to win a specialty.

All the current strains in America, however, are from the English blood. The original Palace dogs brought to America contributed nothing to the future of the breed in this country. Today there are many kennels in the United States raising Pekingese and all are founded on strains quite recently imported from England which can be traced back to the original Palace dogs.

For some time the most celebrated winning Peke in America was the imported Ch. Che Le of Matsons-Catawba, owned by Mrs. James Austin. Now his record has been far exceeded by the Pekingese import Ch. Chik

Right: Ch. Calartha Mandarin of Jehal, father. Mrs. Vera F. Crofton, owner.

T'Sun of Caversham, owned by Mr. and Mrs. C. C. Venable. He has 127 bests in shows of all breeds to his credit, including the great Westminster show of 1960—a great finale to an outstanding show career. It is safe to forecast that many moons will pass before any Pekingese breaks this grand record. Most of today's big pekingese winners are imports with the exception of the author's homebred Ch. Roh Kai Tom-Mi, whose career is just beginning. Americans have, it seems, imported rather than bred their top dogs with a few exceptions. One of the current greatest stud forces to produce well for United States Pekedom is Ch. Wei Tiko of Pekeboro and Roh Kai (a great winner in England and America) whom the author imported at eighteen months of age. Already he has produced 23 Champions with a number of others well on their way to titles. This makes him the top producing living United States Pekingese. It is hoped that we now have in America a sufficient quantity of great English blood so that we can produce our own great Pekingese of the future.

Dandi-Do of Merririch, Mrs. Charles Richards, owner. Sire: Ch. St. Aubrey DoDo of Tzumiao of Bond Hill; Dam: St. Aubrey Sweet Fay of Tzumiao.

II
Your Dog's Heredity

You may be the owner of a single pet puppy and have not the slightest intention of ever being a breeder. Yet the time will come when you will say, "He's been such a wonderful dog. How I'd like to have one of his own pups to take his place when the dreaded day of parting comes."

You may be alone, or a man and wife who have decided to take up serious dog breeding as a hobby. You may be an established breeder who wants to know what is inherited, and how it occurs. Perhaps you want to learn how to breed out undesirable characteristics which, as we have seen, militate against dogs' popularity, and how to breed in all the brains which those little craniums are capable of holding.

THE GERM PLASM

To get down to basic principles, every dog is the product of the germ plasm which created him and his family. It is carried in the male's testicles and the females's ovaries. Biologically speaking, the only reason for the dog's existence, or our own, is the perpetuation of the germ plasm. So much about natural dogs, and about mankind, is a trick of nature to insure its perpetuation.

Under human direction and management our dogs have become somewhat unnatural, but so have all domestic animals. Man chooses the products of certain germ plasm which best suit his fancy, and since in general these products carry the kind of germ plasm which is likely to produce more of the same kind, man produces what he wants by a process of constant selection.

The educated and experienced dog breeder thinks more about the germ plasm than he does about the individual dogs. He combines this and that, hoping that someday there will be a combination that will produce the dog of his dreams, as nearly as possible like the ideal described by the standard.

This brings us to want to know what it is that makes the changes in different generations—what it is in the germ plasm that controls and creates all the characteristics of individuals.

The mechanism is chemical in nature. Microscopically tiny entities called *genes* which are part of the cell nucleus, are the basic factors. At times of cell division (for any animal is a huge bundle of differentiated cells) the genes arrange themselves into pairs of chains which we call *chromosomes* (color bodies) because they take up certain stains which the rest of the cell does not. When the cell divides into two, one chromosome goes into each daughter cell, splits, and becomes two chromosomes.

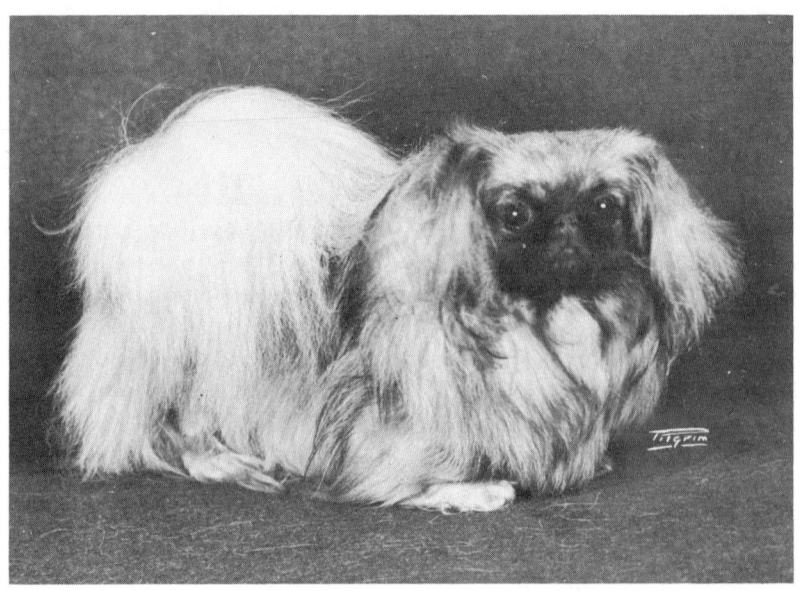

Four-time Ch. Cha-Ming Ku of Chintoi, Miss E. A. Page, owner. Sire: Ch. Caversham Ku-Ku of Yam; Dam: Ming-Tong of Chintoi.

But when the germ cells in the testicles divide to become sperm, only one chromosome of each pair is carried by a sperm. And when the *ova* (eggs) each get ready to unit with a sperm, the egg casts off half of its chromosomes, and, upon combining with the sperm, produces the architectural plans for a new individual. So this new individual inherits half from the germ plasm of each parent.

If you will just remember that *each characteristic of the dog is determined by not one, but two genes in the dog's germ plasm*, it will make it much easier for you to understand this otherwise complicated matter.

Geneticists, the students of heredity, have found that sometimes one gene will be different from its partner in its influence on the production of a given characteristic of the individual. Easiest to explain is coat color, but the principle is the same for many other traits. A dog may have one gene which produces a black coat, and another which produces a mixture of black and white. When the pair work together, the black is able to overpower the parti gene, so the pup this combination produces is black. Therefore such genes are called *dominant;* those overpowered are called *recessive*. If two partis are mated, only partis can result, but if two blacks are mated, each dog having a gene for parti, then some partis might result.

It is all a matter of chance. Here are a pair of genes represented by marbles. The black-producing gene is a black marble, the parti a white marble. Each goes into a separate sperm cell. The dog is mated to a black bitch with the same combination. The chances are the same in her case, so let's represent her genes also by a black and a white marble.

Mix the four marbles in a bowl. Now reach in and take out pairs of marbles. What will you have? You might draw out two blacks, two whites, or a black and a white. The mathematical chances are that from a hundred such tries you would have two blacks 25 times, a black and a white 50 times, and two whites 25 times.

Suppose you mate a black dog, which carries white recessively, with a parti bitch what then? Figure it out: you'll have 50 per cent pure partis and 50 per cent blacks carrying the parti gene recessively, and these of course will be blacks.

So there are six ways, and only six, in which such dogs can be mated.
1. Two pure blacks, which will produce only pure blacks.
2. Two blacks, each of which carries parti genes (hybrid). The expectancy will be 25 per cent pure black, 50 per cent hybrid, and 25 per cent pure parti.

Ch. Tong Tuo of Pekeboro, Mrs. Horace H. Wilson, owner. Sire: Cho-Dee's Jeremy; Dam: Nan Kin Chang. Bred by Mrs. I. M. Jackson.

3. A hybrid black and a pure parti will produce 50 per cent hybrid black and 50 per cent partis.
4. A hybrid black and a pure black will produce 50 per cent hybrids and 50 per cent purebreds.
5. A pure black and a pure parti will produce only hybrids.
6. Two pure partis will produce only partis.

In any single mating these mathematical expectancies may not be realized, but among a hundred matings they would be close. Two blacks have been mated and had a litter of four partis and one black when I expected the reverse, but that does not invalidate the principle, for in the long run my calculations worked out as they should have done.

This principle of dominance and recessiveness in the pairs of genes which determine traits has been studied by many students of canine genetics. It applies to a great many characteristics, not only those of coat color, but of eye color and certain behavior patterns as well.

Then there are other characteristics which are determined by a great many genes. Here is a dog with a perfect gait. Is this dominant over a hitching type of gait? Probably such characteristics are determined by a multiplicity of genes. And the same applies to hunting ability. A poor hunter mated to a good one may produce mediocre workers; the result can't be said to be a

Ch. Sun'ts Imp Sing Lee, Mrs. Horace H. Wilson, owner. Sire: Ch. Sun't Yung Wong Sing Lee; Dam: Singhi's Choncha.

Ch. Linsown Ku-Che-Pet, bred and owned by Mrs. Pownall.

genetic certainty. Half a million dollars was spent studying racing ability in horses, but the results simply showed that it pays to mate the best with the best, and that racing ability runs in families; there is no dominance and recessiveness to it, because racing ability represents the development of so many genes that exact prediction is impossible.

OLD IDEAS

In the old days everybody believed that inheritance came about through blood. Many people who ought to know better still speak of pure-blooded dogs, as if blood had something to do with inheritance. A red blood cell is no larger than a dog sperm. Blood gives one a mind picture of dilution, instead of the correct one of presence or absence. Inheritance in dogs is not a matter of mixing of bloods, which would produce blends. We would be better off without such an idea.

Our grandparents thought that a fright experienced by a pregnant bitch would mark her pups; that the effects of one litter carried over to the next; that some of the previous stud's blood stayed around to mix with that of the next stud and ruin the pups. They often killed bitches which had been mismated, because they thought such bitches were ruined for future breeding.

Yes, and they thought acquired characteristics were inherited. Hunt dogs hard and their pups would be better hunters. Practice dogs in standing for shows, and their pups would stand better at shows. Snip off dogs' coats regularly, and their pups would tend to have shorter hair.

These "aids" to breeding are no longer held in respect by geneticists and certainly those who clip dogs know that their dogs' coats sometimes get longer the more generations are clipped. But this is due to selection, and not to clipping at all. This fact alone should disabuse the mind of anyone who entertains any of these old wives' tales.

MUTATIONS

If not by the inheritance of acquired characteristics, how then did all of these amazing differences among dogs come about? How did the very long bushy coat come into existence? How did the increased station (leg length) develop? Where did the various colors come from? They were mutations.

Mutations are sudden changes. Some occur in the germ plasm and breed true. Some are dominant and some recessive. They are exceedingly rare but they do occur and the dog's owner recognizes one and by selective breeding incorporates it as a characteristic.

I have had several mutations which bred true occur in my own dogs. One had a tight screw tail. Leg length is inherited as it is in breed crosses, the shorter legs being dominant over the longer. But imagine my amazement to find an extra short-legged pup among a litter of pups and then to learn by breeding it, that the characteristic was recessive!

Rokes White Wing of Wanstrow, Mrs. Jean Waring, owner. Sire: Perryacre Bunchi of Redmore; Dam: Ch. Black Wing of Wanstrow.

Ch. Roh Kai Tio, Mrs. Elinor Scott, owner. Sire: Ch. Wei-Tiko of Pekeboro; Dam: Ch. Roh Kai Iwom Jing.

There was no determiner in the germ plasm of the original stock which could produce the ultra long hair some show winners exhibit. It came by steps, each step being a mutation which was incorporated in a strain by breeding.

Most mutations are downward in the evolutionary scale; only rarely is one an improvement. Many breeders consider the long hair an expression of degeneration just as too short legs are.

INBREEDING (mating between cousins or closer relatives.)

Over and over again owners say to me, in excusing the nasty disposition of their dogs, "Too much inbreeding," or "They're inbreeding these dogs too much these days; spoils their disposition." Obviously some of these evil-tempered dogs are badly trained. Actually inbreeding has very little, if anything, to do with the explanation.

All that inbreeding does is to double up the genes in the germ plasm. If there are desirable genes, it enhances the chances of producing desirable traits; if there are undesirable ones, these, too, come out. Usually it wasn't inbreeding which produces temperaments; it is careless, sloppy breeding. The money breeders don't care what the pups are temperamentally, as long as they *look* as they are supposed to. What does a pet-shop owner usually know about the parents and grandparents of the pups in his window? What does the average puppy buyer demand, beyond the fact that the puppy be cute and cuddly? For a fortnight's playing dolls with a pup, he frequently pays with twelve years' ownership of something which is only obnoxious to anyone who knows dogs.

Judicious inbreeding does not weaken dogs: it fixes traits so they breed true. It makes greater uniformity in a strain. But it does reduce vigor to some extent. Yet after long enough inbreeding, after the undesirable and weakening influences have been eliminated, inbreeding having brought them to light, the animals are all so much alike that they are equivalent to identical twins. There are white rats and mice, used in laboratories, which have been mated brother to sister for more than a hundred generations, and no better laboratory animal can be found.

Gwynne's Sun-Nee-Boi, Florence E. Gwynne, owner. Sire: Gwynne's Don Juan; Dam: Roh Kai King Tut's Honey.

Int. Ch. Copplestone Pai-Phu, Mrs. W. Bentinck, owner. Sire: Ch. Cowersham Ku-Ku of Yam; Dam: Ch. Copplestone Petal.

No one has yet announced the inbreeding of dogs, brother to sister, more than four generations. I tried it with Beagles and the litters became very small, screw tails appeared in several, and by the fourth generation the dogs were smaller than the originals. If one had enough money and enough dogs, the dogs could be bred in this fashion without harm to them, provided that one kept up a rigorous selection. But it is impractical for the ordinary breeder. I cite it to show that not inbreeding, but careless breeding, breeding with no thought of selection, is the reason why we have unreliable dogs.

Line Breeding is simply mating dogs reasonably closely related and keeping within a strain. All the great dog breeders combine line breeding and inbreeding. In fact, one must, to establish a strain. All of our modern breeds were inbred and line bred, as you will find if you study pedigrees.

Out Breeding is mating dogs related only distantly, or, as far as pedigrees show, not at all.

TWINS

There are two kinds of twins in human beings, sheep and cattle; that is, in the species which ordinarily produce but one offspring at a time. Dogs produce litter mates and, rarely, identical twins as do the other species.

Identical twins are enclosed in the same fetal membrane and are quite similar if not identical. Several pair have been born among my dogs and since I first reported a pair of identical puppies in "How to Breed Dogs," several persons have written to me. Some have actually found two pups in one membrane and connected to the same placenta. Such puppies result from the splitting of the newly fertilized egg into two cells each of which develops into a puppy.

So much for some basic principles. Now let us take up the inheritance of some of the individual characteristics that interest all of us breeders.

MENTAL APTITUDES

The simple list of inheritable characteristics known for the P e k e is interesting, but some amplification is necessary. Because behavior patterns are the most important aspects of any dog, we shall consider what is known about mental heredity first.

Ch. Langridge Wee Gem, Zara Smith and Anne L. Samek, owners. Here he is winning best of breed; he also went on to win best of group.

Eng. Ch. Black Wing (center) with her daughter Black Maria and son Blackmail, Mrs. Donald Wilson, owner.

Some of the behavioristic school of philosophers tell us there is no such thing as inheritance of mental aptitudes or behavior patterns. But these persons never bother even to glance at what we know about dogs; they work with human beings. But the day of shallowness is passing. One scientist's study of identical human twins upsets all of the claims of non-inheritance made by behaviorists. Yet even this study should not have been necessary to convince the partly-learned psychologists that behavior patterns are just as hereditary as eye color, if in a more complex manner.

The study of the inheritance of trail barking was the first to demonstrate that such behavior is hereditary and independent of training. Dogs of breeds which bay on the trail of game were mated with dogs which trail mutely, and all of the pups barked on the trail. What follows may have no interest to the owner of a pet dog, but will be of considerable interest to a hunter:

Every one of the early "Spaniels" used in cocking "gave tongue" when it scented a bird. For this reason, color in a hunting Spaniel was less important than it is today. You can easily imagine the scene as the early Spaniel was used as an accessory in falconry, the dog busily quartering about in the bush until he scented a bird, then barking as he got closer. A pheasant would run, and the dog would follow him until the bird left the ground.

The hunters would know by the dog's voice that he had "made game" and would remove the falcon's hood. As the quarry shot into the air the incredibly swift falcon would race it and, pouncing down, either injure the bird or catch it in its talons.

If the bird were injured, the Spaniel would retrieve it. Some hunters used to teach their dogs to sit until commanded to retrieve, because if dog, game bird and falcon had met in a free-for-all some damage might well have been expected.

Cocker Spaniels were no exception to trail barking. Indeed we are told that they were bred for a merry tone, and that the tone changed on different kinds

Ch. Sorena of Mathena, Mrs. J. C. Hoynck van Papendrecht, owner.

of game. This is entirely credible. I can tell from the tone of several of my own hounds whether they have treed a squirrel, a porcupine, a skunk or a 'coon.

Stonehenge, in *On the Dog*, which was published in 1790, says, "*A Spaniel possessing a musical but not noisy voice is all the more valuable if it distinguishes in its notes between the various kinds of game.*" The various kinds of game referred to probably included rabbits. A sight hound must not drop its head to find game but pursue only with its nose, so Spaniels were used to "spring" the rabbits which the Greyhounds, seeing, were "slipped" to chase.

But while most Springer Spaniels today open (give voice) on the trail, Cocker Spaniels do not—on birds, at any rate. I have known them to trail up with Beagles and do a little yipping when they saw a rabbit, but otherwise trail mutely. I have known other Cocker Spaniels which ran on deer trails yipping merrily. Just when the change from open trailing to mute trailing occurred in Cockers we don't know. It must have happened through rigid selection, and Cockers were mostly still or mute trailers as early as 1900. In 1899 we find a comment on a field trial by the association's president, Mr. Arkwright: "*All ran mute with the exception of one puppy.*"

A field trial or hunting bird dog who barks as he hunts, even in recognizing the bird, is practically disqualified. If this characteristic follows inheritance in all other breeds, and it appears to, the open-trailing behavior is dominant over the still trailing. So, once the trait is lost, we should not expect it to show up again from any matings of still trailers. If it is desired, the only way to introduce it is to find a dog that opens on a bird's scent and use him in the matings, inbreeding the progeny until they are pure bred for this individual characteristic.

But this does not mean that the dog will open on all kinds of game. A bird dog that opens on rabbits may not do so on birds. By years of selection, Bloodhounds were developed until they never open on a man trail (training has nothing to do with it), but every one will be wide open on a 'coon or fox trail if he is encouraged to run it.

Sun'ts Win Kee of Pekehaven, Mrs. Frank S. Hess, owner. Sire: Ch. Sun'ts Imp Sing Lee; Dam: Tai Tuo Tello of West Winds.

Ch. KoKo of West Winds, Mrs. Horace H. Wilson, owner. Sire: Int. Ch. Tong Tuo of Pekeboro; Dam: KoKet of West Winds.

Other behavior patterns are clearly inherited, and some not so clearly. I can mention the reaction of puppies to a hypodermic. It is amazing to note how similar the reaction is from one generation to the next. The dogs of some strains stand on the table and take the injections without even wincing. Some pups of other strains brought to the hospital for vaccination will turn their heads and snap at the doctor's hand. This variation in reaction occurs in all breeds of dogs. A Springer breeder brought a station-wagon load of 36 pups for vaccination. All were close to three months old, and in one crate there were five pups of a new breeding which he had recently acquired. All of his own pups stood like rocks when vaccinated, but the five of the strain new to him *all* squealed and urinated.

Among all the bird-hunting breeds, the Spaniels are the only ones which are bred to keep their noses close to the ground, hound fashion, when they hunt. Setters and Pointers hunt with heads high. This is definitely a dominant trait. In crosses made of Cockers with Setters, the puppies all hunted with heads up, like Setters. Even in crosses of Setters with Bloodhounds the progeny were useless as trailing dogs. When you see a Cocker hunt with head carried high, he probably has the genes of the English Setter in him.

The behavior pattern of interest in birds and flying objects, which Setters and Pointers generally show so strongly, is not well developed in some Spaniels. When a butterfly flies through pens containing both Setter and Cocker pups, the Setters show intense interest, while the Cockers display only a little more interest than hounds of any breed. This indicates that less selection has been applied to the Cocker to make it interested in flying objects, and in this respect the breed is more houndlike, showing a greater degree of interest in ground and body scents.

Perhaps that is why the crosses of Cocker with Beagle make such excellent rabbit and squirrel dogs. Many run almost as well as field trial Beagles, whereas crosses of Beagles and English Setters were worthless in rabbit trailing.

Some of the smaller breeds as well as the larger are natural tree dogs, and many make squirrel dogs *par excellence*, a use to which only those with shorter coats can be put, and to which not enough are put. Some Poodles tree almost as well as tree hounds bred for the purpose, and this aptitude is not so well recognized as it should be, although it is by squirrel hunters. Crossed with American Fox Terriers, the short-haired pups make grand squirrel dogs, illustrating the inheritance of this aptitude.

Int. Ch. Chia Lee's Tiny Tim of HanLin, Mrs. Marjory Nye Phulps and Mrs. Jerry Hahnlin, owners. Sire: Ch. Chia Lee of HanYin; Dam: Sudah of HanLin.

While most persons never give the aptitude of posing very much thought, observant breeders tell you how much easier it is to get certain dogs to pose as show dogs should than others. There are many who will stand in a show pose when no hand is on or under them. This characteristic quite definitely runs in families.

And there are tremendous differences between the reactions of dogs to an electric clipper the first time one is used on them. No matter how gently a person works, starting on the rear end, stroking dog, talking gently, and taking several times the usual period to perform the task, there are some dogs which are so terrified that they must be anesthetized, in the name of kindness, before the job can be completed. In hospitals and grooming kennels the owners keep special note of the dogs that behave so. Next time they clip them, they may try again to see if they are still panic-stricken. If they are, Pentothal is given again, which the dog enjoys, and he awakens in his new state. Such dogs tend to have the same kind of pups.

Gun-shyness is akin to such temperaments, although occasionally an otherwise temperamentally sound dog may be afraid of loud noises. Gun-shy dogs are invariably thunder-shy. This defect exhibits itself early, and definitely runs in families. At loud reports the dogs really seem to suffer mentally.

Three-time Ch. Kai-Chao of Dah-Lyn, John B. Royce, owner. Sire: Ch. Kai Lung of Remenham; Dam: Griselda of Caversham.

Langridge Sno Tong, Irene Smith Francisco, owner. Sire of Ch. Langridge Wee Gem and Ch. Chun Chu Fu's Chuck-a-Luck, and Grand-Sire of Ch. El Acre Sea Foam.

It is better not to use them for breeding. It is possible to help a gun-shy dog by early training, but such conditioning does not remove the basic defect, and germ plasm which transmits it had better not be perpetuated.

The tendency to piddle is another definitely hereditary weakness which, unfortunately, is generally completely overlooked by breeders. There are many kennels today in which some of the dogs do not wet when approached by strangers, or even by their owners. But there are also too many dogs that show such incontinence. In a kennel of hunting dogs there is less need to be particular about this defect, but in house dogs it should be diligently watched for and eliminated by selective breeding. That it runs in families none can doubt; that it is a matter of simple inheritance is open to question. Probably this failing is concerned with multiple genes.

Fondness for retrieving shows up in all typical retrieving breeds, including Poodles, yet there are strains that show not the slightest natural interest in it and can be trained only with difficulty. This lack runs in families. To me it is amazing to see a dog whose ancestors have never seen any other birds than English sparrows in a city back yard, who have never had an opportunity to retrieve even one of those sparrows for many generations, yet when the pup is given the chance to do his natural work, he usually acts as if he came from a long line of well-trained hunters. So well does his inheritance persist in him.

Ch. Jalna's Pandora of Melana, Zara Smith and Anne Samek, owners. This photo taken at Bellingham Show, where she won Best of Breed and 2nd in group.

Still, there are some who, because of so many generations without selection, have lost the hunting ability. Not from the inheritance of disuse, but because of inbreeding of inferior hunters.

So keen is the desire to retrieve in many breeds, to carry something gently in their mouths, that if nothing is accorded them to carry, they may even pick up stools. This sometimes leads to the filthy habit called *coprophagy* (dung eating). It may be corrected many times, by the simple expedient of leaving a few old tennis balls in the runs. The natural retrievers will be found carrying such tennis balls by the hour. Dog owners sometimes complain that their dogs annoyed them by stealing their shoes, but they really weren't stealing them: *what they were doing was simply trying to satisfy their desire to retrieve.* That is why some dogs learn to "go get things," such as your shoes, on command. Some dogs are more easily taught to fetch your bedroom slippers, bring in the paper, or take the mail from the postman than others. I have even seen a Cocker carry a pound of butter and leave only slight dents in the wrapper. Dogs of most breeds, given such an opportunity, are willing enough to carry the butter, but do so in their stomachs!

Another quite remarkable characteristic of several breeds, Poodles and Cockers especially, used to be manifest in the days when we had great epizootics (animal epidemics) of what was then called *distemper*. When dogs of many breeds have the first rise in temperature which that dreaded disease causes they show it by having fits (convulsions). Almost all Beagles had them, yet Cockers, with the same infection, would not. The subsequent mortality was about equal, but the first symptoms are different in some breeds, a fact difficult to explain.

Pierrot's Sho-Mi of Chun-Cau-Fu, Shirley Stone, owner. Sire: Ch. Thomas' Tombo; Dam: Pierrot's-Jai Kou Chein-Kou.

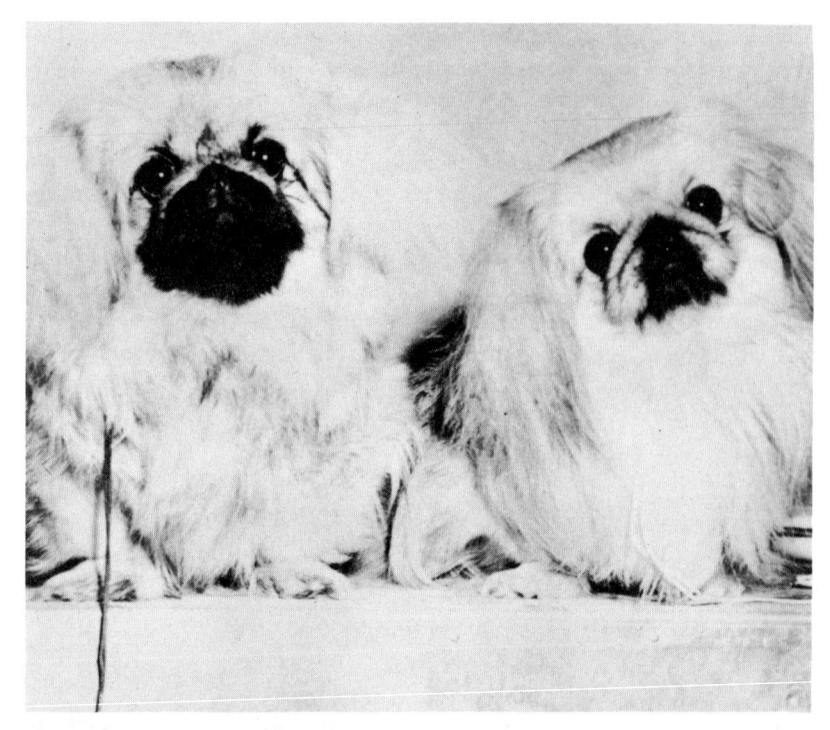

Left: Ch. Cavernock Lydia of Dah-Lyn, John B. Royce, owner. Sire: Ch. Cavernock Fezziwig; Dam: Cavernock Penelope. Right: Ch. Cavernock Fezziwig, Geraldine R. Pearce, owner. Sire: Ch. Philadelphus Antonio of Dah-Lyn; Dam: Jin's Peach of Dah-Lyn.

The propensity to want to swim is also hereditary, and markedly so in specialized water-dog retrievers, or even Poodles and Springer Spaniels. There is great variation among them in this regard, and the water-going aptitude is pronounced in a minority. This is one of the reasons why some dogs make so much better house dogs than other retrievers for families who live near bodies of water or even muddy brooks. When dogs of water-going breeds, like Newfoundlands, are crossed with those of non-water-going breeds, the pups are water dogs, showing the dominance of the characteristic. And quite possibly the inheritance is the same in most breeds.

COAT CHARACTERISTICS

In the pure-bred dogs of many breeds and in breed crosses we find that the *thickness of the coat* (the number of hairs per inch) tends to be inherited with the thinner coat being dominant. Dogs such as Norwegian Elkhounds, whose coats are extremely dense, when mated to hounds with sparse hair produce houndlike coats. When two of these are mated, about 25 per cent of the pups appear with the dense coats.

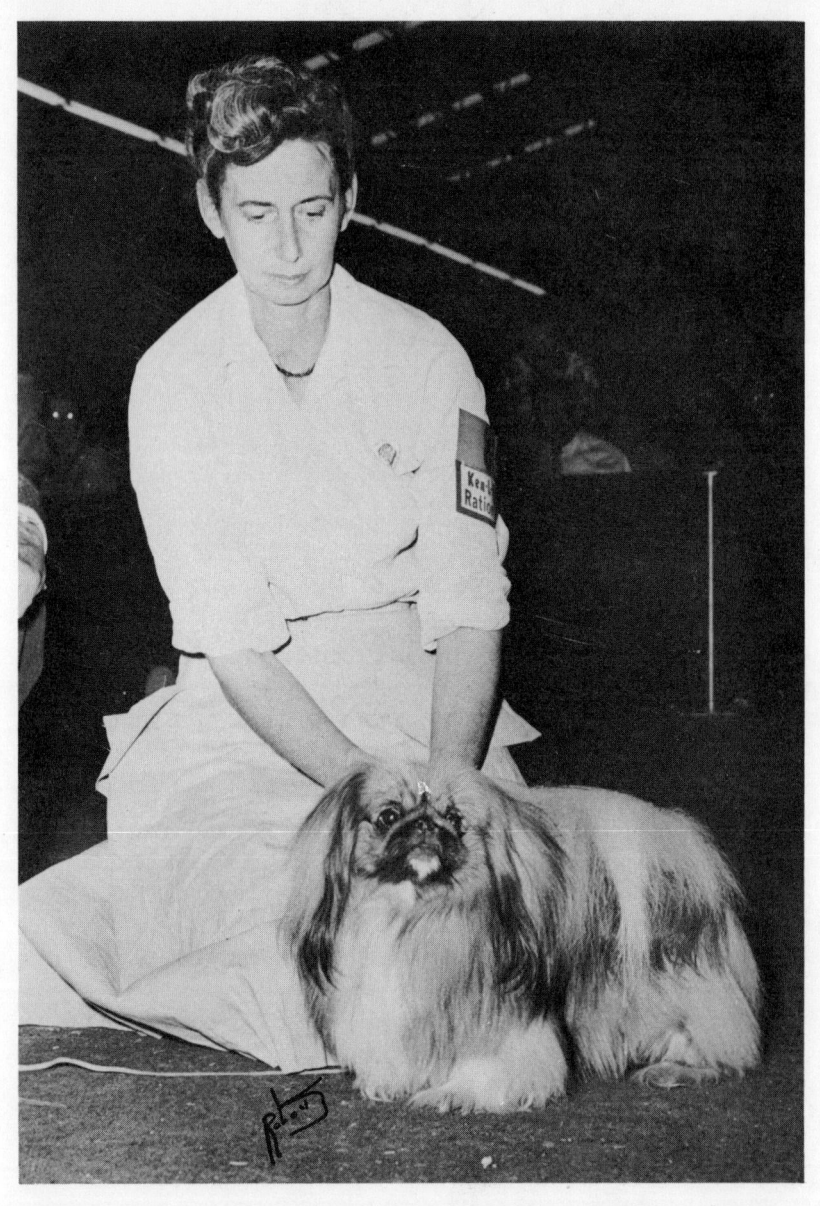

Int. Ch. St. Aubrey Argus of Wellplace, Marvel Runkey, owner. Sire: Eng. Ch. KuJin of Caversham; Dam: Yung Pen of Wellplace.

Ch. Tiko of Pekeboro, an English import, has sired six champions.

In Cockers this holds quite definitely. The woolly-coated dogs often come from parents with proper Cocker coats. This is why it is so easy to breed Woolly Cockers; a pair seldom produces sparse-coated pups.

Wavy hair was dominant over straight hair. The reason dogs have kinky hair or waves in the coat is simply that the guard hair is oval shaped instead of round. This is also the reason why human hair curls.

Length of coat is also inherited, the shorter being dominant, but in all such cases one must realize that color has an effect on hair length. White probably inhibits it; so does red. As I mentioned before, black hair growing in white coats may be many times as long as the white. So the same dog, if it were black, would have a much longer coat. The very long haired Corded Poodle's coat is recessive to the medium length coat, we may surmise, although no studies have been reported. But since Poodles with normal coats have been known to produce pups whose hair "grew in long strings," it is reasonable to assume the long hair is recessive.

This, then, is not a simple matter of inheritance. Coat length seems to be inherited, with the shorter coat in each degree being dominant over the longer. If an American Fox Terrier were mated with the Poodle with the longest, most woolly coat, the pups would have short, smooth coats. If a pure, medium-length coated Poodle were mated to the extreme type, the pups would have medium-length coats. This obtains if the dogs are all of the same color.

How about coarseness of coat? Here again we find the coarser dominant over the finer. It occurs when different strains are crossed within the breeds of Pekes, and this again explains why it is so easy to breed fine-textured woolly coats.

III
Pekingese Standard Interpreted

Every recognized breed has a standard which describes the ideal type of that particular breed. Nearness to the standard determines a dog's value in great part. All judging at shows is merely the selection of the dog nearest the standard of his breed in the opinion of the judge, who is assumed to be familiar with the standard of that breed.

STANDARD OF THE PEKINGESE

EXPRESSION. Must suggest the Chinese origin of the Pekingese in its quaintness and individuality, resemblance to the lion dog in directness and independence and should imply courage, boldness, self-esteem and combativeness rather than prettiness, daintiness, or delicacy.

Ch. Mar-Pat Tiko's Tom Thumb, Martha Bingham and Pat Miller, owners. Sire: Ch. Tiko of Pekeboro.

SKULL. Massive, broad, wide, and flat between the ears (not dome shaped), wide between the eyes.

NOSE. Black, broad, very short, and flat.

EYES. Large, dark, prominent, round, lustrous.

STOP. Deep.

EARS. Heart shaped, not set too high; leather never long enough to come below the muzzle nor carried erect, but rather drooping, long feather.

MUZZLE. Wrinkled, very short, and broad, not overshot nor pointed. Strong, broad, under jaw; teeth not to show.

SHAPE OF BODY. Heavy in front, well sprung ribs, broad chest, falling away lighter behind, lion like, back level. Not too long in body; allowance made for longer body in bitch.

LEGS. Short forelegs, bones of forearm bowed, firm at shoulders, hind legs lighter but firm and well shaped.

FEET. Flat, toes turned out, not round, should stand well up on feet, not on ankles.

Ch. Caversham Black Queen of Orchardhouse, Bettina Belmont Ward, owner. Sire: Kinbourne Morning Glory of Chyanchy; Dam: Helenes Black Sprite of Orchardhouse.

ACTION. Fearless, free, and strong with slight roll.

COAT, FEATHER, and CONDITION. Long with thick undercoat, straight and flat, not curly nor wavy, rather coarse, but soft; feather on thighs, legs, tail and toes, long and profuse.

MANE. Profuse, extending beyond the shoulder blades forming ruff or frill around the neck.

COLOR. All colors are allowable. Red, fawn, black and tan, sable, brindle, white, and parti-color well defined; black masks and spectacles around the eyes with lines to ears are desirable.

Definition of a Parti-color Pekingese. The coloring of a parti-colored dog must be broken on the body. No large portion of any one color should exist. White should be shown on the saddle. A dog of any solid color with white feet and chest is *not* a parti-color.

TAIL. Set high; lying well over back to either side; long profuse straight feather.

SIZE. Being a toy dog, medium size preferred providing type and points are not sacrificed; extreme limit 14 pounds.

PENALIZATIONS. Protruding tongue, badly blemished eyes. Over shot and wry mouth.

DISQUALIFICATIONS. Dudley nose and weight over 14 pounds.

Scale of Points for Judging Pekingese

Expression	5
Skull	10
Nose	5
Eyes	5
Stop	5
Ears	5
Muzzle	5
Shape of body	15
Legs and feet	15
Coat, feather, and condition	15
Tail	5
Action	10
Total:	100

INTERPRETATION OF THE STANDARD

The written word can be interpreted differently by individuals, and each person in his own mind feels positive his is *the* correct one. It is these differences in opinions and interpretation of the printed Standard that often makes

Ch. Tuppence of Dah-Lyn, John B. Royce, owner. Sire: Ch. Philadelphus Antonio of Dah-Lyn; Dam: Millie of Dah-Lyn.

for different placings of the same dogs at different shows. The Pekingese dog should be judged as a whole—it must present a picture of balance and type. It must be evaluated for its good points rather than torn apart for its faults. In evaluating a Pekingese, one must keep in mind that it is a toy dog of great substance and character for its small size.

Head. If we look more closely at the scale of points, we shall notice that 40 points are allotted to the head alone plus the portion of the ear fringes that go into consideration of "coat, feather, and condition" (evaluated at 15 points entirely). Therefore, nearly half a Peke's value is in his head, and a poor headed Peke is essentially a poor Pekingese. The head should be large compared with the rest of the body and should be broader than long, that is, measuring more from ear to ear and cheek to cheek than from chin to top of head. It should be an elongated rectangle resting on its side rather than the often suggested square. The top of the head should be very flat and very wide between the ears. Under no circumstances should it be curved or dome shaped, which is characteristic of the Japanese and English Toy Spaniels. When examining a show Pekingese, the head should be *felt with the hands* to ensure that a good haircut or stripping job hasn't fooled the eye. The head should *feel*, as well as appear, massive and bony without curve when handled. The slope from the forehead to nose leather should be deep. The occipital bone should not extend outward.

Eyes. Pekingese eyes are perhaps the largest of any animal for its small size and should be very large, round, lustrous, and dark. They should never be any shape but round, rather full but not bolting, and there should be *no white visible*. Popeyes are incorrect even though they may be large. The darker the eyes the better they are. They should appear black when indoors and dark brown in the bright sunlight. We are told light eyes are very difficult to eliminate once such a fault creeps into a kennel. The eyes have much to do with the "condition" spoken of in the Standard, for health is so often displayed by eye appearance. Certainly the eyes have much to do with the expression of the Peke mentioned in the Standard. When you gaze into the eyes of every good Peke, there should appear a little "devil." They should have a fire and aliveness and give the expression of a little rascal rather than the docility that one meets in many other breeds such as spaniels. A Peke should never appear sweet and pretty. It should be more virile and combative —perhaps even a bit crafty and knowing—as becomes a lion dog and should

Eng. Ch. Silverdjinn Splash, Mrs. Nora McFarlane, owner.

have the grotesque oriental appearance of an old Chinese war lord—but with round, not slanted, eyes. The eyes should be placed wide apart yet facing forward on the front of the face, not set at its sides. All dogs look alternately out of one eye and then the other. And although the impression of being cross-eyed is not desirable in a mature Pekingese, it is sometimes present in pups. Eyes rimmed in black with shaded dark rings and lines to the ears resembling spectacles are the ideal.

Nose. Placed high up between the eyes with a slight upward tilt should be the jet-black short flat nose with wide-open nostrils. Pinched nostrils, a common fault of the breed in recent years, are not only unattractive but account for difficult breathing in some cases. Unless a Pekingese has a perfectly flat nose, he can be completely discarded as a show specimen in this modern age. (A shade more nose than is desirable for a show specimen may make for a good brood matron provided she is surrounded in her ancestry and littermates by flat noses. This is especially desirable in the warmer climates.)

In examining the photographs of champions of the past, one is surprised to find that they did have considerably longer noses when compared with our modern Pekes, but this is where the breed has improved. It is to be hoped that the nosey Pekingese can be eliminated entirely and replaced with one having a flat nose with very wide open nostrils. Good nose placement is in the center of the face with the top of the nose touching an imaginary line drawn between the two eyes. The nose should be set in an unbroken wrinkle which frames it and the top of the muzzle and extends out to the edges of the face. All older authorities to the contrary, the unbroken wrinkle is here to stay, and unless a Peke has it, his chances of winning in modern shows are slight. Of course the exaggeration of it—the heavy roll over the nose covering it—is neither correct nor attractive. Nose leather should be tilted slightly up, giving a rather snobbish appearance in keeping with our tiny aristocrat's character. Viewed from the side, the Peke should look completely flat faced with a very slight upturn; when you are looking down at him from the front, you should be able to see his face without his stretching his neck too much. It is important that facial features should never seem crowded.

A Dudley Nose, spoken of as a disqualification, is a very light colored nose, often spotted. While no other color but black is permissible, it should be mentioned that there are times when an otherwise black nose goes *slightly* off color, for example, in cases of illness, injury, and undue exposure to cold, and also when some bitches are in season. In all these cases the nose usually comes back to good color as soon as the offending condition is remedied or the season is past. All puppies are born with pink noses that turn black usually by the time their eyes are opened or within a month. However, there are cases where dogs with too light a pigmentation have been bred thus producing a faded nose color. This is a definite warning to such breeders to outcross immediately to a dog strong in such pigmentation and black markings that he is known to give to his offspring. This faded pigmentation and nose color should definitely be avoided.

Ch. Gee-Mai's Tum Tum, Jean M. Thomas, owner. Sire: Vahti of Goshems; Dam: Tong's Mi Sherrie of Chin Se.

Ch. Roh Kai Tom-Mi. Best in Show winner.

Muzzle and Mouth. The muzzle of the Peke should be broad and well cushioned with the wrinkle at the top, extending around the nose. It should extend almost as far to the sides as the skull width and should preferably be black, the more velvety the better. The upper lips, however, should *never* overhang the lower ones as in spaniels. The lower jaw should be very broad and also with the slightest of upturn—not weak—yet not too strong as to be suggestive of the bulldog or to crowd the features. A narrow scoop type under jaw is most unattractive. The mouth should appear level so that the lips just meet. The under jaw should be as broad as possible and level—not giving a twisted or off center appearance. In spite of much discussion it is impossible to have a correct Pekingese mouth without the teeth being slightly undershot. The average Pekingese specialist judge does not feel it is necessary to examine the teeth when judging the Peke provided his teeth and tongue do not show and the mouth looks to be satisfactory, that is, neither too weak nor too strong in the under jaw. However, in looking at the lower front teeth and noting how they are crowded and placed, one can more easily compare the breadth of the under jaw in two otherwise close specimens. Pekingese of recent date often have too weak under jaws and many judges do not sufficiently recognize this defect. It is this fault that often accounts for the lippiness that spoils the correct combative expression and grotesqueness that is so characteristic of the breed.

Wry mouth, which is really a crooked under jaw, and the protruding tongue and overshot mouth, occurring when teeth of upper jaw extend beyond those of the lower jaw, are both penalizations according to the Standard. Protruding tongue refers to a tongue that cannot stay in the mouth. It should not be confused with a Pekingese panting in the hot weather or during excitement.

There should be a shallowness of the brow, and the distance between the eyes and top of the skull should be at a minimum. A deep forehead is undesirable, although common to many present-day Pekes.

Ears. The ears should be heart shaped, drooping, and attached at the outermost edges of the head on a level with the top of the head—not too high or too low—hanging along the side of the face and slightly forward. Thus they give the impression of added width to the top skull and face, forming a frame. The leather of the ear itself should never come below the muzzle although of course the fringes will do so. The ears should be heavily fringed, the more the better, provided the ear leather is not oversized and below the muzzle. However, there seems to be a tendency in the current craze for

Ch. Rosy Ridge Wei Chu, Merritt Olds, owner. Sire: Ch. Sun't Yung Wong Sing Lee; Dam: Ch. Rosy Ridge Ah Chu.

Champions Roh Kai Tyrone and Roh Kai Too Chi.

beautiful fringes to have an exaggeration of ear leather which is, at this time, definitely incorrect according to the Standard. Since it is attractive, it may be indicative of a trend in the breed for the Peke to emerge with exaggerated (Cocker Spaniel type) ears. Nevertheless, the Standard is quite explicit as to the actual size of the ear leather, and any exaggerated feature should be discouraged. It should be further mentioned that some Pekes have small tufts of fur standing up and out at the base of the ear which are known as "aigrettes." These are most attractive but, unfortunately, are increasingly difficult to find in our present-day Pekes.

Before we leave the face and head points of the Peke, attention should be called to the desirability of wide-open faces with uncrowded features. The monkey-type face in which features are crowded together and the under jaw usually has too sharp an upturn is undesirable. Other poor type faces are the long narrow face, no matter how flat otherwise, and the "down-faced" Peke whose nose is low and is generally accompanied by lippiness and a weak under jaw.

Body and Legs. A Peke's head should be attached to a very *short neck*. Actually the head should sit right into the Peke's very firm shoulders. The body should be broad in *chest* with *deep* broad barrel ribs, tapering at the waistline to a more narrow and delicate but sound rear quarters. The body viewed from the front should present a broad chest actually slung between— rather than perched upon—well-bowed, heavy, short, fat legs.

The *front legs* should be very heavy in bone with a firm attachment at the shoulder and a bow or curve to the upper bone; front feet should be large (but not round) with toes pointing slightly outward. The Peke should stand well up on his feet (not on ankles or pasterns). Far too many Pekingese are unsound in shoulders, and this fault if very bad leads to arthritic and rheumatic pains in old age. The easiest way to determine a sound front is to have the dog gaited straight toward you. *If* his legs are *bowed* and he *toes out*, he has tight shoulders. However, this is not necessarily a true test if he is straight legged. *The Peke that toes in always has defective shoulders.*

The *rib cage* is very important to the health (since it houses heart, lungs, and vital organs) as well as to the appearance of the dogs. Pekes should have *broad* and *deep* ribs and be as full there as possible. Flat sidedness is to be avoided in the breed for health purposes as well as being atypical of the lion dog.

A Peke should have a *short level back*. Exception is made for the bitch in which allowance is given for some additional length. This is useful for carrying and nursing a large litter of wide-faced pups. However, it should be kept in

Ch. Mar-Pat Lil Chin Clipper, Martha Bingham and Pat Miller, owners. Sire: Ch. Jalna's Lil China Boi.

A Puppy Show Pekingese guarding his trophy. Photo by Louise Van der Meid.

mind that long backs are difficult to eradicate once that fault has emerged in a kennel. The back should be as level as possible, neither roached nor swayback. Although tail carriage often masks this fault for judges in the show ring, it should be checked by the careful and conscientious. Length of back is measured from the base of the neck at the shoulders, or withers, to the base of the tail. The Peke in today's show ring must have compactness if he is to win over his competitor.

Rear legs should be firm, muscular in thigh, with straight hocks well let down, definitely lighter and closer together than front legs. Toes of the rear legs should point straight ahead. The Peke should stand with legs directly underneath him—not stretched out as in some of the sporting breeds. His rear legs should be rather close together but knees should neither turn in (cow hocked) nor out (bandy legs). The rear legs should move freely straight forward. Toes should be tufted with fringe; however, beware of too much fringe lest it be indicative of lack of exercise. Although fringe may tend to cover up splayed or poorly shaped feet, too much fringe may also emphasize any poor movement. Never sacrifice exercise for fringes. Rear quarters are difficult to judge when gaiting because of the long skirts of the show Pekingese. They are best judged while on the table where a slight pressure on the rear quarters will indicate their firmness.

Coat. Although counting in full 15 points, Pekingese coat is perhaps the most coveted single item. It can make a beautiful picture and can cover a multitude of defects. Even though a good coat can cover many faults, a truly good, properly textured coat is a joy to behold. It consists of the long straight overcoat on the coarse side yet soft to touch and the undercoat which is quite soft and fluffy and makes the longer coat stand out rather than lie flat. The curly or wavy coat is never correct, and fortunately it is becoming increasingly scarce except for a few colors in which there has been too much color breeding. The ideal Peke has a profusion of the coarse, thick hair known

Ch. Orchid Lane's Ku Banchee, Merritt Olds and David Bevers, owners. Sire: Ch. Caversham Khi Ku of Pendarvis; Dam: St. Aubrey Wanee of Raymode Dah-Lyn.

as a "ruff," or "mane"—really a ruffle about the neck and shoulders. Unfortunately it is fast disappearing. A good ruff adds to the illusion of breadth and the tapering of body that is so important. The coat on the rear quarters is often flat, which contributes to the appearance of a pear-shaped body. When the Peke matures, there is a soft, long feathering around the cuffs of the front legs that extends from ankles to body. Long feathering also appears on the thighs of the hind legs, the tail, and toes. The feathering on the skirt or panties of the mature Peke should be profuse and reach just to the ground. Feathering and fringes on the ears should be absolutely straight in texture and as long and profuse as possible.

The *tail* should be set high on the body. It should have long straight feathering in great profusion. The feathering often reaches (in the adult dog) to the Peke's head when the tail is posed in a stretched position along his back and nearly covers him completely. When gaiting, the tail should curl loosely over the back and fall carelessly to either side. Screw tails and chrysanthemum tails (more of a double curl or tightly curled) are not in current favor with most breeders although nothing is mentioned about them in the Standard. They are acceptable if they are carried correctly, which they always are. Tails carried flat on the back straight along the spine line when gaiting are *incorrect*. according to the Standard; they are too suggestive of the Pomeranian breed. Gay tails are those that wave high above the back and do not curl to the side.

The *color* of a Peke's coat is of no consequence. All other points are far more important. However, the Standard only states the desirability of black mask and spectacles which add considerably to the grotesque expression so important to the breed. There is a difference, however, in black mask and black muzzle only. Fawns, reds, and sables tend to win more in shows these days probably because more are bred, and more are bred because they tend to win. Those who breed for color in Pekingese will find their road fraught with disappointment for in the same litter there can be quite a difference in coloring—ranging almost from white to black. Also, those who breed for a definite color, such as white or black, are of necessity often bound to disregard other far more important structural points in an effort to secure the clear desired coloring. While beautiful blacks and whites do exist, they have, as a general rule, been the result of breeding for more than just the actual color alone. It is recommended that the novice breed Pekingese for their good points and try to stay away from color breeding, leaving it for the expert. Most Pekes have a number of colors in their fur with lighter markings on chest, skirt, feathering, fringes, and tail, but a true parti-color must have white and color broken on the saddle. When a dog has a white spot on its forehead (as frequently happens in the parti-color) it is often called the "kiss of Buddha"; tan spots above the eyes of black dogs are called "dragon marks"; white feet on an otherwise solid colored dog are called "standing in the snow."

Ch. Lin Tong of Rosedowns, Mrs. Evelyn Ortega, owner.

Ch. Dah-Lyn Rosette of Wangza, John B. Royce, owner.

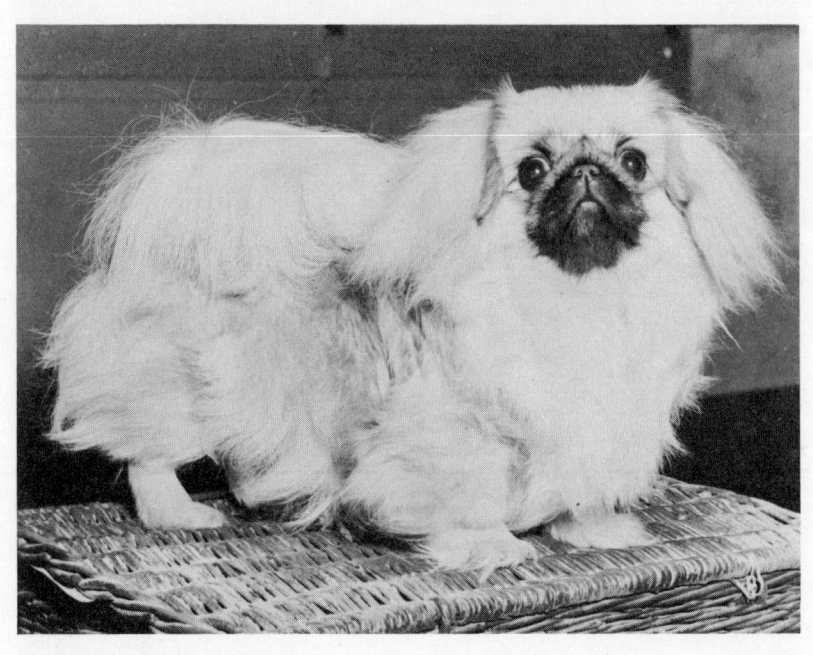

Size. It should be kept in mind at all times that the Peke is a toy dog; therefore, it should be of medium to small size. The Standard sets a definite limit of 14 pounds, and this is a good sized Peke. Those which, when mature, weigh under 6 pounds are said to be sleeve specimens; while the miniatures are those weighing more than 6 pounds yet under 8 pounds. The Pekingese should be a very sturdy and heavily boned dog and for that reason the compactness and appearance of smallness is most desirable with actual weight a secondary factor. Of the two, the author prefers a small male and larger female. Bitches that are too small (under 6 to 6½ pounds) are more prone to whelping difficulties, and although there are always exceptions, at Roh Kai we do not breed bitches weighing under 7 pounds. For a long time in this country, most of the Pekingese were very coarse and up to size. Then suddenly very small Pekingese started to be exhibited. The change was a little too drastic. Now, recent big winners have been larger dogs than most breeders desire. It always seems that, although judges may prefer a larger Peke, breeders and even pet purchasers prefer them smaller. It is to be hoped that the Pekingese which win at the shows of the future will be more of a medium size—a dog of compact dimensions but of heavy bone and large head.

Eng. Ch. Charterway Ung T'Sun, Mrs. E. B. Partridge, owner. This beautiful dog is the only black champion in England.

Ch. Derrie of Rosedowns, Mrs. Evelyn Ortega, owner. Sire: Ch. Whitworth Knickerbocker; Dam: Plum Blossom of Rosedowns.

Action. The proper action of the Pekingese is a fearless rolling gait which comes naturally to a well built Peke. If a Pekingese is wide in front and tapers to a narrow, lighter but firm rear, is sound and has a level back and bowed legs, he will walk with a *smooth* roll to his gait. If he is out of shoulder and is higher in rear than in front, or walks on his pasterns, he will have more of a "rock and roll" as do so many these days. The straight-legged Peke has a more trotting gait. Some people feel it takes a longer backed Peke to roll; however, the short backed one will also roll if he is otherwise put together properly.

THE PERFECT PEKINGESE

Of course the perfect dog described in the Standard and described in this chapter in greater detail is a myth. He is what we are striving for and will of course never fully attain. He is only on paper. No matter how lovely and great the winner, there are always some little things that one would prefer different before perfection could be reached.

IV
How to Purchase a Pekingese

When purchasing a Pekingese, selection depends on the ultimate purpose for which you plan. Every Peke is an ideal pet and charming companion which will add untold joy to an otherwise lonely or humdrum existence in return for comparatively little personal responsibility. It is truly a joy to be owned by a Pekingese! However, regardless of your reason for annexing this animated furry charmer to your household, it is desirable that he be healthy in mind and body.

RELIABLE BREEDERS vs. PET SHOPS

When purchasing a Pekingese there is no substitute for a reliable breeding kennel or good pet shop. Pekes of pet type are occasionally for sale at pet shops, but these dogs are often lacking in inoculation and the superb care including vitamins, wormings, care of coat, etc., that a first class kennel might give to its pups. Furthermore, the average Pekingese breeder of the dog has a great interest in its welfare beyond the selling price. Dogs of this type are usually bred because the breeder personally has an emotional attachment above and beyond his monetary investment. For this reason most breeders are especially glad to give helpful advice on care and problems. They know that if each dog they sell gives satisfaction to his owner, the dog itself will attain happiness. As a general rule, pet shops are impersonal on such matters and often do not really know many of the fine points about the breed. They usually have many dogs of various breeds, all of which are raised for a wholesale market. The main advantage of buying your Peke from a pet shop is that the price is lower and the pet shop is more dependable should any future problems arise.

If you plan to purchase stock for exhibition purposes, then you really have no hope of securing it except from a first class reliable breeder. It is the breeder who knows that his foundation stock can give only pet quality offspring who will sell his entire litters of puppies to shops for resale at very young age. Rarely will a reliable breeder sell his dogs wholesale to a local pet shop for resale. However, occasionally a breeder will purchase dogs of his own bloodlines—usually from offspring he has sold—from other breeders for resale in his own kennels.

Advertisements in local newspapers may bring you into contact with a breeder for securing pet stock, and it will usually be of a better cared for and bred variety than in the average shop. The best way to secure really the best type Pekingese puppies is to contact breeders at local dog shows or to look for advertisements of the larger kennels in the dog magazines such as *Pure-*

bred Dogs American Kennel Gazette, in which only A.K.C. registered stock is advertised, *Popular Dogs, Dog World, Dog News* and *Kennel Review.* There is no substitute for shopping around for seeing personally all the dogs available, and for examining the environment and ancestors from which they come. Making an advance appointment is always desirable and more courteous than an unannounced visit as well as less disappointing. However, in the event the kennels are too distant for you to visit personally, you need have no qualms about long distance buying over the telephone or by mail. Some reliable breeders will usually send snapshots and will try to describe their dogs accurately. Many very satisfactory sales are made in this manner.

Ch. Pierrot's Bei Ying Sing Tsai. Sire: Ch. Thomas' Tombo; Dam: Pierrot's Kou Chein Ku.

Ch. Pierrot's Jai Me. Sire: Langridge Wee Lin; Dam: Pierrot's Rozetta Lu.

A PEKE FOR PET, BREEDING, OR SHOW

In purchasing a Pekingese, as in purchasing any breed, it is well to define in your own mind the purpose for which you require your dog and to convey this to the seller. A great deal of disappointment and dissatisfaction can be avoided merely by a meeting of the minds between seller and purchaser. When inquiring by mail, always give as much detail as you can regarding your needs, plans, and preferences. Purchases are essentially divided into three categories: for companionship or as a pet, for breeding, or for exhibition. It is always well to give your preference as to sex and even color if you have one; if it doesn't matter, that, too, should be mentioned. Inquiries including such information are more quickly and efficiently answered and satisfaction is the more likely result. It is the person who asks and pays for a pet and then tries to exhibit it that is most unhappy when his doesn't win. This tends to build up occasional resentment on all sides including that of the seller whose reputation may unwittingly suffer from such action. Every breeder is delighted if an ugly duckling he has bred turns into a show specimen, but if it isn't a *really good* show specimen, others may think that it was sold at a higher price for exhibition purposes and that the buyer was cheated. It is this kind of misunderstanding that may account for so many poor imports being exhibited today. Some persons may not state definitely at purchase time that they desire a show specimen because they feel it will be more expensive, which it will be; but it will also, in all probability, be of different quality, too.

FOR A PET

Although every well-bred healthy Pekingese is an ideal companion and will make a superb pet, actual pet stock is usually the least expensive of purebred registered stock. It is least expensive because it is often a dog who will be unsuitable for breeding or exhibition.

A wicker basket full of six-week old black Peke puppies. Photo by Louise Van der Meid.

People usually prefer to obtain pets at a young age. However, it is recommended that a puppy should never be purchased earlier than between three and four months of age. At this age the puppy should be inoculated with vaccines (not just the temporary serum). Also, the puppy will be old enough to have had a good start in life from its mother and initial environment so that it will not be too fragile to care for or too difficult to train. If funds are limited and if you find yourself captivated by this great little breed, this is the type dog to purchase. Every Pekingese breeder was probably first the owner of a pet Pekingese.

Every Peke puppy between three to four months is adorable, and it is easy to understand the person who doesn't want to miss those precious hours of puppyhood even though they may entail a bit of mopping. In purchasing a pet, your main consideration should be the obtaining of a delightful, charming, beautiful, and healthy companion who will remain so for a number of years with average luck and good care. While it is true that females as a whole are exceptionally devoted, you may discover that they are often expensive unless they are too small to breed safely. These tiny ones, however, will probably not be for sale until they are nearly a year old, because breeders always hope

Eight-week old Mai Doll of Tsingtau and Ka-Nee being inoculated. Photo by Louise Van der Meid.

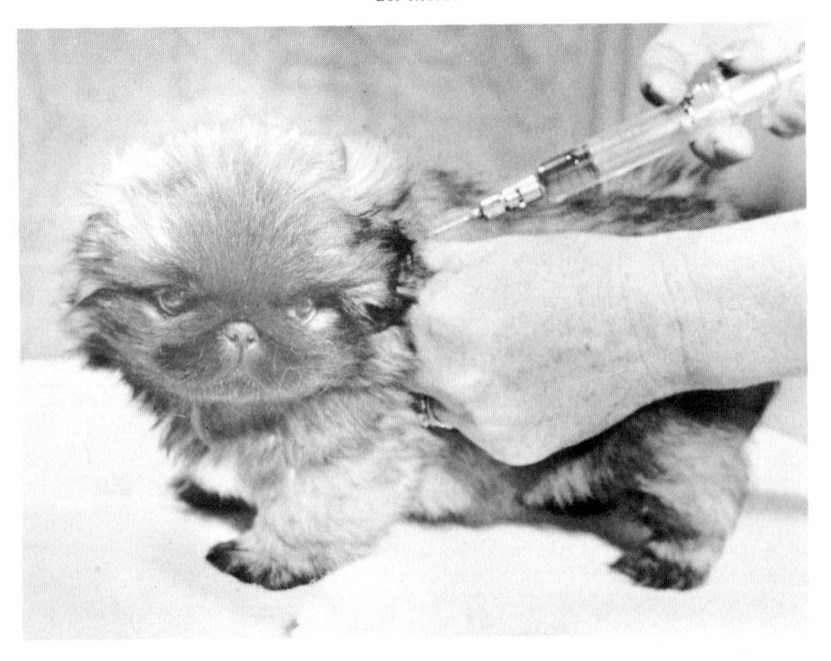

All young pups need a lot of sleep, and this one is no exception. Photo by Louise Van der Meid.

for a last spurt of growth. Males can be just as charming and devoted and as easy to train as females, provided they are not used as studs. From the breeder's viewpoint, pets are those dogs which are suitable for loving companionship yet which, for some reason, will not be ideal for breeding or exhibiting. Among the latter and probably the most beautiful are males who are not entire (monorchids or cryptorchids) and females that are too small to whelp safely. Such dogs will, in all probability, not be sold until they have matured since there is always hope for improvement until that time. Also included in this group are dogs that have certain leg or head faults which a breeder feels would be best not propagated into future generations and yet which in no way affects their health or ability to love and be loved. Sometimes a dog for which hundreds of dollars has been refused as a puppy ends up selling for a pet price when a year old. Although a few months of enjoyment in puppyhood are lost to the purchaser of such dogs, they are wise purchases. A Pekingese, because of its toy size and playful nature, remains puppylike throughout its usually rather long life.

Older kennel dogs often make ideal pets because they are so grateful for home life and affection, and it is surprising how well they adjust to new homes

Choosing a puppy isn't easy when they are as alike as these three. Photo by Louise Van der Meid.

Ten-day old pups whose eyes have just opened. Photo by Louise Van der Meid.

and people. Their innate cleanliness gives them a sense of decorum, and their desire to please is such that even older kennel dogs have been known to enter new homes and behave faultlessly. In fact Pekes purchased at any age will usually make ideal pets.

In selecting a pet, one should select a puppy that is healthy. Often veterinarians themselves cannot detect some conditions at too early an age, and a physical examination by them merely brings the pup into contact with germs left by any really sick dogs which shortly preceded him. On the other hand *if the puppy is ill, there can be no substitute for a veterinarian*. For this reason, the most important thing in purchasing a pet Pekingese is to purchase it from a good, reliable individual. Usually the established kennels of good reputation are the best places because they have had experience in puppy rearing, because they have bred the pup and reared it in the hope of making it a show specimen, and because they usually have top bloodlines. Also, when you go to such a kennel, you can see for yourself parents, perhaps even grandparents, as well as the conditions of sanitation, and so on, which make for healthy happy puppies. Reliable kennel owners usually know from their own experience if the puppy is healthy. Such breeders are quite willing to offer advice and help should you require it. Novice breeders who are sincere and have an occasional litter are also good sources from whom to secure pets, but sometimes in ignorance alone they have neglected certain points of inoculation, worming, check of stools for parasites, etc. At under three months, Pekes all look tiny, flat-faced (even those who will ultimately have noses), and charming.

Pet shops do, at times, sell Peke puppies . . . but it is rare. The advantage of dealing with, or through, a pet shop is that they have a reputation and good will to maintain and many sell dogs at a break-even price just to make a new customer for accessories and food.

Different types of puppies are more suitable for different individuals and their households. For a home with active children, only an older (nearer to a year), lively, larger, and sturdy type of Peke is recommended. For an older lady who wants a companion with whom to watch TV at night, one with a more quiet and subdued temperament of perhaps sleeve or miniature size may be more suitable.

It is not recommended that the prospective purchaser enter a home or kennel and view an entire litter in the hope of selecting the liveliest specimen. Often the liveliest one day or even one hour is the quietest the next from sheer exhaustion. Some dogs react differently to strangers, although all Pekes would ultimately respond when given a little time to adjust. All dogs, no matter how spirited, are a bit upset or subdued when strangers are around. Dogs, and in particular Pekes, are creatures of habit and dislike their routines disturbed. They are usually quiet in any unfamiliar surroundings and circumstances. Many of the so-called "quiet ones" in the kennel become absolutely charming spirited companions and exude good health and happiness once they have adjusted to their new homes. It is better to rely upon the advice of the breeder or kennel manager as to the personality of the puppy than one's own judgment.

FOR BREEDING

In addition to good health, good breeding stock should have good bloodlines. The best available specimens are the best to breed, but occasionally a well bred dog of mediocre show points can prove an exceptional producer.

Age at which to buy. Stock for breeding should be purchased definitely at six months or older, because at that age one can tell better what the dog will be like—at least as regards size. Starting at around four months of age is the "awkward age" when the puppy coat is dropped and the adult coat is not yet grown in. A dog who looks good at this time without his coat will usually tend to improve with maturity. However, those who have "gone to seed" at this adolescent age will often come back and become beautiful specimens when mature. Keeping this in mind, stock for breeding can be purchased most wisely at this age provided you have reasonable assurance that, if it is a bitch, she will mature at 7 pounds or over and not be too small for safe whelping. However, an over 7-pound weight is no guarantee of self or free and easy whelping because larger females have been known to encounter whelping difficulties. Most breeders agree that too small a bitch should not be used for breeding. In some kennels, probably because they have been given adequate vitamins throughout their lives, the dogs mature as to size around nine months of age. Furthermore, it is not unheard of for a dog to continue growing to as late as 18 months of age.

Purchasing a bitch. If possible it is a good idea to purchase a bitch that has already had a season, although you may discover an increase in price the nearer the bitch is to breeding age. The average well-bred bitch is like money in the bank as she nears her second season, for with average luck, she will more than pay for herself with her first litter. If you can purchase a well-bred bitch that has been bred for the first time or arrange that she be bred in your behalf when she comes into season to a good linebred male, there is no better way of starting a kennel. However, purchasing a bitch who has already had a litter is not recommended unless the reasons for sale are extenuating and *known absolutely*. Good brood matrons of good bloodlines are in the *greatest demand* and may be of far more value than even show bitches. A good brood matron is one who is in good condition and whelps a good or average size litter naturally, is a good mother, has no milk troubles, has no losses, and whose puppies are as good quality or better than herself. An average Pekingese litter contains three pups; five living pups is considered a good sized litter. While litters of eight and nine Pekes have occurred, any containing more than six pups is unusual. Remember in breeding, quality is always far more important than quantity. Very few breeders care to sell a young bitch answering to the above description; usually they sell them if their puppies are disappointing or if they have had some difficulties. This isn't always true of an older bitch who is sometimes sold to obtain a good home for her in her old age and at the same time will give a beginner a chance for several good litters. However, a young bitch is strongly recommended because if one considers the actual depreciation of the purchase price over the number of productive years to be expected, an older bitch may not be so attractive in price as it may first appear. If one is starting out, he will find that young stock ages only too soon in dogs, so why start out with one who has already depreciated half or more of her productive (approximately eight years) life. However, some bitches will whelp more in number as well as more valuable puppies in one or two litters than others will in a lifetime.

How does one select the best producing bitch? This is a difficult question to answer. One big breeder told the author that he had known the author's first bitch, Ch. Mao-Ling, as a youngster but did not purchase her. Then he added, "How was anyone to know she was a gold mine!" Ch. Mao-Ling is just over eight pounds yet under nine pounds in weight, compact in stature, and quite low to the ground. She has regular barrel ribs and a perfectly flat face, is red in color with shaded muzzle, and has the blackest pigmentation and broad wide-open nostrils. As a show specimen today she would be considered rather mediocre for she has never carried a heavy coat, has a bit of weakness in one shoulder, and although her head isn't truly domey, there are dogs with heads more flat on top. Her mouth was good before she dropped a few teeth and even yet is level, and she has about the sweetest most placid disposition encountered. Perhaps the greatest brood matron owned by the author is her granddaughter Ch. Roh Kai Ri-Mona. She is a rather doggy type bitch of good heavy bone, very wide-flat face, very good coat, and a superb showman. Red with black muzzle and large dark eyes, she is 100 percent sound in leg. She is herself really a top show quality bitch and proved it by becoming a Pekingese Club of America Champion (all wins at major shows including winners at one of the specialties of the Pekingese Club of America) as well as whelping seven champions (including the best-in-show winner Ch. Roh Kai Tom-Mi), two more of her offspring have both majors and another two are about ready to go out and win, thus making her the top living producing United States Pekingese female. She does have what some consider an exaggerated overnose wrinkle, slightly heavier than the ideal. However, she has never had a single puppy who didn't have a beautifully flat face, and only one had the exaggerated wrinkle.

From the above you can see that it is possible to purchase a bitch for breeding purposes who has a superb pedigree but who may be just a bit lacking as a top show specimen yet who will give lovely puppies when bred to a good stud. The rib cage is most important in a bitch. Heavy bone and soundness are also important. Wide-open nostrils are particularly desirable. Anyone who has seen a new mother pant during whelping and after nursing and licking her babies will understand the desirability of wide-open nostrils (and perhaps even a bit more nose than desired in a good show specimen). In hot weather and warmer climates this is even more of a must and should be kept in mind unless puppies are reared entirely in air-conditioned surroundings. The best bitch obtainable is the best one to select for breeding. If funds or selection are limited, select a bitch for breeding purposes that is surrounded in her pedigree (and *immediately* surrounded, not watered by two or three generations of pet stock) by top quality show specimens even though she herself may have a fault or two. Good health and stamina in a bitch are of paramount importance for this is often transmitted to her puppies.

Purchasing a male. In selecting a male for prospective stud purposes one must again purchase as good a specimen as he can afford and as is available. Occasionally a prospective stud can be purchased at a younger age than the bitch since his mature size is not so important. Often it is better to avail oneself of outside stud services rather than use a mediocre one. However, the main consideration other than points of structure should be pedigree and line breeding to the bitch. There is a tendency of dogs to throw offspring more like their parents than themselves; so if a male is well-bred and has good health he will produce best when bred to a line-bred female. Often a tiny male will sire puppies of larger size and conformation than his oversized counterpart. Sometimes the poorest male of a beautiful litter will sire better puppies than his show type littermate. For these reasons pedigree and freedom from outstanding transmittable faults are the main considerations beyond good personal health in purchasing a prospective stud dog. Nevertheless it should be kept in mind that puppies sired by the male must ultimately be sold and the dog who is a champion and makes a name for himself in the show ring creates a demand for his own offspring at good prices as well as his services. For that reason a wise breeder, if funds permit, will select for purchase as a stud dog one that he hopes will be a first class show specimen even though the show points of the dog itself are not always transmitted by him to his children.

When purchasing a proven stud, it is important to know how he was used to prove him. Whether he was trained properly to serve the bitches he bred or whether he was just left with one which he happened to breed on his own. A well-trained proven stud dog of good type puppies is indeed a jewel which is rarely for sale until the breeder has a number of his pups on hand, which is usually not until middle aged. Such older studs if they have been known to produce good puppies make excellent buys for new breeders since they regularly have a long period of usefulness.

FOR EXHIBITING

A dog purchased for showing should be as near to the Standard as possible and should be mature enough so that it won't change considerably for the worse from time of purchase. It should be of a quality and type that will definitely win at shows when in good bloom and condition. Of course it won't win at every show but it should have a measure of success.

Ch. Choo Lin of Ber-Gum, William Bergum, owner. Sire: Langridge Wee Lin; Dam: Choo Bee of Ber-Gum.

Rosy Ridge Ku Chi, Merritt Olds and David Bevers, owners. Sire: Hu Ra of Alderbourne; Dam: Ch. Orchid Lane's Ku Banchee.

Age at which to buy. For exhibition purposes it is advisable to purchase at over ten months to a year of age, at which time nearness to the Standard can best be evaluated. It must be remembered that in the previous chapter our description of the ideal Peke was of a mature dog. Puppies appear differently. It has been said the best time to select the best puppy from the litter is at the age of 11 months, 29 days, and 23 hours. In other words one can never really be positive of how a puppy will mature until he has already done so. The breeder of toy dogs has the advantage that he can more easily and with less cost "run on" full litters for longer periods of time than those breeds which require more room and are more costly to feed and maintain. However, although it is recommended that those who are purchasing stock for exhibition purposes purchase at as near to mature age as possible, such high grade stock is of necessity much more expensive and difficult to locate. If funds are limited and the desire is great, the following suggestions on how to pick the best puppy from the litter at a young age may be followed. Even *experts have erred in such selections*, but there are always exceptions, which probably prove the rule.

Selecting the best puppy. Select the puppy which has the best head for a head start. Nose placement never gets worse and even in some strains tends to "bed up" and improve considerably but the "up-faced" puppy is the safest bet. This would mean the nose appears flat and well up between the eyes, preferably with a slight upward appearance; mouth should be level, teeth not overshot or too much undershot, for under jaws have been known to grow. Strong under jaws have also been known to appear less so as face broadens and cushions with maturity. Breadth of face changes and one cannot be sure on this point until the dog is mature. Eyes that are dark do not lighten, but in the very young puppy, there is sometimes a bluish tinge that is difficult to forecast either light or dark. Light eyes at five months don't usually darken. Rib cage and spring of rib if good usually remain constant. Length of back and length of legs change with maturity and are difficult to forecast. Front legs can be felt for bow in very young pups and their correct bone structure and strong shoulders do not usually go astray, but exercise very often strengthens many leg weaknesses.

The puppy with the best puppy coat often has the best adult coat, but this criterion is not by any means absolute. It should be kept in mind that puppies change constantly from the time they are born. At that time they have a very flat coat. Then around six to eight weeks they develop their puppy fuzz or more fluffy or woolly type coat which they start to shed around four months of age, some going almost coatless shortly thereafter until their adult coat begins to come in around nine months of age and they start looking like Pekingese again. It should be kept in mind when purchasing that puppies do go through these changes for even experts of long standing can forecast incorrectly the ultimate appearance of the Pekingese when viewed at a young age. Puppies that have a tight black curl around the ears usually have fairly nice ear fringes, but these can be lost by poor care or rough littermates especially during puppyhood. A flat topskull and flat face is indicative of one throughout life. Pups will often outgrow a bit of curve in the occipital region. Size at maturity, often so important to the show prospect, cannot be forecast. As a show prospect the largest puppy in the litter is not recommended although at a young age he may well seem the best one. Such puppies often mature too coarse and large. The medium sized pup is the better selection (especially in males) even if lacking somewhat by comparison with his larger brother. The smallest one may mature too tiny for winning at shows and then may not. The dog which looks mature when young is often a sleeve or miniature. The true sleeve Peke of under 6 pounds is most appealing but he should be a miniature of the lion dog and not just a "flat faced Chihuahua" with long coat as so many unfortunately are with straight thin legs, rounded topskulls, and lacking substance completely. Miniature Pekes are those over 6 pounds and under 8 pounds. All Pekes are toys and none should weigh over 14 pounds—this weight being larger than general preference. Ideal weight for a show Pekingese is between 8 and 11 pounds; however, structure and compactness of body should be coupled with heavy bone. Ears and tail may go off a bit during teething, both flying and going gay. Sometimes with maturity both ears and tail carriage improve considerably.

Show temperament, which seems to be a problem in the Pekingese, can sometimes be overcome by training. For example, a dog considered too timid for exhibition turned into a lovely fearless show dog by proper training and change of environment. On the other hand, a dog that started out as a superb showman sustained a fright from a large dog at a show, and it took years for him to recover. Health of course is a must in a show specimen.

Remember if your puppy looks good during the "awkward age" of adolescence when growth is in spurts and different parts grow in varying degrees (four to nine months is this awkward age usually in Pekes), the chances are he will grow slightly more and only improve after this time. Often the poor specimen during this period will suddenly blossom forth into a beautiful dog; but more often the beautiful young puppy will at this age show a mediocrity from which he will never emerge. Any Peke who looks good at this time will be a "world beater" when mature. For this reason purchase show stock preferably when mature but certainly not under six months of age; even at this age you will still be taking a gamble. The price will in all probability increase correspondingly with the age at which your gamble becomes less. Remember *different strains mature differently*—some points developing early in one strain and late in another. It is the wise breeder who has experienced such developments in his own strain that will be able to help you select the best puppy in his own litter for exhibition purposes, but even so there is a gamble involved.

Usually one must *either breed or exhibit a female Pekingese*. Once she is bred, it takes nearly a year before she is back into coat and condition suitable for exhibition. If you are sincere with the breeder and give him assurance that you will exhibit a good dog if he sells it to you, the chances are that he will be very glad to assist you in your selection.

V
Reproduction in the Bitch

In order to be a fairly successful breeder it is not essential that you understand the processes of reproduction. You can proceed by hit-or-miss, by reliance upon tradition, which stems from a conglomeration of old wives' tales and general attempts to explain phenomena without the underlying knowledge we have today. Or you can leave it all to your veterinarian; but that will be unnecessarily expensive.

One of the most attractive features of dog breeding is the fact that those who get the most out of it are those who travel down the bypaths into which it leads them in search of knowledge. There are so many of these temptations, and they are all intriguing. Reproduction is one of the most rewarding and fascinating of them. Many people who know very little about human reproduction have considerable information about canine, and of course they catch the implications. Many parents find that letting their children learn about reproduction from watching the phenomenon in dogs, and helping with a few bits of information as the children acquire knowledge, is one of the finest ways of dealing with the matter. Our children learned in that way. We

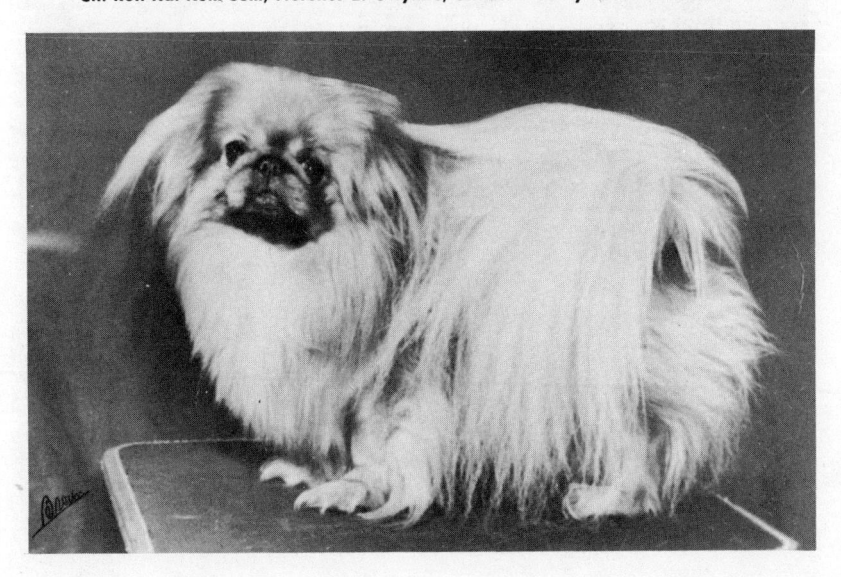

Ch. Roh Kai Kum Sum, Florence E. Gwynne, owner. Bred by Rose Marie Katz.

explained, when they asked, about the inside happenings, ovulation, gestation, and so forth, and they never did ask the silly questions so often put by children who acquire their information on street corners, or behind the barn, from other children.

Despite today's broad education, the public know practically nothing about their own reproduction, and what they think they know is mostly erroneous, so how can they be expected to understand it in dogs? I have often asked women clients, to whom I am about to explain the "facts of life" about their bitches, if they know what day of the cycle the human female ovulates. Surely 95 per cent of them never heard the word, judging by their expression of bewilderment.

Probably this is all "old hat" to you; if so, skip it. If not, read it, because if you are a serious dog breeder it may save you time and money.

The female ovaries, that part of her for which all the rest of her exists, are located inside her abdomen, high up and just behind her last ribs. They are about as large as a yellow-eye bean but a little more compressed (flatter). Each ovary is encircled by a capsule, in one side of which there is a slit, with spongy tissues along its edge, called fimbria. Starting from this tissue, a tiny

Ch. Roh Kai Terek, Alice Knox Scobie, owner. Sire: Ch. Wei Tiko of Pekeboro and Roh Kai; Dam: Ch. Roi Kai Ri-Mona.

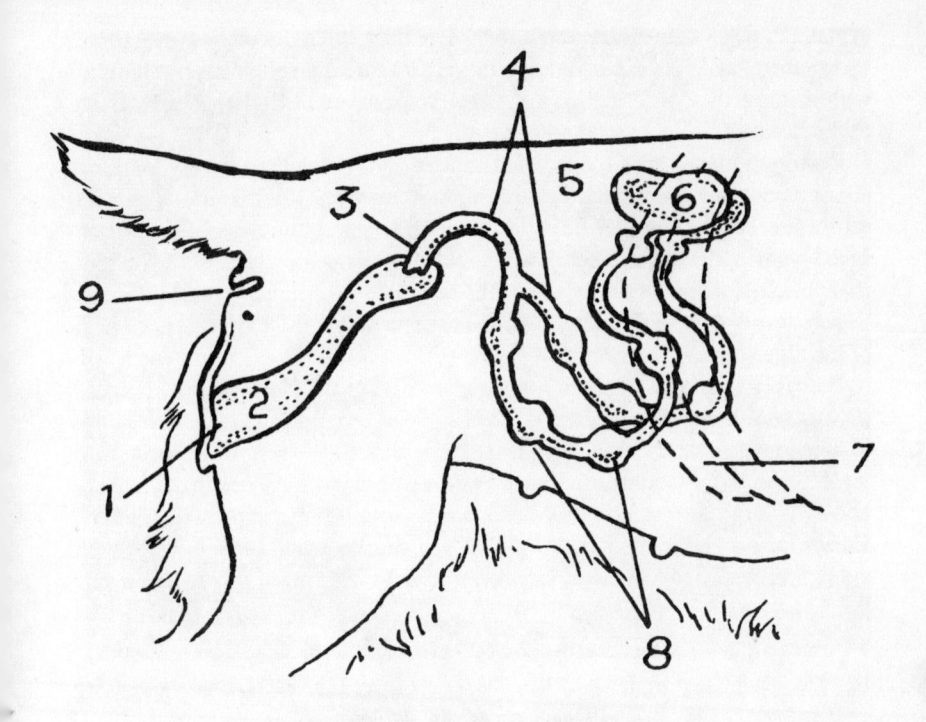

Female organs of reproduction. Reproductive system of a bitch. (1) Vulva. (2) Vagina. (3) Cervix. (4) Uterus. (5) Ovary. (6) Kidney. (7) Location of ribs. (8) Lump consisting of embryo and placenta. (9) Anus.

tube runs in a zigzag course over each capsule and terminates at the upper end of one of the branches of the uterus (womb). These tubes are called Fallopian. The uterus is constructed in the shape of a letter Y. The illustration shows the difference in anatomical construction between the human and canine reproductive tracts. It is considerable. Many of those persons who have some knowledge of the human tract think the long arms of the uterus in the bitch are Fallopian tubes, but such is not the case.

When a bitch becomes pregnant, the fertilized eggs nest at various places along the uterus, which expands to accommodate their growth and to protect them as well. A bitch with a dozen pups in her uterus will have developed each of its horns to perhaps thirty inches long and two inches in diameter.

When *copulation* (the mating of dog with bitch) occurs, sperm are transferred and are moved up the uterus by the same sort of movement (peristalsis) that occurs in the intestines. Within a few minutes after tieing (sexual fusion) occurs, the sperm are already up the uterus, through the Fallopian tubes, and in the capsule surrounding the ovaries.

Ch. Roh Kai Ladin's Genie, Alice Knox Scobie, owner. Sire: Ch. Roh Kai Aladdin of Elsdon; Dam: Roh Kai Ual Tong.

THE MATING CYCLE

Within the ovaries of the bitch there is a rhythmical period transpiring, very much like the human. But while the average human female has thirteen periods in a year, the chief difference in canines is that only two of these periods come to full development during a year. It is interesting to know why.

The changing length of the day is apparently the chief influence in inducing a cycle which brings the female reproductive tract into a condition where she will, during part of it, "accept the dog." As the days grow longer in the latter part of winter, and when they get noticeably shorter in late summer, the vast majority of bitches come into heat.

This fact can be used to bring a bitch into heat. If the length of her day is increased by artificial light, one hour a day for the first week, two hours the second, three the third, and four the fourth, she will usually be in heat. Or shipping a bitch from, say, the vicinity of Boston to some city in Georgia will usually accomplish the same result in less than six weeks. The reverse produces the same effect, especially when it is done during the winter when days are short, and provided the bitch is not kept in a lighted kennel or in your home.

The germ plasm stored in the ovaries, ripens eggs which develop in blister-like pockets that grow toward the surface of the ovaries. Of these there are a great many more than there are eggs which become puppies. At a certain time, about the fourteenth to sixteenth day (much as is the case with the human female), these pockets, called follicles, are as large as small peas, and protrude from the bean-shaped ovary. The follicles produce *follicular hormone*, which acts to prepare the uterus. When they cannot stand the internal pressure any longer, due to the thinning of their walls, most of the follicles which have protruded from the ovary burst and liberate the eggs (ova) into the capsule around it.

They are beset by a multitude of male sperm, provided, of course, the bitch has just been bred. It was formerly thought that one sperm was sufficient to penetrate an egg, but we now know that a large number of sperm are required to break down the egg's resistance, because the sperm have an enzyme which weakens the egg's coating, and then one sperm can get through.

The eggs, whether fertilized or not, are moved through the Fallopian tubes down into the uterus and there, if they have been fertilized, they become attached to the uterine lining (endometrium) and grow. If they have not

Ch. St. Aubrey Ku Kuan of Jehol, Mrs. W. A. Bailey, owner. Sire: Ch. Caversham Ku Ku of Yam; Dam: Anne of Jehol.

joined with sperm already, they may meet them in their downward passage and, becoming fertilized, nest in the uterus.

Since ovulation does not occur before the middle of the acceptance period (which starts at the eighth or ninth day from the first showing of swelling of the vulva and bleeding), the ideal time to mate dogs is close to ovulation, either a day before, or any time during the rest of the period. The fragile sperm do not live more than three days in the female tract, and perhaps are not able to fertilize when they are more than two. This is the reason why bitches mated the first day they will take the dog so often fail to become pregnant: the sperm cannot live until the eggs have been discharged from their follicles.

As soon as the follicles rupture, the pits made by this phenomenon fill with blood, thus forming bloody plugs called the blood bodies (corpora hemorrhagica). These soon change their characteristics and secrete a hormone, the luteal hormone, whose effect is almost opposite from that of the follicular hormone. The blood bodies become quite tough and, since they take up yellow stain when prepared for study, are called the luteal bodies. These corpora lutea persist during pregnancy and for some time thereafter.

The luteal hormone puts the brakes on the whole mating cycle. Shortly after the luteal hormone enters the blood stream, the bitch's vulva, which has

Ch. Japeke Stormy's Di-Nah II, Marjory Nye Phulps, owner. Sire: Japeke Stormy Weather; Dam: Japeke Snow Mist.

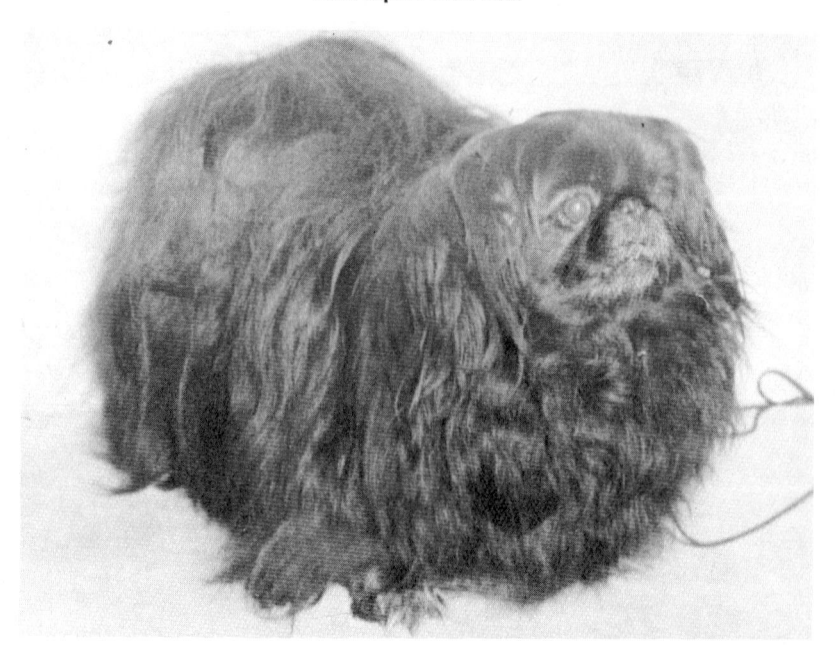

Ch. Wei Tiko of Pekeboro and Roh Kai, eleven-time winner of Best in Show, all breeds. Imported from England, he has sired twenty-three champions.

become firm and greatly swollen, loses its firmness, and within 36 hours becomes flabby and soft. If you own a bitch but have failed to note her first day, perhaps even being appraised of her condition by the action of your male dogs or of neighbors' dogs camping on your lawn, then watch for this sudden softening of the vulva. It means she has ovulated, and that you had better not delay many days before mating her.

When she has conceived, in other words when the male sperm and eggs have joined and a new pup has been started, the egg with its complete pairs of chromosomes divides into two. Each of the daughter cells formed from the fertilized egg has complete pairs of chromosomes. This process of cell division continues until about the sixth, when one pair of cells is set apart to become the germ plasm of the pup.

The dividing cells become a hollow globe, which finally pulls in one side, just as if you let the air out of a hollow rubber ball and pushed one side of it in until it touched the other side, then squeezed it together until you made a canoe-shaped body, squeezing further until the two gunwales of the canoe touched and stayed together. What was the outside of the ball is now its inside.

Ch. Mar-Pat Tei Cup Tu shown winning award for Best of Breed at Grand Island, Nebraska, 1961. Mar-Pat Pekingese, owner. Sire: Ch. Pierrot's Jai Me. Dam: Ch. Mar-Pat Tiko's Wei Tei Cup.

This new formation grows and grows by cell division, until by the twenty-second day it is a very tiny object surrounded by protective coverings and the placenta, which connects it to the uterus. If you have a delicate sense of touch, you can feel it through the abdominal wall. You must put your thumb on one side of the bitch's belly, your fingers on the other side, and, feeling very gently, you will discover several lumps. They feel like tiny marbles, round and uniform.

By the twenty-fourth day they will be noticeably larger, and every day they will grow larger until the thirty-fifth day. After that the lumps will be so soft that they will be difficult to feel, but one scarcely needs to anyway, because the size of the belly is a good indication.

If your bitch ovulates and does not conceive because she was not bred, the stud was sterile, or the mating took place too early, she will develop enlarged breasts, an increased appetite, and, 60 to 63 days from the time she ovulated, will go through most of the activity of a bitch about to whelp, yet not produce pups. She may steal other pups to mother; she may produce some milk, so don't think she is sick. Rather, if she does not do these things, consider the probability that she did not ovulate. She will not retain the *corpora lutea* and may come into heat two months earlier than you expect.

In the days when Carre's disease was the great scourge of dogs it was very common to find bitches pregnant at the time they contracted the disease resorbing their puppies. I reported this fact many years ago in a veterinary journal. The interesting thing was that when the bitch did this, the pregnancy protected them against the disease so that its effects were so mild one often would not normally know they were sick. This accounted for the survival of many more bitches than dogs in epizootics of that horrible disease.

Have you ever listened to discussions among dog breeders on whether to breed a bitch on her first, second, or third heat? If not, then if you are at all scientifically minded, get such an argument started and sit back and listen. I have done it, many times, to learn all the ideas dog breeders have. In every such discussion the ideas most often expressed are based on thoughts about human beings. An adroit *why* interjected here and there soon brings out the fact that nearly all of the ideas are also based on rationalization and not knowledge. Here are some:

"You wouldn't want to see a thirteen-year-old girl have a baby, would you? Answer: a thirteen-year-old girl is not grown or physically mature when she first menstruates; a bitch doesn't come in heat until she is mature. Time of marriage is a social convention. Moreover, a woman obstetrician tells us that the thirteen-year-old girls she has delivered have had their babies much more easily than older women.

Roh Kai Wee Ti Ku, owned by Miss H. Louise Ruddell, bred by Rose Marie Katz. Sire: Ch. Wei Ti Ko of Pekeboro. Dam: Roh Kai Lu Lina.

"Puppies from older bitches will be better puppies than those from young ones." Anyone who makes this claim should present evidence, and all scientific studies show it to be without foundation. Many champions have come from bitches bred their first heats. Those who support the view with arguments should realize that they are also supporting the argument for the inheritance of acquired characteristics, a viewpoint pretty well vitiated by research. It is probably true that one can find more champions from the second heats of bitches than from the first, but this is because many breeders skip breeding the first heat through mistaken notions.

"A bitch isn't old enough to take proper care of puppies before she is two years old." More rationalizing. True, she may take better care of her second litter because of experience, but that is a very different matter. Mother love in a bitch is based on hormone production (prolactin). The second litter is no longer novel to her. She may take better care of her fourth. On the basis of the above argument she should never have her first litter.

The scientifically minded dog breeder wants to know why, and when he inquires of those with experience, he learns that many breeders have found (that a bitch bred her first litter) may have better spring of ribs than one bred later, because while her bones are "less brittle" they are pushed outward and tend to "set that way." How much of fact or fancy there is in this idea we do not know from research, but it is the opinion among a wide segment of fanciers who breed their bitches the first heat on this account, and find it does them no harm.

Alert and inquisitive Pekingese pups at 10 weeks of age. Owned by Roh Kai Pekingese.

Ping Wan (right) and Missie-Ku-Chi, both owned and bred by Marion McVega. Both dogs sired by Fee-Che II; dam (for both) Sueann V.

The person with an open mind also asks those who, like myself, have bred dogs in studies, and learns that we always breed the first heat and have had no bad results.

Then there is another point too often overlooked, namely the possible loss of unique, valuable germ plasm which a puppy may carry. Dogs are subject to so many perils that their average age is probably not over five, and it is best to have litters as early as possible to be sure of getting any.

Besides, where space is limited it pays a breeder to know what kind of puppies a dog produces, so he can keep the best producers and eliminate the inferior. Why keep a bitch an extra year to find this out?

Many breeders owning valuable bitches have one or more miss, and want to have pups from them. Or certain bitches fail to come into heat, and the breeder wants to bring them in. This may be done with hormones, but it is a veterinary matter. The combination of drugs which has produced best results in bringing a bitch into heat is stilbestrol. It may be given in pill form, or right in the food, or it may be injected. After about five days' treatment with five milligrams a day, a 25 lb. bitch will be in heat. After she comes in heat, two milligrams a day will continue the heat normally, but she probably will not ovulate. To produce ovulation we inject her with about 20 units of pregnant mare serum and breed her the next day. Our percentage of fertile matings has been high.

VI
Reproduction in the Male

In the preceding chapter we discussed the part the female plays in reproduction, and mentioned the sperm from the male. These very minute bodies are actually shaped like polliwogs. They are oval and flattish, each having a tail about nine times as long as the body. Each sperm, as we have seen, has half the normal complement of chromosomes.

Sperm, short for *spermatozoa*, are manufactured by the germ plasm of the dog, and this basic mass of cells is part of the *testicles*. The testicles are, in many ways, interesting organs.

They develop within the puppy's body but move outward through slits in the abdominal wall, and are already out of the body and just forward of the sac which holds them later, the *scrotum*, at the time of birth. Sometimes people who should know better compare the descent of the puppy testicles with those of boys', whose testicles do not descend until puberty, but there is no real basis for comparison.

Regal bearing and imperious glance aid this Pekingese in being the champion he is. Owned by Mrs. Ray Chandler, this is English Champion Berar of Ifield.

Ch. Snowball of Rosedowns, owned by Mrs. Evelyn Ortega. Sire: St. Aubrey Snowball of Tzumiao & Rosedowns. Dam: Taffy Supreme.

While we are on this subject, we should know the terms which are used for the conditions in which the testicles fail to descend at all. When they remain in the abdomen, or when they have come through the abdominal rings but have not progressed far enough to occupy the scrotum, the condition is called *cryptorchidism*.

A *monorchid* is a dog which has only one testicle, or a dog in which only one testicle has grown into the scrotum.

An *anorchid* is a dog without testicles, or one in which the testicles have not grown into the scrotum.

The word grown here may puzzle some readers who have the idea that testicles simply slide down a passageway into a sac. Not at all. The process is one of growth. The testicle, while inside the abdomen, becomes adhered to the tissue lining the abdomen—the *peritoneum*. This then grows downwards through the abdominal slits (rings), and drags the testicle with it. This growth is under the influence of a hormone made by the anterior pituitary gland. It is now manufactured synthetically, and sold under such terms as A.P.L. (Anterior Pituitary Like). If this is injected early in the growth period into a cryptorchid puppy, it often stimulates the descent and renders him normal. In some older pups, when the testicle was close to the scrotum, it has also

The Mighty Atom of Roke, bred by Jean Waring.

brought about the desired result. But dogs which have to be treated thus can still pass on the condition to their pups, and are bad risks as breeders. Cryptorchidism is rare in some breeds, and common in others.

When testosterone was first offered veterinarians, it was used repeatedly in an effort to correct cryptorchidism, and several reports of success appeared. Later reports indicate that its use is substitutive therapy, and that it is not only useless, but tends to degenerate the testicles.

Sperm are of two kinds: male-forming and female-forming. This capacity is due to the number of chromosomes the sperms possess. Bitches have only one kind of chromosomes, but in a male dogs a pair of them differ. One is called the X and the other the Y. And this is the explanation of sex, for when a male with a Y chromosome combines with an egg possessing a Y, the product is a bitch pup. When the X chromosome combines with a Y chromosome, the pup will be a male.

So theoretically there should be an equal number of dog and bitch pups born, but there are not. There are many more males than females. Those interested in following this study further can consult the book *How to Breed Dogs*. Conceptions occurring in the cold months result in a much higher ratio of males to females. There are influences at work, which we do not as yet understand, modifying the expectancy. But today we have no way of producing sex to order.

The males' testicles are outside the body because the heat inside would prevent the production of sperm. A muscle pulls them close to the body to keep them warm in cold weather and lengthens to permit movement of air and some sweating from the scrotum in hot weather.

The penis of members of the dog family is unique in that, besides being capable of becoming enlarged with blood, it has an area which enlarges much more than the forepart does. When there is no enlargement of the penis, it is quite small. The dog's penis contains a pointed bone which may be felt in the front part, just behind this bone is located the section capable of great enlargement. When the dog copulates with a bitch, the penis is thrust into the vagina, where it instantly swells. The huge enlargement of the bulbous part takes place due to its filling with blood, and it becomes at least three times as large as the rest of the penis. In this way, the dog is tied to the bitch; it is entirely due to the male, the bitch having no part in the initial tieing.

When tieing has occurred, the semen is pumped by spurts into the vagina. Probably then the bitch helps keep the penis enlarged, because there begins a series of peristaltic waves, which causes a slight tightening and relaxing of the

Pekingese Club Champion Beh Tang, owned and bred by Dorothy P. Lathrop. This dog made her championship in three five-point shows, and won the group at the Garden.

American Champion St. Aubrey Jin T'son of Holmvallee, owned by Charleen Prescott, bred by Mrs. M. E. Birks and Mrs. E. Rhodes of England. Sire: Ch. Ku Jin of Caversham.

vagina. Some males will remain tied (or hung) for five minutes, some for 60. A five-minute tie is just as satisfactory as a longer one, because the semen has been moved up through the uterus and Fallopian tubes to the ovarian capsules by the end of five minutes.

How often may a vigorous stud be bred without harm? Probably once a day will not hurt him. The week before he died, at thirteen years of age, Red Brucie bred seven bitches, all of which conceived. Nature is most generous with sperm. In one good mating a dog may discharge millions of sperm, though a smaller amount is produced by dogs frequently mated. Rams offer an excellent example of the possibilities, for a single ram has been known to impregnate sixty ewes within 24 hours. I have seen a vigorous stud, left with a bitch, copulate five times with her, and remain tied at least 18 minutes each time. The dog showed no signs of weakness. It probably harms the dog not at all, but more than one breeding a day would produce questionable results in the ensuing litters. Some stud-dog owners refuse to permit their dogs to be bred more often than once a week, surely on sentimental, not on scientific grounds.

VII
Rearing Puppies

At the end of her gestation period the expectant mother dog lets you know that she will soon deliver her puppies. You can tell by such behavior as this: She seeks a nest. It may be a hole she digs in the ground, or her kennel bedding may be scratched up and rearranged. If she is a house dog, she may push your shoes together in a corner. If she is loose, you may find her in a secluded corner of your garden. She plainly shows that she wants to be by herself. If you wait for her to have her puppies and then move her to a place of your liking, she may turn against her pups. Even the best mothers become poor ones when disturbed during the first week after whelping.

Just before she whelps, a long haired bitch's hair can be clipped from her breasts to good advantage. If she has been allowed to lie in a run infested with worm eggs, she may have thousands of them stuck to her nipples and to the waxy secretions on the skin. If she is thoroughly cleaned a day or two before she whelps, it may prevent early infestations of her pups by intestinal parasites, and thus remove an obstacle to raising the litter.

Ch. Chun-Chu-Fu's Comet Chan To (bitch) at 7 months. Bred and owned by Shirley Stone, she is the eighth champion offspring of Langridge Wee Lin. Dam: Al-Za's Kung Chu Taza.

Most bitches are good mothers. It is seldom necessary to help them, but when you see a bitch straining and accomplishing nothing for several hours, a call to your veterinarian is in order. The average bitch will require about three hours to complete her whelping, but if she has a pup every 90 minutes, or takes six or eight hours to complete the task, it is not necessarily abnormal. Even 24 hours labor can be considered normal in the case of slow whelpers. A tiny amount (1/10 cc.) of Pitocin injected under her skin will hurry a slow whelper remarkably.

If she fails to chew off a sac in which a puppy is born, you must rupture it and slip it off the pup, folding it back over the umbilical cord so she can consume it along with the placenta. She will do as well if you cut the cord off an inch from the puppy and dispose of the placenta as if she were permitted to be natural and eat it. There is doubt that she obtains anything of value from it. Very likely it is a holdover from the days when bitches were their own janitors and kept the nests clean in this way, just as they do when they consume the urine and feces of their puppies.

In this matter of elimination by puppies, it is not generally understood that they tend to hold their urine and feces until the lapping of the mother's tongue causes a relaxation of the sphincters. Persons rearing orphan puppies can keep their boxes perfectly clean by simply wiping the pups with a moist piece of cotton until they eliminate.

Dah Lyn Hei-Jin of Caversham, owned by Miss H. Louise Ruddell, bred by Miss I. M. de Pledge. Sire: Ch. Ku-Jin of Caversham, Dam: Caversham Ku Yamei of Tissans.

Ch. Wee Jock of Hesketh-Toytown, owned by Del-Vila Kennels.

DEWCLAWS

The extra digits on the feet, equivalent to the human thumbs, are called dewclaws. Breeds used for retrieving in water find them useful, but in pets and those used only for upland bird hunting they are often a source of trouble. This is due principally to the fact that the nails on the rear dewclaws do not reach the ground to wear off, and so may grow in a circle and penetrate the toe.

Only a small percentage of dogs possess them anyway, and they are inherited, so may easily be bred out of a strain. If your pups are born with dewclaws which you feel will never be useful to the grown dog, trim them or have them trimmed off early.

Occasionally a bitch will lap a puppy's surgical site and keep it bleeding until she may weaken it greatly. Remember that there is almost a complete absence of iron and some other minerals in bitches' milk, a puppy being born with all he will have until he begins to eat solid food. If he hemorrhages early in life, his precious iron and sodium won't stretch out enough to enable him to live, and he will either be unthrifty or die.

The first food other than milk which puppies receive, if their mothers behave normally, will be partially digested stomach contents. The wild bitch kills rodents or obtains other food, comes home with it, digesting it as she comes, and then vomits among her litter of pups. They wallow in it, eating all they can. When they are done, she eats the remainder and laps them clean.

Champion Jai Atom Mieke of Orchard Hill (female). Owned and bred by Mrs. Hermine W. Cleaver, this Peke won at the Pekingese Club of America competition in March of 1961. Sire: Jai Atom of Orchard Hill. Dam: Penny of Delaware. At that time she was just about two years and one month old, for she was born on February 10, 1959. The lady at left is one of the judges at the show, which was held at White Plains, New York.

First prize at the Hutchinson Kennel Club show, held in Hutchinson, Kansas, in April of 1961, is being presented to Champion Ku-Chi Tan Wo of Su-Yin. This Peke is a black and tan male weighing seven and a half pounds. He was sired by Champion Gordon's Wei Khi Ku, and his dam was Lah-Nei Mei-Loy of Su-Yin.

Champion Jiri of Elacre being presented with an award at a show held by the Lake Shore Kennel Club (Indiana).

So, if your bitch acts doglike and unhumanly, don't imagine that she is sick, but accept her actions as natural. You'd be amazed to know how many experienced breeders have brought bitches that behaved in this manner to veterinarians, because they thought the dogs were sick.

WORMING

In Chapter X you will learn about parasites. But here a warning: Puppies can be and often are born infested. The embryonic worms remain dormant until birth, when they start to grow, and by three weeks of age the pups may be anemic from loss of blood to hookworms, or so poisoned from roundworm toxins, that they succumb.

There is no harm done to three-week-old puppies by deworming them if it is done properly. I deworm all of mine then, and again eleven or twelve days later, and have reduced puppy mortality a great deal in this way. In Chapter X the safe doses are given. But if your pup is anemic and weak from worms, no dose is entirely safe. Don't blame the drug or the method then, but blame yourself for permitting the ravages of worms to weaken your pups. If you find the pups prostrate after deworming give them heat and it may revive them. Starvation is extremely necessary, because tetrachlorethylene is soluble in fat, and since bitches' milk is half fat, unless rigid starvation has preceded the drug, you can kill pups with it. But no method I know is so efficient or harmless when properly used.

WEANING

Weaning is a crucial time in all puppies' lives, and it is a good time to commence weighing your pups to determine whether their growth is satisfactory. By all means start to wean them, and at the same time start to spare their mother, as soon as you can get your pups to eat. By using the right foods, this can be as early as 15 or 16 days.

A black Pekingese mother nursing her pups. Start to wean pups as soon as they are able to eat. Photo by Louise Van der Meid.

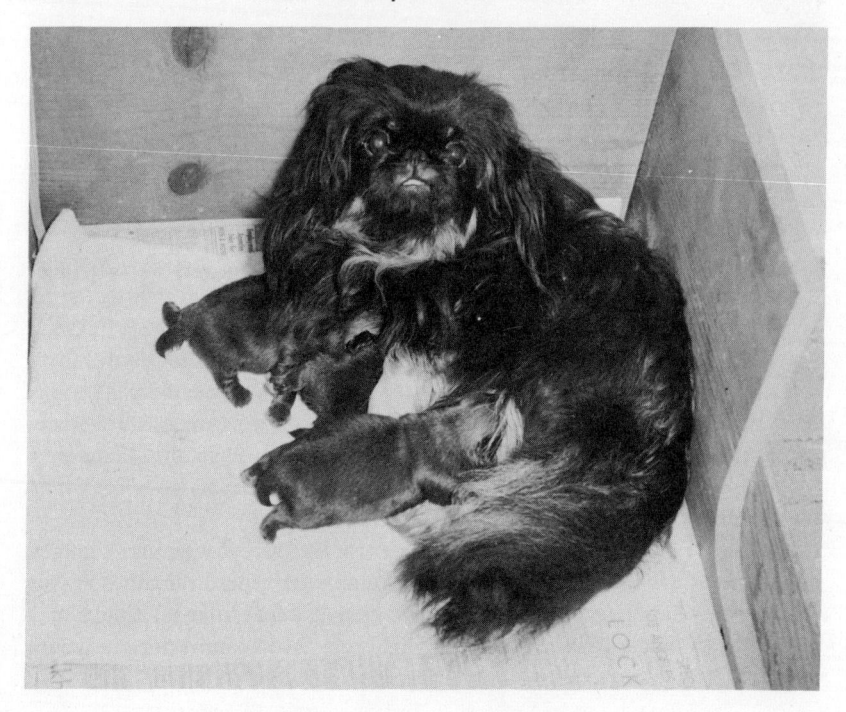

Experience has shown that puppies do best on rich milk, to which foods containing good-quality protein and some minerals are added. If no Jersey milk is available, add some coffee cream to evaporated milk. And whatever you do, try to modify cows' milk toward bitches' milk, and not toward human milk. Almost all of the older books gave us formulae for simulated human milk, whereas bitches' milk is the very reverse. This table shows the difference:

The Difference in Composition in Bitch, Cow and Human Milk

	Bitch	*Cow*	*Human*
Water	77.0	86.3	87.3
Protein	7.3	3.5	1.3
Sugar	3.7	4.7	7.5
Fat	11.0	4.0	3.5

Instead of adding dextrose (glucose) and lime water, we must add more fat and more proteins, and subtract sugar. Dextrose is sugar, as is lactose, which is milk sugar. Puppies have been raised on such improper diets, but not nearly so well as on one such as this:

Lactogen ....2 oz. by volume
Heavy Cream (30 per cent butter fat)................2 oz. by volume
Water ....4 oz. by volume

If you make such a mixture, the sugar in the lactogen will be a little higher than the ideal, but I have raised hundreds of pups on it, and so have others. Now don't spoil it, when the pups are old enough to eat solid food, by adding baby cereals to it. Remember that babies require seventeen years to grow, whereas puppies have explosive growth, your pup will be grown in seven months. There are excellent puppy meals to be had, designed for rapid puppy growth and containing all the necessary minerals and vitamins, besides the complete proteins and fats which the explosive growth of puppies requires. For those selling puppies, such a good puppy food is a Godsend, because a small supply may be given or sold with each puppy, which foresight upon your part prevents digestive upsets. You will find that many buyers return puppies to you because of loose stools, which are due only to change of diet. It is well to have the buyer continue on the food your puppies have been eating. If that can be arranged, one source of worry will have been banished.

Some puppy sellers give with each puppy a stupid yet elaborate set of feeding instructions embodying the feeding of a great variety of foods, and causing a lot of trouble in preparation. These lists are entirely unnecessary, and simply show the buyer that you are a generation behind the times in your knowledge of dog feeding. Science has demonstrated that all this fuss is absurd, and that a high-grade meal food, plus fat and milk for the young pup, will do a better job, and that variety is not necessary.

Five Roh Kai pups showing the ideal flat nose and the overnose wrinkle. All of these dogs became champions.

HERNIA

As the puppy grows, you may note a small lump over the umbilicus or navel. A high percentage of pups fail to heal across completely, and the bulge you feel is a hernia. In such a slight deformity there is no danger unless the opening through the abdomen is sufficiently large to permit a loop of intestine to work out into the sac you feel. If it is small, the sac will eventually harden into a lump which never harms the dog and is not noticeable. If the orifice is large enough to allow the intestine to work through, have your veterinarian repair it before a strangulation occurs.

TEETH

At very close to fourteen weeks of age the two upper middle incisors will loosen and be pushed out by a new pair. Then the teeth will gradually all fall out and be replaced. If, at this crucial time, the puppy has any sickness which disturbs his metabolism, the enamel will not be deposited on the teeth. If they are partway in, you will eventually find a ring around the teeth. If the sickness occurred earlier, only the tips of the teeth may be pitted and discolored. It used to be thought that only "distemper" caused such disfigurement, but today we know better; many ailments can cause it.

Champion Bettina's Kow Kow, owned by Bettina Belmont Ward, has captured (up to April, 1961) 31 Group firsts and 10 Best In Show awards. This Peke was bred by Miss I. M. de Pledge. Sire: Ch. Caversham Ku Ku of Yam. Dam: Ch. Caversham Black Queen of Orchardhouse.

In Chapter IX we shall consider vaccinations against various diseases, so we need not go into the problem here.

The kennel clubs insist upon litter registrations before the individual puppies of the litter may be registered. Since this process requires several weeks, it is well to send in the application, properly filled out, and have the litter registration in your hands by the time the puppies are old enough to sell. You can thus be ready to give each buyer a completed individual registration application with the litter. This foresight, too, saves headaches.

It is highly important to sell your pups at as early an age as possible, be-

Ch. Bey Li Shaman, owned by Bettina Belmont Ward, made his championship at the age of eight months. He was bred by Mrs. W. A. Bailey. Sire: Bey Li Kish Mi Kuku. Dam: Bey Li Kuku Kween. He has been shown only once as a special, when he went Best In Show at the Pekingese Specialty at White Plains, N. Y.

cause you will get no more for them once they are out of the cute puppy stage than you will when they are seven weeks old, and often less. So advertising should be planned well in advance to appear at the proper time. Newspaper ads seldom bring the buyers willing to pay what those who read the national magazines will pay. In the former case you will answer many phone calls from those wanting $5.00 pups; in the latter, there will be voluminous correspondence from those who want to know the ancestry back to Adam.

Have some photos of the parents and litter if possible. This will save hours of writing.

VIII
Care of the New Pekingese

So you've purchased your Pekingese and have brought him home for the folks to admire! If you have a choice, the best time to bring a puppy home is in the morning so he can have all day to accustom himself to his new surroundings before bedtime. Do please consider *him* first and let him accustom himself to his new surroundings slowly and at his own pace. There will be plenty of time later on to show him to your friends. Too many people accompanied by too much noise and confusion merely complicate matters.

If you are wise, you will have prepared a special place for your Pekingese that he can call his own.

After transporting your Peke on a journey, you should offer the dog a drink of water when you reach your destination. Photo by Louise Van der Meid.

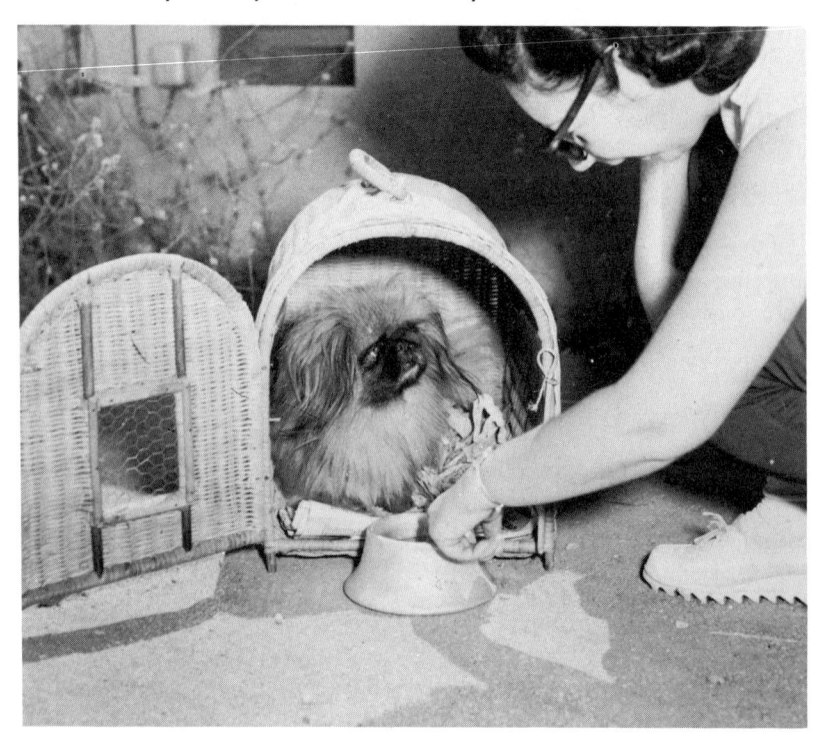

A combination basket-cage such as this is a good carrier for transporting your Peke, for either a long trip or a short one. Photo by Louise Van der Meid.

NEW QUARTERS

Immediately acquaint the pup with his spot or the place where he can feel at home. Such a place may be a pen in the kitchen or bathroom where you will perhaps confine him when you are away or until he is trustworthy. There he should have a little bed even though it is a blanket and paper box with one side cut out for easy entrance. It should be large enough so that he can stretch out in comfort yet small enough to make him feel cosy. At least he will feel it is his and will probably retire to it until he takes over the entire house. Even if he is later to share your own bed, which every pet Pekingese should do, his own bed will be good for daytime naps and give him a place where he can relax and keep from underfoot at busy times.

At all times he should have access to a large deep dish of cool water. Water in deep dishes stays fresh longer, and please don't forget to change it at least twice daily in cold weather and more often in the summer when you can kindly add an occasional ice cube. It is important that his water dish always be kept immaculate. Give him time to settle down and familiarize himself with his new environment before offering him any food. Remember when you are upset from travel and excitement your own appetite is often temporarily impaired, so why should your new Peke be different?

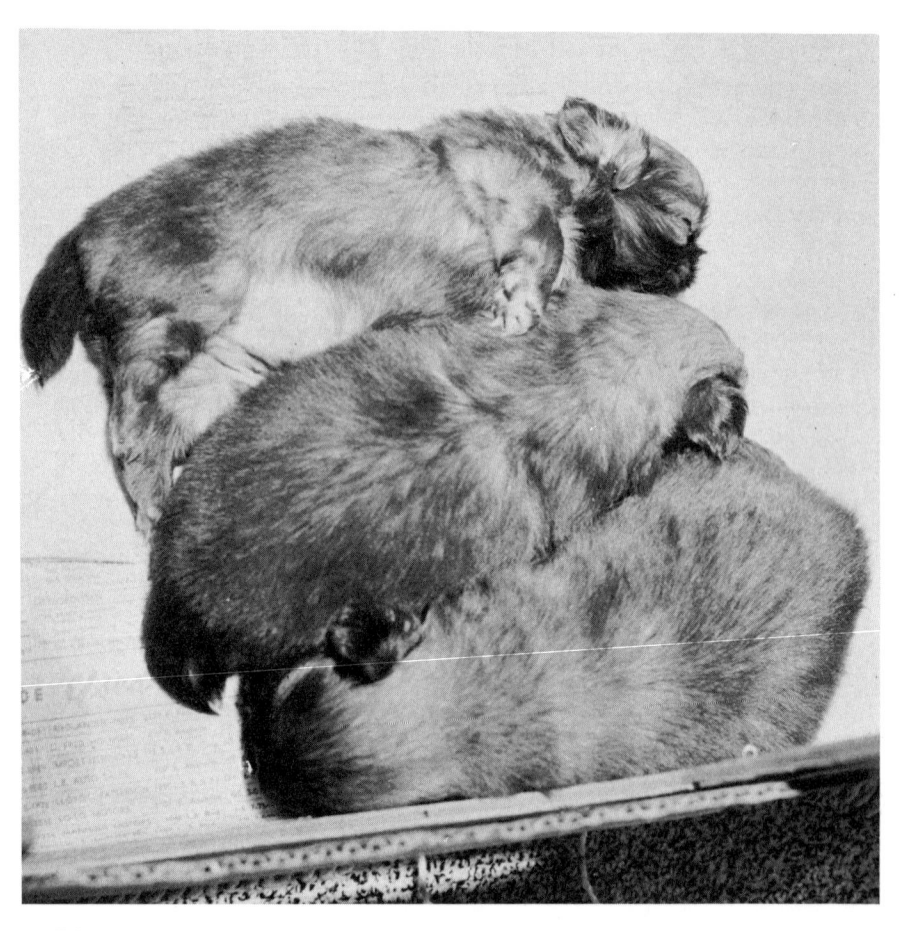

Pekingese puppies cuddle against one another to keep warm. Although young Pekes like warmth, adults do not take kindly to too much heat. Photo by Louise Van der Meid.

If your puppy is young, he may cry when left alone the first night. All he wants is companionship. If you take him to bed with you, he will be perfectly content. He is just lonely for his littermates. An alarm clock wrapped in a blanket and a hot water bottle for warmth placed in his bed may comfort him considerably. Young pups like companionship and to be warm although adult Pekingese cannot stand too much heat. The Pekingese is said to be the sturdiest of all the toy dogs—he needs no coat in winter, has legs strong enough to permit jumping from chair or sofa without danger of a broken bone, and in fact can stand almost anything but hot sun in hot weather.

FEEDING

It is to be hoped you were given a feeding schedule by his breeder so that the food can at least seem familiar amidst the strange environment. Such a schedule giving the exact diet to which the dog is accustomed in the kennel is often furnished with temporary supplies for the first meals so that the change in diet will be as slight as possible in the beginning. After a week or two in the new home, the new owner can slowly change the diet to fit his own needs and preferences. It is good to remember that *all dietary changes* and even at all ages should be accomplished *slowly*.

For example, when changing from one brand of kibble to another, it is best started by putting about one-quarter new brand with three-quarters old, and after a few days add more of the new brand making the mixture about half and half. After a few days of half and half, increase the mixture to three-quarters of the new brand with one-quarter of the old until finally the new brand alone is being fed. It is also well to keep in mind that food should be served to dogs neither too hot nor too cold—*never directly from the refrigerator*. Food should be lukewarm or at room temperature in order to avoid intestinal upset. Pekingese dislike their food being sloppy in any way and are exceptionally selective regarding it.

This little Pekingese puppy is being trained to eat solid food. All changes in your Peke's diet should be accomplished gradually. Photo by Louise Van der Meid.

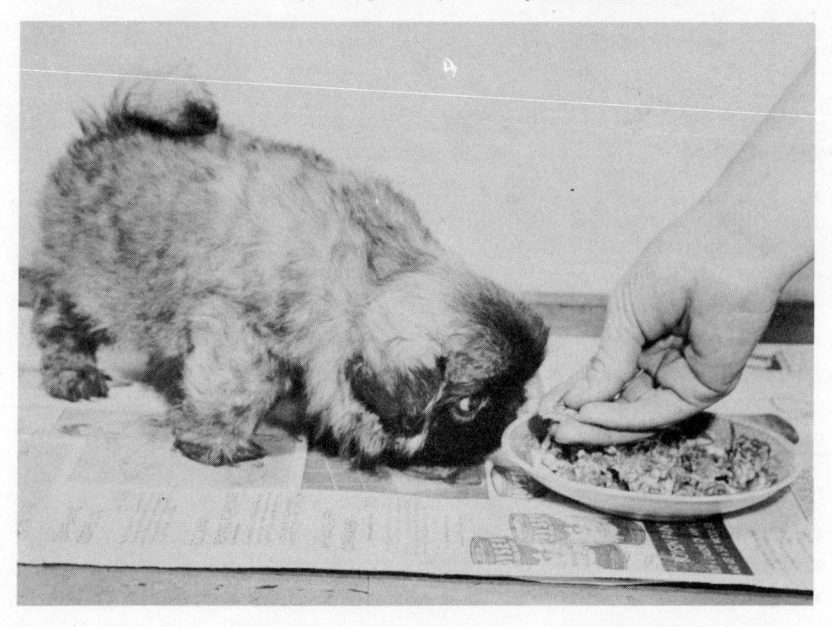

This little fellow is getting an auxiliary feeding from a baby bottle. Peke puppies occasionally need supplementary feedings. Photo by Louise Van der Meid.

Puppy schedule. The following feeding schedule is given to Roh Kai puppies from weaning until six (to sometimes eight) months of age:

8 A.M. Milk ($\frac{1}{2}$ Pet milk, $\frac{1}{2}$ hot water, little honey) with puppy meal
Noon Raw hamburg with warmed strained baby vegetable
4 P.M. Eggnog (milk, honey, and yolk only of raw egg)
8 P.M. Raw hamburg mixed with puppy meal previously moistened with vegetable soup or stock and left to stand. Optional for flavor, mix in cooked strained baby meat.

Milk is left all night with very young puppies.
Daily: Feed into mouth of each dog by dropper: $\frac{1}{4}$ teaspoon *liquid* Pervinal and $\frac{1}{4}$ teaspoon Rex wheat germ oil.
1 Diostate D pill, which they eat like candy.

Pet milk is used in the kennel because it means no change of milk for the puppy when he is sold to a new home. Also, it is easier to keep fresh in quantity at the kennel. Milk kept in the refrigerator is mixed with hot water so that the complete mixture is lukewarm when served.

Adult schedule. The following schedule is for all dogs over six months of age:

    Morning   Milkbone biscuit (for small dogs)
                      Milk is offered to those dogs that enjoy it, but the majority of adults refuse it.
    Noon   Hard boiled egg yolk (only yolk) lightly salted

This Pekingese puppy is being weighed to check his growth rate. Photo by Louise Van der Meid.

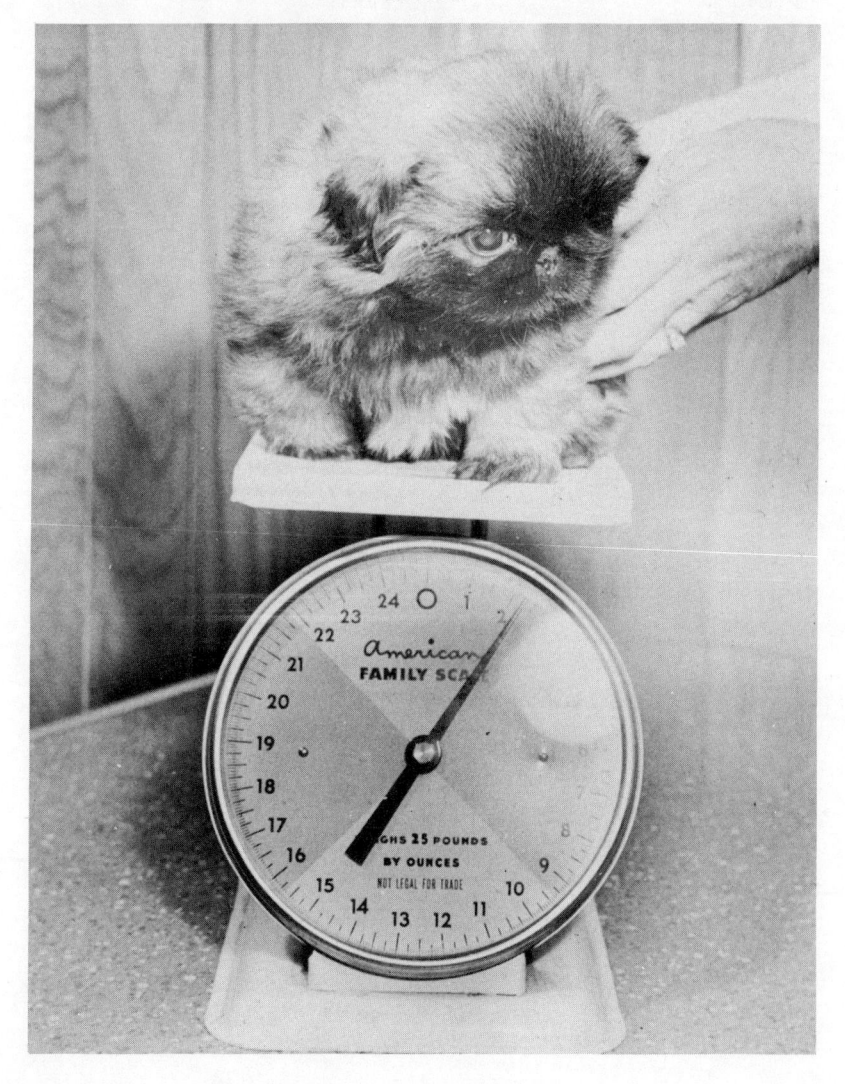

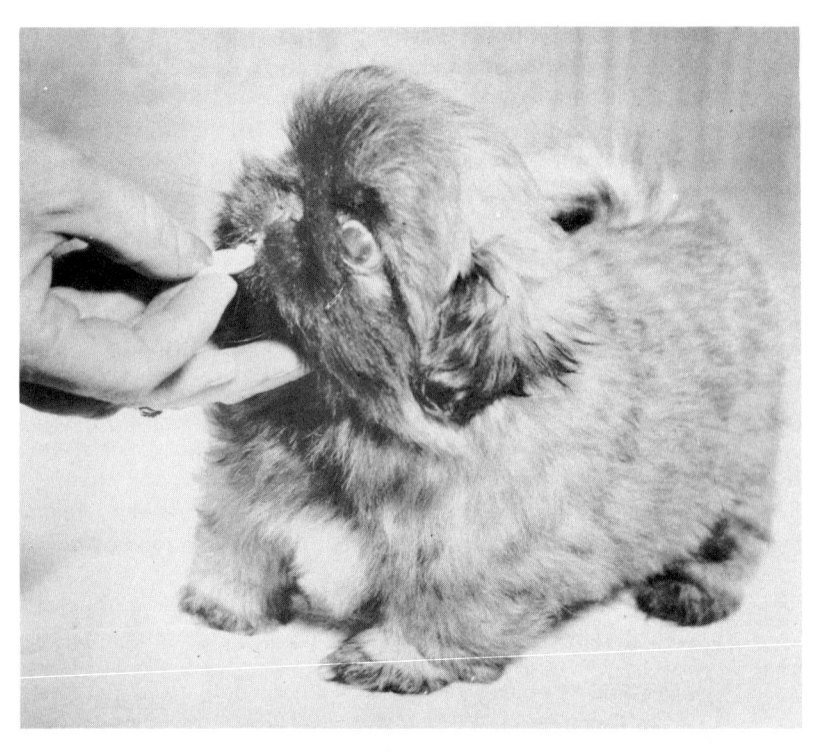

In feeding pills to your pet, care must be taken to see to it that the dog's mouth is not injured in the process. Rough handling in this regard might lead to difficulty in other areas of dog care. Photo by Louise Van der Meid.

Night   Chunked beef cooked in vegetable soup mixed with raw suet and kibble that has been previously moistened with vegetable soup in which meat was cooked and left to stand at least an hour. Include any vegetables from the soup. Several times each week in place of beef, feed heart, kidney, or liver with cooked rice (Minute Rice) and the kibble previously moistened with the stock.

Additional Milkbone biscuits can be given adult dogs in the afternoon and at bedtime if this feeding does not interfere with regular meals and if their weight permits. Puppies may also have a Milkbone biscuit at night if it doesn't interfere with their evening meal. It is an excellent toothbrush and aids teething.

Vitamins. Adult dogs should also receive daily doses of one-quarter teaspoon liquid Pervinal and one-quarter teaspoon Rex wheat germ oil. These doses should be given with a dropper directly into the mouth—not included with the food. Pekingese are so discriminating in their taste that they do not eat as much food when a vitamin-mineral supplement is mixed into it. They eat much better if given their vitamins early in the morning at the end of the day opposite to their largest meal. As valuable as such vitamin supplements may be to show dogs, there is nothing so good for a Pekingese as good food and in particular red meat. If the vitamins are mixed in the food, the dog who eats the most receives the most vitamins and he probably needs them far less than the one who does not eat well and gets less food and, therefore, less vitamins. By giving the vitamins directly to each dog you ensure that each dog gets his proper share. There are a great many vitamin supplements which are probably adequate, but at Roh Kai we have used with great success Pervinal in the *liquid form.*

Pekingese should have a regular change of diet every day or two in order to whet their appetite and thus maintain food consumption at a maximum.

Your puppy should be provided with his own bed. Often, when a puppy is first introduced into a new home, he is lonely and starts to cry. In such a case, it might be best to take him into your bed. Photo by Louise Van der Meid.

Now after all the above advice so carefully given to the owners of a new puppy, it is not uncommon for a Pekingese to refuse to eat one single item on his feeding schedule. He has come into a new home and this little oriental aristocrat has decided he might as well hold out for the delicious roast the smell of which is emanating from the kitchen of the new palace which he plans to rule—and believe it or not, he will usually get it. One lady related that she regularly cooks three suppers for her Pekingese every night—he usually refuses the first, tastes the second as an accommodation, and eats the third! To say this dog is a spoiled tyrant is to put it mildly; yet he is a most charming, sweet, lovable, and adored companion to his devoted mistress. This is of course a rare circumstance and exaggerates the point that even though a Peke has been accustomed to a definite diet, he may not eat well in his new home and may hold out especially for good or tempting tidbits—usually liver or chicken (*never* the chicken or fowl *bones* which splinter but the *meat only*). Once you start this catering on the food subject, the chances are you may have to continue it, so *beware of spoiling your Peke's eating habits.*

House pets have been raised and kept in good health and condition on a diet of yolk of egg at noon and table scraps of almost entirely meat at night, eating Milkbone biscuits morning, noon, and night, which they enjoy so much and in such great quantity that kibble does not seem to be needed. Pekes may thrive very nicely on an all meat diet, although it can be expensive. Discussion with nearly every Pekingese breeder will reveal that some members of every kennel are excellent eaters while others are quite particular about their food and require special coaxing, attention, and in some extreme cases even hand feeding to maintain in proper show weight and condition.

Never feed Pekes bones once they have acquired permanent teeth. This is especially true if you have more than one Peke. Bones ruin their digestion and disposition alike. A large beef bone that does not splinter may be given to teething puppies, but beware of quarrels arising from an over possessive puppy. Biscuits seem to do the teething job adequately for most Roh Kai pups.

PAPERS AND REQUISITE INFORMATION

When you purchase your puppy, you should receive from the breeder the American Kennel Club registration paper, his pedigree (both of which may be sent along shortly after purchase), and the dates and type of vaccination the dog has had whether serum or vaccine. The vaccination information should be *in writing*—not just verbal. All dogs over three months of age should be inoculated with distemper and hepatitis vaccines, preferably of the longer lasting type. If your dog has only had serum from his breeder, he is only protected from these dreaded diseases for approximately ten days once his

The first six Sing Lee Peke champions. From left to right: Champion Chu Chi Sing Lee, Champion Wee Tu Sing Lee, Champion Wong Sing Lee, Champion Starlett Sing Lee, Champion Yung Wong Sing Lee, and Champion Stars Tan Gee of Ramsey.

mother's protection has run out. Unless it is discovered otherwise from a seriological study of the mother, many puppies cannot be vaccinated to protect properly with the longer acting vaccines until after three months of age. So until your dog is inoculated with vaccine and for about two weeks after, great care should be exercised in permitting strangers to handle him or any contacts with adult dogs going to shows, etc., since puppies are most susceptible to these dread diseases. (In many states you may need to give him a rabies shot in order to obtain a dog license, but if possible postponement is advisable until he is nearer his first birthday.) If your pup has only had serum inoculation it is important to know the date it was injected so that you can take him to your own veterinarian for continued protection.

A two-month old Peke puppy poses on his pillow. An aristocrat to the core, the Peke is truly a creature of comfort. Photo by Louise Van der Meid.

CARE

Toys. A source of great enjoyment both to the dog and his owner are toys. For the Pekingese they should be small and a little soft with an ear or tail that he can grasp easily in his tiny mouth. The rubber toys with the large squeakers or whistles are preferable as the Pekes don't get them out so easily as the small whistles and, therefore, are not so likely to swallow them. Toys made of rubber should be *examined frequently* and discarded when rubber starts to peel, because even a small piece of rubber can cause intestinal upset. Pekes love balls especially, and the small size used for playing jax or those that come with a rubber band attached (always be sure to remove the rubber band) are of ideal size and inexpensive. Pekes never tire of chasing these little balls and carrying them about. They have been known to develop a game of their own playing with them. Leather toys are also loved by them if they are not too hard and if they can find a small enough part to grasp with their little mouths. Often the first toy given a young Roh Kai puppy is an old nylon stocking knotted up. This they seem to adore.

You will discover if you have many toys for your Peke, he will be much like a child with a lot of playthings, tiring of them quickly. This can be avoided by leaving with him only one or two different toys every day. Then they will seem new and important to him.

Regular inspection of all toys to make sure that any with sharp edges are discarded is important.

Daily care. Each and every day you should look carefully at your Peke's eyes. With a piece of cotton moistened with boric acid solution or plain water gently wipe off eyelid margins, training the hairs away from the eyes. Working along the lids, move any foreign particles in the eye to the inner corner where they can be wiped away with the wet cotton. DO NOT TOUCH THE EYE ITSELF. The wrinkle should be washed and *dried very carefully* each day to avoid any soreness. This drying of the wrinkle is even more important in hot weather. In event there is any inclination to soreness, use either Neo-Sporin ointment (just a tiny bit inserted with the little finger into the wrinkle),

Daily care includes treatment of the face and ears with a piece of cotton moistened in water or a boric acid solution.

boric acid powder, or Fuller's earth. The latter two, although considerably less expensive, are not so efficient as the ointment and they make the nose white. Skirt and extremities should of course be cleaned daily to avoid odor.

Soiled skirts are easiest to clean before they dry by letting water from the faucet or a spray float soil away. Dry by towel or dryer, and when slightly damp, sprinkle talcum liberally on the hair, let dry for a while, massage in, then brush off. This procedure completely restores cleanliness as well as keeps your Peke sweet smelling. If stools are regularly a bit soft, include some extra rice in the diet.

At least twice weekly you should groom your Peke as described in Chapter XIV.

Children love Pekes and the Pekes, in turn, respond to and return the love and attention lavished on them. Here a little girl carefully grooms her pet with a brush. Before being allowed to handle the Pekingese, however, a child should be instructed in the fundamentals of good dog care. Photo by Louise Van der Meid.

Pert partners: this little miss has dolled up in her Oriental costume to display her pet with pardonable pride. Photo by Louise Van der Meid.

Cold weather. A Pekingese that is in good health never needs a sweater or blanket in the cold weather, because he is well protected by nature with his beautiful luxurious coat. However, he should be carefully and completely dried to the skin in wet weather. Snow, which a Peke adores, may form balls (if there is much of it) under the forelegs and in the groin. Such balls can be easily removed by dipping a wide-toothed metal comb in hot water and gently teasing them off before they melt and chill the dog. A good hand dryer is

The Pekingese should be allowed outdoors, but he must be protected from the hot sun. This girl is prepared to put her dog into the shade should he become too warm. Photo by Louise Van der Meid.

also very useful. When the Peke is partially dry, sift a little talcum powder into his coat near the skin, work it in with your fingers, and then brush it out. This will help to dry him thoroughly as well as remove any doggy odor caused by dampness. It is a good idea to keep a "thirsty" towel handy near the door so that your Peke can be dried off immediately when he comes indoors.

No dog should be permitted to be in a draft, and none should be left to lie around outdoors in inclement weather.

Hot weather care. In hot weather your Pekingese should be kept as cool as possible for he really cannot stand the hot sun or excessive heat. Indoors is perhaps the best place during hot weather. Certainly your Peke should be permitted outdoors but *only* in a *shaded* area. Keep in mind that the sun shifts, and the shaded spot in the morning may be sunny by noon. A Peke should have access to clean cool water at *all times* in an immaculate dish. He will enjoy an ice cube in his water and one to lick occasionally when the weather is especially warm. Exercise in hot weather should be confined to the early morning and sundown, when it is cooler. If you have an air-conditioned room, please let your Peke share that room in the summer.

Protection from pests. Although protection from fleas, ticks, and lice is important the year round, it is most important in the hot weather. The easiest procedure is to *act* as if your dog has fleas and use a good spray or dip on him the year round, thus *preventing* fleas *before they arrive*. It is so much easier to prevent fleas, and it is far less worry for you and less agony for the dog. Such vermin bring with them to your dogs worms, skin disorders, and sometimes even disease. There are a number of good commercial powders, sprays, and dips, the best of which your veterinarian will probably recommend. During the winter months, an application every four to six weeks is adequate if your dog has no infestation and if you live in the part of the country where there is a constant frost. But from April until the frost in November (Sep-

Going for a walk, this Peke puppy really has his work cut out for him, for his legs don't cover much ground.

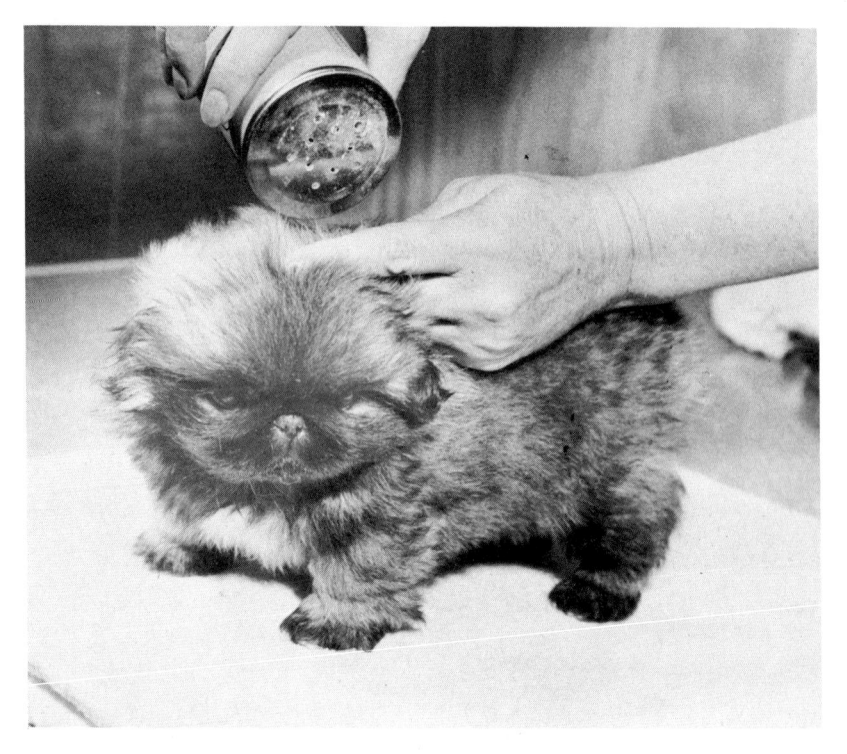

The judicious use of flea powders and sprays is a necessary part of the over-all care of your Pekingese. Photo by Louise Van der Meid.

tember, October, and until heavy frost in November are the worst months) your dog should have some flea protection every ten days to two weeks.

Dips are very easy to use because one need only submerge the dog to wet him completely to the skin and then permit him to "drip dry." A dryer may be used, but a towel may wipe the preparation off. It should be remembered that such dips are washed off by rain, dew, or any other type of contact with water. In fact, when you wash a skirt of a dipped dog, you have created an Achilles' heel!

When using such powders, sprays, or dips, completely encircle the dog around his neck to prevent fleas from rushing into his ears or wrinkle, then cover his head and ears. Work straight down the center of his back to his tail, then work on either side, and do the tail. Then turn the dog on his back and spray thoroughly underneath from the neck downward—particularly under the fore legs, the groin, and the pads of his feet.

Some dogs are allergic to individual preparations, particularly powders, that tend to be somewhat drying during hot weather. You will need to experi-

David and Goliath: this Peke puppy and his Great Dane friend hit it off remarkably well.

Located in a shady corner of the yard, this playpen is a good romping area for the Pekes it houses. Photo by Louise Van der Meid.

Carrying cages must make a provision for a locking device. Notice the transverse locking bar, which is doubly secured. Photo by Louise Van der Meid.

ment to find out which preparation is the best for your particular Peke. The current favorite dip used for the past three years at Roh Kai has been Tritox. It seems to be especially kind to coats and gives adequate protection.

It is easy to sponge a dip on your dog as a good *preventive* procedure, provided you know the dog does not already have fleas. If an actual cure is necessary, you must completely submerge your dog for best results.

Exercise. A Pekingese should never be permitted to run loose, because he becomes the easy prey of large dogs who may play too roughly. No Peke should be allowed out unless on a leash with a responsible individual or in a fenced-in area. Because of their size and build, they do not require excessive exercise, and it does not become burdensome to keep them fit. Watch when you leave your Peke outdoors in a tremendous yard or in an average size run; he will take only a moderate amount of exercise and then perch himself on something high for a rest. It is always better to curtail exercise than to endanger the life and limb of your Peke.

Teeth. The Peke's teeth should be checked regularly and be scaled by a veterinarian when indicated. The baby teeth should be entirely shed so that the adult teeth will come in straight and correct. Once in a very great while, baby teeth need to be removed, but usually a large bone given to a pup to gnaw at during the teething period will help prevent the need for this. Hard biscuits are helpful in keeping teeth clean because they act as a toothbrush. Pet Pekes of the author used to have their teeth cleaned semi-weekly with a cotton moistened with mouthwash, but they disliked it very much. When one Peke resented it so much that she popped an eye (which immediately went back into place by pulling the lids over the eye), it was decided then and there to forego this item of care. The cleaning of teeth is now left to the veterinarian.

Nails. Examine the paws of your Pekingese and cut nails when they grow too long. Long nails may cause sore feet and interfere with proper gait. Some owners prefer to use the claw-type nail cutter purchased from the pet

The owner of a Pekingese should learn to cut the dog's toenails. Be careful not to clip into the vein!

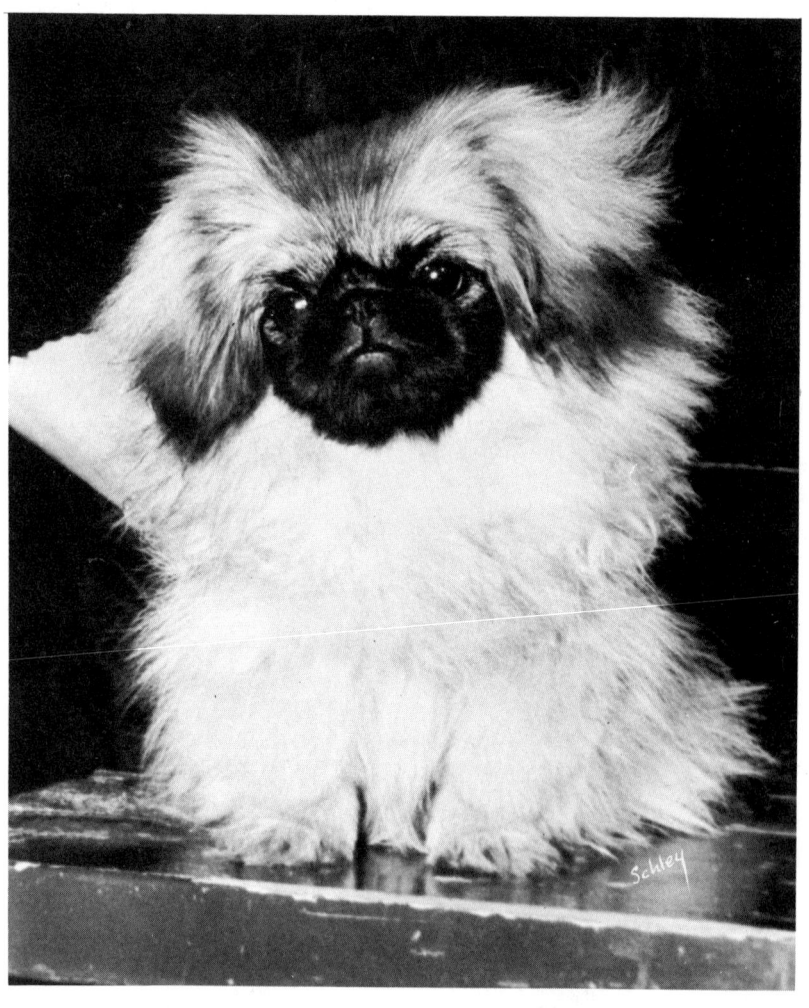

A puppy bitch sired by Ch. Pierrot's Jai Me. Dam: Ch. Mar-Pat Tiko's Wei Tei Cup.

shops. If nails are light in color, you can see where blood vessels end and avoid them. Dark nails present a greater problem and should be cut in small increments to avoid pain and bleeding. A moistened styptic pencil held at the site of bleeding for a full minute or two will usually stop the bleeding caused by too close a cut.

Dogs kept indoors on rugs and exercised on grass outside tend to have excess fur on the pads of their feet and nails that need frequent manicuring.

Do not hesitate to trim fur from under foot pads; it will cut down on the mud and dirt carried into the house. On show dogs try to leave some toe fringes as recommended by the Standard. Dogs exercised on cement rarely need their nails trimmed; the cement wears down the toe fringes and the fur on the pads of the feet as well as the nails.

Pet owners should learn to take proper care of their dog's feet. To take your dog to a vet to have nails trimmed is like asking your doctor to give you a manicure—it is a bit degrading.

Watch your Peke. If you see your Peke sliding or scooting his rear along the floor, check to be sure his skirt is clean. If his skirt is clean, the chances are his *anal glands* need expressing. These small glands on either side of the rectal vent need emptying at various times from monthly to semi-annually depending on the individual dog. When filled, they can cause extreme discomfort for the Peke. This service is best performed by the veterinarian.

Always check your Peke's *ears* to be sure there is no odor or dark discharge. Any irritation of the ears will cause loss of the delicate fringes. In the past some breeders recommended a pinch of boric acid powder dropped into the ear once each week as a preventive measure. However, some veterinarians feel any foreign matter even though antiseptic can set up an irritation. For this reason it is recommended that ears not be medicated unless the need is definitely indicated. A Pekingese's ears should be checked constantly.

The Peke's ears should be checked for odor or discharge, but medication should be attempted only when definitely needed. Photo by Louise Van der Meid.

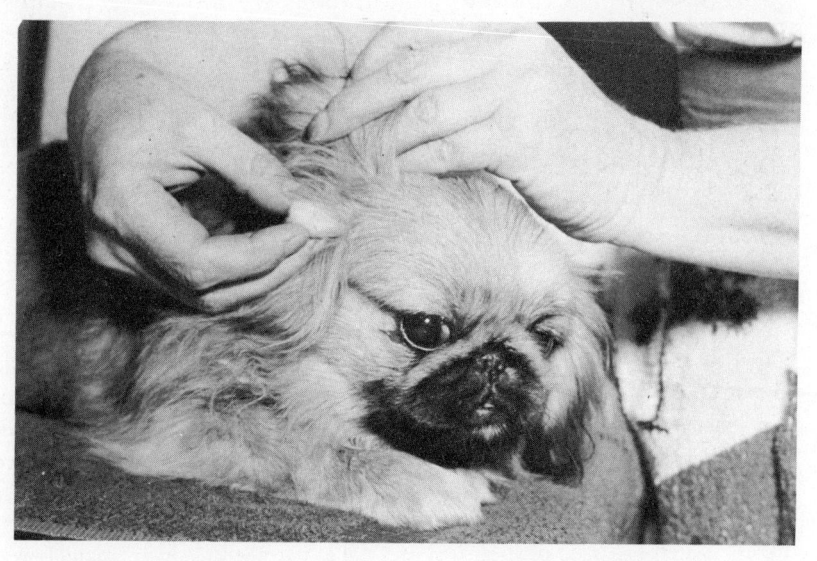

Stools should also be watched by the new owner; they are often indicative of the health of the dog. It is important for a new owner to realize when his dog is ill. This is discussed in detail in Chapter X.

TRAINING OF A TYRANT

House manners. Your young Pekingese should be confined to one room until he shows indication of reliable habits. The best procedure is to train your dog to use newspaper first. You may find him almost automatically papertrained if he has been kept from puppyhood on newspaper in the kennel from which he came. The amount of paper should be slowly cut down in area. When Pekes trained in this way get older, they tend to hunt for newspaper for elimination purposes.

When training a young Peke, always keep some newspaper *near* at hand and do not have the pad of papers entirely clean; keep one soiled piece with the fresh pad so that the puppy will get the scent. Slowly the number and areas covered by the paper pads can be diminished. As your male grows old enough or if purchased at an age when he likes to raise his leg, turn up the edge of the paper. Do not let a very young and inexperienced puppy run

When your Peke has relieved himself in the proper place, pet and praise him for his good performance. Photo by Louise Van der Meid.

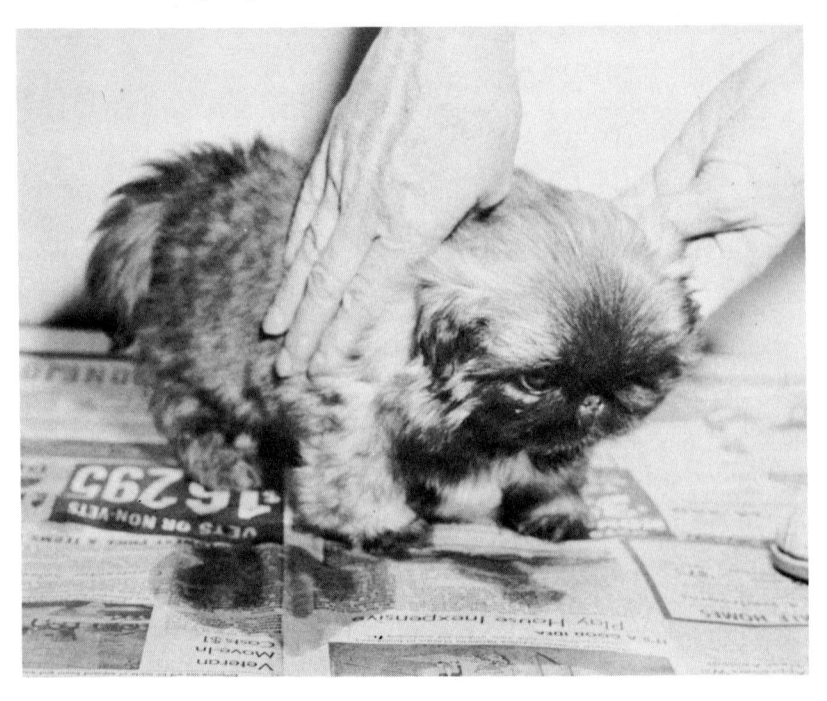

This Peke is being trained not to bring bones into the house. Photo by Louise Van der Meid.

through the house on his short little legs and expect him to always get the great distance (for him) to the door before an "accident". Older dogs can of course hold longer before eliminations. Be patient with your young Peke and permit him the freedom of the house slowly, after you have seen that he has relieved himself and is not likely to do so again in a hurry. Try to *prevent* an accident for such *positive training* is so much easier than trying to break a bad habit once it is formed. Reward him with praise and love when he has done his job in the correct place. Once a Peke has chosen a particular spot, it is indeed difficult to get him to change it. Remember you are training a born tyrant.

When training for outdoors, the dog should be taken on *frequent* excursions regularly timed *under supervision*. When he has done his duty outside, he should be praised and loved just as he was when he did such "duty" on newspaper indoors.

Scold *immediately* when an error is made—Pekes have short memories and unless you catch them almost in the act the scolding is wasted; then place the

It is easy to teach a Peke to stand on his hind legs, because this ability comes to him naturally. Photo by Louise Van der Meid.

dog on the paper and pet and love him. He will soon associate love and affection with the newspaper and a scolding with the carpet.

Patience, understanding, and perseverance are necessary to train a Pekingese. When he finally understands your requirements, he will try hard to please you in order to earn your love, affection, and praise. Most Pekes are very clean by nature, and once a bit of effort is expended with your dog, he will remain immaculate in habit throughout his lifetime. So a little effort in this direction when your Peke first enters your household will prove worthwhile, with average luck, for a very long time.

Some people are a bit particular about their furniture. If you are and if your Peke is not to be allowed the full use of every item in your house, it is well that you acquaint him with this fact while he is still very young and new to your home. Common sense in training is more important with this breed than with some others, for each Peke has a certain stubbornness of character. Once he has decided for himself that he wants to do something, it is indeed difficult to change his mind. For this reason, new owners are urged to give a Peke his freedom slowly and to try to help him form good habits when he is young—habits that will not have to be changed later. When older, some Pekes will just not accept a scolding, and *all training must consist of reward and association with something pleasant.*

It is important to accustom your Peke to letting you groom and handle all parts of him, such as opening his mouth, examining him in various ways, and under the tail. If you start when he is young and continue such examina-

Your Peke should be trained to stay away from the dinner table, or he might become a source of annoyance during mealtime. Photo by Louise Van der Meid.

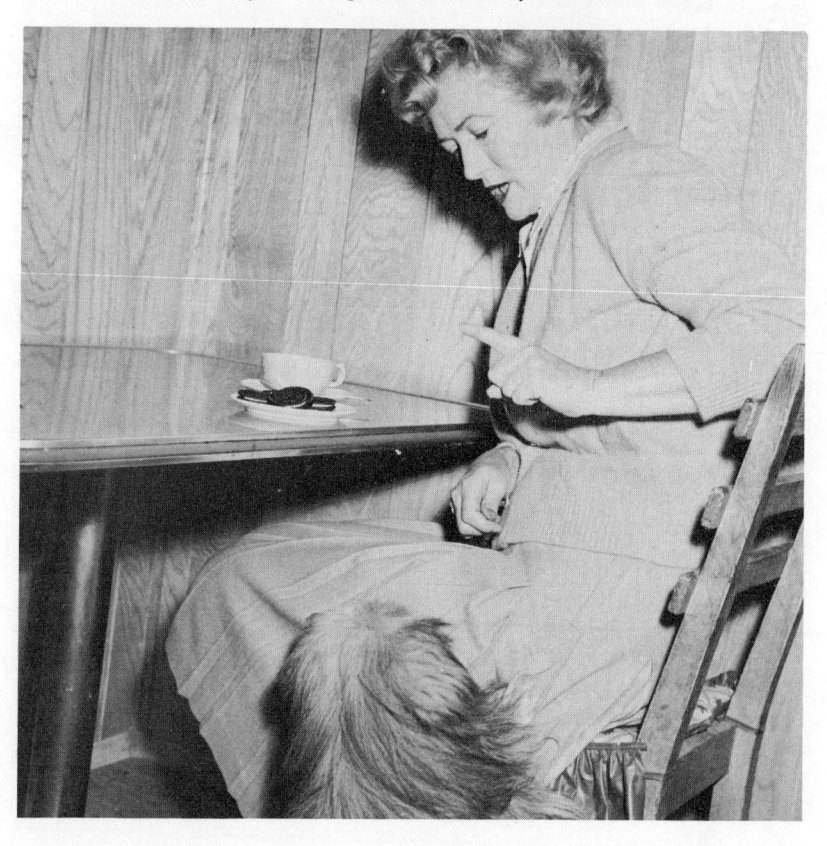

125

If you don't want your Peke to have the run of the house, teach him to stay off the furniture. Photo by Louise Van der Meid.

tions regularly, he will accept them as a matter of course. If you give in to his displeasure in such matters, his desire for privacy will tend to progress steadily as he grows older, and in event of illness, necessary medications and ministrations can become a great problem.

Lead training. Every Peke should be trained to walk on a lead. This should be done at a fairly early age—three or four months is not too young to begin such training. Place a soft collar around his neck, such as a nylon show lead, and let him wander to suit his own taste. As he becomes accustomed to it, hold one end of the lead and go along with him where he wants to go. The next step is to get him to *want* to go where you are going. This may come naturally to him, loving you devotedly as he will. However, you may need to coax him with a bit of liver or tidbit until he learns that the lead is not unpleasant so long as he follows you nicely at your side. Sometimes he will follow you on the street or among strangers better than in more familiar surroundings. Training periods should always be of very short duration and end on a favorable note so that he will remember only the pleasantness of the excursion. Collars (never a harness for the Pekingese) should be rounded rather than flat so as not to cut into the coat and should be as lightweight as possible.

Every Peke should know his name. Whenever you pick up your dog and caress him call him by name. Let him associate the sound of his name with affection and pleasantness, and you will soon find him running to you for this affection when he hears it. In spite of the fact that other dogs are successfully trained to come when called by attaching a long lead to them and pulling them to you when called, Pekes aren't naturally subservient and some will not accept graciously any such indignity. However, because they have such

Start to train your Peke to a lead while he is still young. Photo by Louise Van der Meid.

At first a Pekingese pup will rebel at being held on a leash, but promises of reward and affection will soon teach him that it is not at all an unpleasant experience for him. Photo by Louise Van der Meid.

great love in their tiny hearts, they will often almost leap into your arms for affection when called. Always make it a point to praise and display affection when they do heed your call, and soon you will have little difficulty.

One need never teach a Pekingese to stand on his hind legs or sit up and beg, for these are things he does without any instruction whatever—it just comes naturally to the breed. Several Pekingese in the author's kennel will sit for long periods of time with their front paws in the air with no apparent effort or discomfort. Never teach Pekes to "speak." One house pet so trained proved most annoying by barking, or "speaking," for food throughout dinner. This annoyance was overcome by putting him in a child's highchair so he could view the dinner table, be on a level with the family, and enjoy an occasional snack to his great delight. This, too, proved a great error, for when he passed away, nobody in the family could enjoy dinner for some time. Pekingese enjoy being made to feel like "little people," which indeed they become in your household if given the opportunity.

Obedience training. Many are surprised to find that Pekingese do very well in obedience training. Roh Kai Slo Shan was shipped to Spokane, Washington, after having won 9 points (3 major shows under different judges), and his owner, Miss Marvel Runkel, has trained him to a C.D. and C.D.X. degree. Miss Runkel first noticed the trainability of Slo Shan when he started to bring her bedroom slippers to her upon her arrival home from her work as a nurse. She also noticed that he seemed to understand much of what was spoken to him and found that it was very easy to train him to the obedience exercises. Pekingese are intelligent, and their desire to please those they love makes them obedient without becoming subservient. However, intelligence differs within the breed as it does among humans, and there is probably a tendency for such intelligence to be inherited among certain strains or families within a strain. There are now a number of Pekes with C.D. degrees, and there would probably be many more if there was as much *need* for the obedience training of them as there is for the larger and harder to manage breeds. A Pekingese is such an aristocrat, he is usually a lady or gentleman automatically.

This puppy has now been trained to the leash and enjoys going for a walk with his owner. Photo by Louise Van der Meid.

IX
Diseases

Not according to their importance, but according to their time of appearance, will the diseases of puppies be considered. Nor have we the space to consider them in detail. Books specializing in diseases and treatments can be consulted. The veterinarian is available to you for the specialized help he is prepared to give. Here we consider the important features of the different diseases so that the breeder may recognize the fact that illness is present and needs treatment.

At the outset, let us confess that we know very little about the many diseases of puppies. One of the reasons for this sad state of affairs has been the reluctance of those interested in dogs to think that any disease which causes sniffling and runny noses in puppies could be anything other than distemper. But today, with the real distemper recognized, and the realization that it is becoming less prevalent in some communities, it behooves us all to try to learn what these diseases of puppies really are.

The celebrated Ch. Coronation Kai Jin, bred and owned by Mrs. Marilyn Allen. Sire: International Champion Dah-Lyn Kai Jin of Caversham. Dam: Wee Chee of Dah-Lyn.

Ch. Tarka of Drakehurst, a Pekingese Club Gold Medalist, one of the most famous of all English Pekes. His owner, Mrs. L. R. Drake, turned down an offer of almost $5,000 for this beautiful animal.

NAVEL INFECTION

When puppies lie on soft beds this trouble practically never occurs, but when they are left on rough boards or on concrete, it is likely to kill every one of a litter. Infection enters through the unhealed navel and spreads rapidly under the skin. There is a moisture and an obnoxious odor about the spot. The bitch cannot lick it clean because her tongue cannot reach as far as the infection has penetrated, and the infection continues to spread in an ever expanding circle. Constant wearing on a rough surface may also penetrate the abdomen until the organs are exposed. The puppy becomes dehydrated and feels stiff to the touch. He may cry more than he should and usually dies in about three days.

Once you observe such a spot in one puppy, you must look over every puppy and see that those surfaces which are worn, even though the infection has not penetrated the skin, are medicated. You should also see that there is plenty of bedding under the puppies in order that no further irritation can occur. Finally, the infected pup or pups must be treated surgically. No halfway measures seem to cure the malady.

The veterinarian will lift the skin and scrape every bit of infected tissue away. He will then apply disinfectant medicine to destroy any bacteria and if

Swedish and Norwegian Champion Chiquita of Mathena, bred by Mrs. Y. Hoynck van Papendrecht, owned by Mrs. Doy Hamrin.

the opening is not too wide, may suture it so that the skin can heal together. It is the lowest layer of skin which has the power of joining with the same on the other side when the two are approximated. If the infection has eaten away this layer, as it often does, there is no point in suturing the dead skin. It is better to trim the skin away up to the point where it is alive and let it grow together from the sides.

Taking care of a puppy with a navel infection sounds easier than it is. You get precious little cooperation from the puppy who seems compelled to lie on this point of his belly. It is essential that the raw spot be well medicated with some healing lotion. If you cannot obtain the services of a veterinarian, try one of the household remedies such as Unguentine, sulfa salves or mild healing powders, etc.

Cover the spot with a bandage. The results of treatment are better in females than in males; because the bandage on males comes so close to the penis that it is constantly wet, and the mother licks it more than she does a bandage on a female. I have had best results from putting adhesive tape around the puppy's body over the bandage. Then each day I cut the tape lengthwise across the belly, change the bandage, and put more tape to hold it in place. This obviates hairs pulling out of the pup's back in removing the tape daily. While the area is healing, the puppy is growing. It may take ten days to heal, by which time the pup is twice as large as he was when treatment was begun. All of the tape around his body will not need to be changed during that time; only that which applied daily over the dressing.

Canadian Champion Puff's Halo of Wangza, owned by Mrs. B. Howlett, bred by Mrs. C. de P. Doniphan. Sire: Ch. Sannell Hai Puff of Acol, Imp. Dam: Starlin of Wangza.

EYE INFECTIONS

In the very young puppy, sometimes one not over seven days old, a bulge will occasionally be seen under the eyelids, possibly on both eyes. If you make a small opening at the nose end of the slit between the lids with a not-too-sharp instrument, a few drops of pus will run out. This infection has always been due to a *Staphylococcus* type of organism in every affected puppy which I have treated.

Anyone can see that such a swelling is developing. If it is not removed, the pus may damage the eyes, so that it will remain blue and opaque for several weeks, or may destroy the eye completely. Fortunately the eye starts to open at the tenth day and there are not many days in which the pus can do damage. Nevertheless, it should be removed at the very earliest sign.

Several of the mild germ killers which are not harmful to eyes may be used to clear up this infection, but you must be judicious in selection of the proper

Ch. El-Acre K'Buse, bred and owned by Vivian H. Longacre.

Champion Ir-Ma-Mi Ten-Mits Ilov Ting, owned and bred by Irene Marie Miles.

one because when it is applied, it will be in a pocket with the eyeball. It does not wash out, as ophthalmic medicants do when they irritate. Let your veterinarian direct the treatment. He may use 5% sulfathaladine or sulfathiazole ophthalmic ointments. Both have proved 100% effective in my experience, as has penicillin.

An eye disorder of puppies, though not an infection, is the inverted third eyelid (nictitating membrane) which causes the protrusion of a gland in the nasal side of the eye, giving the appearance of a little oblong tumor. Sometimes the membrane can be tipped back and the gland tucked in so it will stay. A little zinc sulphate ophthalmic ointment may be sufficiently astringent to shrink it so it will stay. If this measure is unsuccessful, snipping off the gland usually ends the trouble.

Tri. Int. Champion Ditto Shanling Sing Lee, the only Tri Int. Champion in the West during his lifetime. Owner: Mrs. Ruschhaupt. Sire: Int. Ch. Shanling Sing Lee.

Most puppy eye disorders are caused by scratches of other puppies whose sharp little nails are almost like needles. Trim your puppies' nails regularly from the time they are three weeks old. Many otherwise lovely puppies are ruined by eye scratches.

DIARRHEA IN VERY YOUNG PUPPIES

Sometimes as early as the third day, you will hear your little puppies crying pitifully and find them pushed away from their mother who practically disowns them. There is a foul acrid odor about them. The area around the anus, hind legs, and tail is wet. The mother has refused to lick this, and the puppies have become increasingly repulsive to her. They soon are dehydrated, lose their appetites, grow stiff and die, usually emitting pitiful cries almost to the end. Indeed the process is quite pathetic, and you may become frantic wondering what you can do, while watching your puppies dropping away one at a time.

This symptom of diarrhea is probably characteristic of several diseases. So little work has been done on it we know very little about it. It used to be said that acid milk was the cause, but acid milk is normal, as we have seen.

One terrific siege in my kennels killed about three-fourths of all the puppies born one spring. Bacteriologists undertook a study, located the responsible bacterium and found it in all the organs and blood. It has never before been described as accomplishing such devastating work.

Another different bacterium caused a similar attack recently and many puppies were lost in three litters. When a fourth came, three puppies began to show the wetness around the tail and gave off the characteristic odor. They died, and might be said to be checks against the next two puppies which showed it. A mixture of sulfathaladine powder and apple pectin has been most successful in my kennels. It is hardly likely that either sulfaguanadine or sulfathaladine will destroy organisms which have left the intestines and are in the blood and organs. It is necessary to have these drugs administered very soon after the trouble starts.

Another remedy which seems to help materially is giving acidophilus milk instead of mother's milk. When I used this method, two feedings of the acidophilus milk put a number of puppies on their feet, but those which were far enough gone to refuse food were not helped even when it was given via a stomach tube.

This is Ch. Sun't Yung Wong Sing Lee, sire of at least sixteen Champions. Breeder-Owner: Mrs. Ruschhaupt.

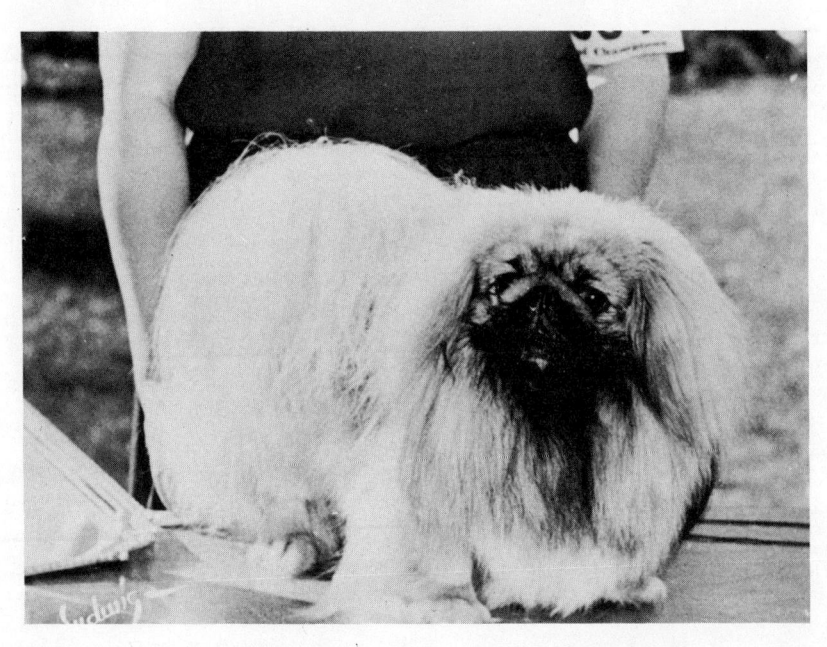

DIARRHEA IN OLDER PUPPIES

Diarrhea in older puppies can be caused by such a wide variety of things that we must admit a whole book could be written on this subject alone; this is not an exaggeration. Diarrhea is more often than not a result of disease, parasitic infection or laxative diet, but some bacteria which we shall consider can also produce the symptom. Carre distemper, heavy roundworm infestations, and skim milk or improper fiber in the diet are among the chief causes. All but the first are easily corrected.

We should try to eliminate every possible cause before we treat for diarrhea and we often have to learn the cause by the process of elimination. This takes time and puppies are often lost through the best of intentions. I often think, when I hear veterinarians criticized for not having at once hit upon the true cause of a diarrhea, of an experience I had with an outstanding doctor. The patient, a woman had a most unusual ailment and a consultation of eight of the foremost physicians in New York City had been called. Each of their diagnoses was written on a sheet of paper, which my friend gave me to observe while he was making his diagnosis. Every diagnosis was different! Remember that diarrhea has a multitude of causes, and don't condemn your veterinarian

Mrs. Alma L. Helm's puppy Ka-Nee's Jai Toi of Tsing Tau. The toe fringes are in evidence.

Mirabile Visu, owned by Mr. William H. Blair and bred by Mrs. W. A. Bailey. Sire: Ch. St. Aubrey Wi-Ja of Elsdon. Dam: Mirabel of Elsdon.

because he can't say within five minutes of seeing your puppy exactly what the trouble is. The competent doctor will explore all possibilities before starting treatment.

Bacteria of various types have been implicated in the diarrhea of puppies between one week and eight weeks of age. This is sometimes curable, and sometimes not. Whole litters are often wiped out when the wrong organism obtains a foothold.

In seven litters which came to my attention within one month, cultures of the stools showed large numbers of a *Salmonella*, a bacterium which produces hydrogen sulphide. This substance causes fits, pains, prostration, loss of appetite and together with the toxins elaborated by the organism, death. However, the period of sickness in the puppies is quite prolonged. The little fellows start lying around in their pens crying pitifully and day by day become weaker until they die. You may hope to see at least two or three recover, but it is generally expecting too much.

An often lethal type of diarrhea has recently been found to be caused by one of the *Shigella* class of bacteria. It has not as yet been named. It produces almost the same symptoms as coccidiosis does. No drug has been found to cure it, but palliatives materially help the puppy to live. Constipating foods and rich foods all help.

Jean Waring and four of her all-white Pekingese, photographed in the garden of her home in Surrey, England. Some of her pure white Pekes have been shown on television.

Champion Black Wing of Wanstrow, owned by Mrs. D. Wilson. Photo by C. M. Cooke.

Segregation is imperative. The puppies that seem well must be quickly taken away to uninfected places. The sick ones may be treated with any of the older remedies such as collodial, iodine, silver preparations, intestinal disinfectants and constipating foods, after a thorough initial physicking. None of the sulfas seems able to effect a cure, nor does penicillin. Streptomycin and auremigrain have now been tried with considerable success in cases of diarrhea in older pups.

Food poisoning organisms are frequently found affecting little puppies, after they have eaten spoiled food, such as garbage. One litter was brought to our hospital showing pains and prostration. The puppy was given hydrogen peroxide, and it promptly vomited canned green string beans.

POISONING

Poisoning is surprisingly rare in puppies, but you may know from experience that those energetic little animals will do crazy things if given the opportunity, lick spray material, eat paint, swallow soap, chew the top of an automobile battery, consume rat poison, roach poison, or an ant button. All these items, as many more, are poisonous and prompt treatment is necessary.

Symptoms. Pain, panting, trembling, vomiting and occasionally diarrhea are all symptoms of poisoning. The trouble is, of course, that they are

Champion Toydom Ts-Zee, owned by Mrs. A. C. Williams. Photo by C. M. Cooke.

symptoms of other ailments, too. You can usually make a definite diagnosis, though, by finding remains of the poisonous material or by knowing that your puppies had access to a source of poison.

Treatment. Call your veterinarian immediately. Be sure to let him know what poison the puppy ate if you know, before he leaves his office so that he may bring the proper antidotes. While he is coming, empty the puppy's stomach as quickly as possible. The best way to do this is to mix some peroxide of hydrogen, the drug usually called "peroxide", with an equal amount of water, and pour some down the puppy. Make him swallow it. A teaspoonful of the mixture will make a very small puppy vomit, while it may take 2 or 3 tablespoonfuls for a large puppy. He will vomit in about two minutes. Peroxide is an excellent antidote for phosphorus, which rat poison often contains. It is harmless, changing into water and oxygen when it fizzes.

If the puppy has eaten paint, as soon as his stomach is emptied and he stops vomiting, give a large pinch of Epsom salts, which is an antidote for lead poisoning and causes physicking as well. Leave further treatment up to the veterinarian.

PARASITIC DISEASES

With one exception, these have been considered in detail in the chapter on parasites. Because they produce disease symptoms, they are of great importance in themselves and must be treated in both mother and puppies (early in the life of the latter) and much hinges on this treatment. The only important parasitic disease which should be stressed now is *coccidiosis*. This is because coccidiosis usually occurs in puppies, at the earliest, when they start running around.

COCCIDIOSIS

There are three chief forms of the organism causing this disease in puppies and dogs, *Isospora begimina*, the smallest; *I. rivolta*, a middle-sized organism; and *I. felis*, which is the largest.

They seem to be harmful to puppies in the reverse order of their size, the smallest doing the greatest damage. *I. felis*, the cat form is found as often in dogs. The organisms or coccidia are so small they are almost in a class with bacteria. When they are passed out in stools in their infective form, they appear as you see them in the illustration. Sometimes the nucleus is doubled

Champion Hanya of Alderbourne. Miss Ashton Cross is the owner of this Peke.
Photo by C. M. Cooke.

because of the first stage in cell division. The puppy becomes infected by getting some of these organisms into his mouth. As soon as they are ingested, they begin to change their forms and go through a cycle of changes. At one stage they possess a boring form and are able to bore through into the cells lining the intestine. There they multiply in enormous quantities, doing damage directly proportional to their numbers. The infectious form of the organism is then spewed out into the intestines and passed out in the stool. Your veterinarian can look at a sample of stool with his microscope and diagnose the presence of coccidia without guesswork.

The symptoms of coccidiosis are almost the same as those most people think of as distemper. About the only difference is that puppies do not shun light as they do in Carre distemper. The eyes fill with pus, the nose discharges, the temperature often goes to 104, the stools are fluid.

Treatment. Probably more medicines have been reported to cure coccidiosis than any other known disease. The cure notices continue to be circulated, but so far the truth seems to be that no known drug has the least effect on the disease. It improves of its own accord. Any drug which could kill the infecting organism would probably kill the tissue in which the organism lives.

Champion Alderbourne China Doll of Kaytocli, owned by Miss Ashton Cross.
Photo by C. M. Cooke.

Champion Copplestone Phudie-Puff, owned by Mrs. Y. Bentinck. Photo by C. M. Cooke.

One drug tested was sulfaguanadine, and it proved, in safe doses, to be useless. In poultry, where heavy doses can be given, it has been shown to be effective though expensive, but such doses are harmful to puppies.

VIRUS DISEASES

We very likely have not scratched the surface in our knowledge of the virus infections to which dogs and puppies are heir. Time was, not so long ago, when everything that made a dog sick was called "distemper." Now, in some sections, true distemper has almost ceased to be a problem and is one of the rarest of diseases. In other sections it still kills thousands of dogs annually.

Often litters of puppies have been brought into my hospital with diarrhea. Bacterial examination by competent bacteriologists show no pathogenic or disease producing bateria and no parasite eggs. Some of the puppies die, and some live. Chances are that an unknown virus disease has done its work. The whole field of such diseases offers a wonderful opportunity for study, although we do know something about some viruses and how to control them.

CARRE DISTEMPER

What was once called distemper, before vaccination became prevalent is now called Carre distemper in honor of the man who discovered that it was

Miss Ashton Cross's Champion Goofus le Gisbie. Photo by C. M. Cooke.

a virus-caused disease. Carre was the first to start unscrambling all the diseases of the "distemper complex."

Symptoms. Carre distemper was thought, some years ago, to be a disease of weaned puppies only, since it was held that puppies obtained some maternal immunity. Recent research however, shows us that four-week-old puppies often contract the disease. It is a question how little puppies would obtain immunity, especially if their mother had never had the disease. So it is of particular concern in cynidiatrics.

Differentiating or diagnosing the diseases of mature dogs is a very simple matter compared with doing the same thing for puppies. There are so many puppy diseases, each producing similar symptoms, and causing early death, that the very best specialist may make mistakes, especially if he is given only one opportunity to observe the puppy. Then, too, the puppies may die so quickly after being infected with a disease that there is no time for lesions to develop. In such cases, even a post-mortem examination is of no avail. When one has a litter to observe, the situation is different.

In small puppies, Carre distemper causes great prostration about the seventh day after the initial infection. Then follow running noses, mucous-filled eyes, dry hacking cough, loss of appetite, fever of 103 or over and loose stools, becoming darker as the disease progresses. The eyes become very sensitive to light and the puppies will try to remain in a dark or dim place blinking and squinting, if forced into the light. The younger the puppies, the higher the mortality rate.

Breeds differ greatly in their resistance. Some will survive in better than a 50% proportion, while others, like Bloodhounds, will usually all die. Breeds vary in their symptoms also. The first observable symptoms of Carre distemper in Beagles are usually running fits. Cockers, as soon as the first rise in temperature occurs, seldom have fits. Poodles seldom have the fits either.

Treatment. If the disease breaks out in your litter of puppies, call the veterinarian at once. He will procure serum and inject every puppy with large amounts. Research has shown that the 10- and 15-cc doses which used to be given are generally useless in larger puppies. The longer the disease has progressed without treatment, the greater the amount of serum needed. Some large puppies need 100 cc. of serum to benefit. Laidlaw and Dunkin claimed better results with small doses, but our commercial serum, under practical

Mr. W. Hindley Taylor's Champion Mignonette of Kyratown. Photo by C. M. Cooke.

Bertha L. Worl stands behind her Bon Jai Sunny of Orchard Hill. Bred by Mrs. Richard S. Quigley from sire Champion Bonray Tony of Orchard Hill and dam Champion Jai Pansi of Orchard Hill, this Peke has a total of 11 points.

Champion Tong-Tuo of Pekeboro. Owner: Mrs. Jackson. Photo by C. M. Cooke.

field tests, has not shown enough value in small doses to warrant its use, in my estimation. Globulin, a component of serum, is coming to be used a great deal.

Once the disease has been aborted or prevented in your early infected puppies, you must not live in a fool's paradise. The protectiveness of the serum has not immunized your puppies for life. Laidlaw and Dunkin said that serum protected for 9 days. Therefore, after a large initial dose, it is quite necessary to administer small protective doses for many weeks. Then some time must elapse, during which protective substances furnished by the serum are lost before permanent immunization is practicable. Vaccine, if given too soon, is neutralized and little benefit is derived.

Prevention. We have been talking about treatment when distemper makes its dread appearance. Now, how can we prevent the disease?

There are at least 10 successful methods of immunization against Carre distemper. Some have more to recommend them than others. Some have distinct drawbacks. The most important factor to consider is the state of preservation of the biologics used. If they are fresh and have been kept at proper temperature, any of the ten methods listed below is satisfactory. The IF is a very large one.

Champion Ping-Yang of Coughton, owned by Lady Isabel Throckmorton. Photo by C. M. Cooke.

Laidlaw and Dunkin's original method was the use of a dose of fresh vaccine followed in a week by a dose of live virus. But procuring live virus today is a gamble. Other research has shown that the virus is not at all necessary; that if enough fresh vaccine is given, one dose, graded to the size of the dog, will immunize him for life, or at least for many years. It is doubtful if any better method has yet been devised. Vaccine is safe, fairly certain, produces no ill effects, and is inexpensive.

The newest method is the use of live virus grown on hens' eggs. This is dried by a freezing method in a vacuum and reconstituted before use. This kind of virus, but called vaccine, is easily obtainable in a live, effective form. And it is an excellent method of vaccination.

An expression which has come into vogue of late years is "puppy shots." This is a vague term usually referring to injections of serum. Possibly your veterinarian may favor them. I hope not, unless he is *sure* there is distemper in the neighborhood and flies are abundant. Flies spread the disease. If serum is given, then time must elapse for the effects to wear off before the puppy is in a condition to be vaccinated. Why should serum be given when vaccine could just as well be given starting permanent vaccination while the pup is, say, one month old? A week after such an inoculation the puppy is able to throw off the distemper virus. Even if he did contract it, he would have a very light case. Then later, if he has not been exposed and he is much larger, a full dose, graded to his size, can be given and he will be immunized for life.

The Green method has been much publicized and has considerable to recommend it. This method consists of injecting live virus collected from ferrets which have had the disease and attenuated or aged the virus. It is even claimed that the virus injected into dogs just starting with the disease will help bring about a cure. The Green method depends for its success partly on the fact that the virus is alive. If assurance can be given that it will be alive when injected, it should be a great boon because it can be used on puppies as well as grown dogs. If it is alive, it should cause the disease in a very mild form. If it is not alive, the dog owner does not know whether his dog has been successfully immunized or not.

Champion Toydale Jin-Jah, owned by Mrs. Bagshaw. Photo by C. M. Cooke.

METHODS OF SUCCESSFUL CARRE DISTEMPER IMMUNIZATION

1. Fresh vaccine alone, one dose, graded to the size of the puppy.
2. Vaccine, followed by live virus.
3. Vaccine, vaccine, and live virus.
4. Vaccine, followed by Green virus.
5. Serum and live virus, simultaneously given.
6. Serum and exposure to true Carre distemper.
7. Vaccine with dead complicating organisms.
8. Blood virus alone.
9. Vaccine followed by blood virus.
10. Green virus alone.

The author's preference is the first. The others are not given in the order of their value or of preference, but more or less in the order of their use as they have been developed.

Champion Calartha Wee Bo Bo of Ecila, owned by Mr. S. North. Photo by C. M. Cooke.

Champion Fee-Bee of Kyratown, owned by Mr. W. Hindley Taylor. Photo by C. M. Cooke.

INFECTIOUS HEPATITIS

This is the newest of the distemper complex diseases. It is caused by a virus which, in mature dogs, produces a mild disease. Every serious student of it has remarked that if a dog sick with hepatitis lives one day after the symptoms show up, he does not die of the disease. If he does die it is because of some other disease or a combination of diseases.

While this is true of mature dogs it is not so in the case of puppies which often die when they are in the early stages. Some die so soon that the disease has had no chance to leave any telltale marks.

Puppies which survive a few days show a thickened gall bladder, turn yellowish and if they survive often have the transparent front of the eyeball turn to a bluish color. Often only one eye is affected and in a few weeks this color changes back to normal.

Dogs which are sick can be helped by giving them glucose in such a form as corn syrup or powdered dextrose made into a thin syrup.

It seems advisable to have all puppies vaccinated against hepatitis while they are quite young. This, in the opinion of veterinarians of my acquaintance, will carry them long enough so that, if they should become infected later the disease wont amount to much and they will be immune for life.

Champion Kyratown Josephine of Wanstrow, owned by Mr. W. Hindley Taylor. Photo by C. M. Cooke.

There are vaccines now available which will immunize against three diseases at the same time.

PHARYNGO-LARYNGO-TRACHEITIS (P-L-T)

This is a relatively new disease, having been described in 1943 for the first time under the name of Housedog Disease. It often masquerades as Carre distemper, but the symptoms are sufficiently different to eliminate too much confusion.

The first symptom is a phlegmy cough as contrasted with the dry light cough of Carre distemper. The pup seems almost to be trying to raise something which is stuck in his throat. This cough can easily be confused with that exhibited when puppies are gagging up the larvae of round or hookworms, if they are heavily infested with worms. The temperature is low, staying between 102 and 103 and being predominantly 102.6 F. The stools become somewhat loose and the appetite diminishes, but to no such extent as in Carre's disease. The nose may run and the eyes fill somewhat, but neither of these symptoms are as pronounced as in the real distemper.

One of the really noticeable differences between Housedog Disease and Carre distemper is in the appetite. Once the throat phase of Housedog

Disease is over, if encephalitis ensues, the dogs eat normally right up to the approach of death. They do not do this when affected with Carre distemper.

The younger the puppy is, the more likely he is to develop encephalitis. In a series of dogs studied over a year, only 9% developed the brain symptoms, while in puppies under six months 36% developed them.

Pneumonia may follow the throat symptoms; and whether it does or not, the causative virus often invades the puppies' brains and causes encephalitis. This may take many forms although the most common are convulsions and twitches. The former may be no more than a slight frothing from the mouth, or it may be so violent that the puppy races about screaming and ends up in a tetanic convulsion which may last many minutes. These usually occur more and more frequently until the death of the pup. On the other hand, they may slacken and the puppy may appear to be recovering, only to start crying and slowly or suddenly to develop a twitch. The twitch may affect only one small muscle, a large muscle, or groups of muscles. Sedatives are indicated; your veterinarian will know best how to treat such a dog.

It is typically a disease of dogs kept indoors and so far seems to be confined almost entirely to the northeastern part of the United States.

Champion Yu Wei Lad of Kyratown, owned by Mr. W. Hindley Taylor.
Photo by C. M. Cooke.

INFLUENZA

Rare, except during outbreaks of severe influenza in human beings is this explosive disease. It sweeps through a kennel like Carre distemper. Puppies are prostrated with but little warning. They remain sick with fevers over 105F. for about 5 days and suddenly seem almost well again. Occasionally bacterial diseases follow. Pneumonia is a common one, but with protective drugs, you need not worry too much about that. Many cases in puppies and dogs were reported for two years when influenza ravaged humanity, but that type of influenza has not been seen since, to my knowledge.

A unique fact about the disease is that dogs having had it are not immune to Carre distemper, but dogs which have had distemper are immune to this influenza. This fact is another excellent reason for Carre distemper immunization.

BACTERIAL DISEASES

Leptospirosis. The principal form of this bacterial disease is called *Cavicola fever*. And here is a disease transmissible to human beings by dogs.

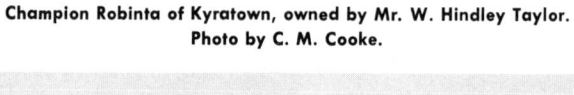

Champion Robinta of Kyratown, owned by Mr. W. Hindley Taylor.
Photo by C. M. Cooke.

Champion Berar of Ifield, owned by Mrs. R. Chandler. Photo by C. M. Cooke.

It is contracted by us from dogs' excreta. It is much more common than people generally realize. In dogs it sometimes is mild. In man its symptoms may seem like influenza. Proper diagnosis from blood tests can only be made after the disease has subsided. If a person has a sick dog which is recovering, and that person becomes sick, the dog's blood may be the best means of diagnosing the disease. Prompt treatment with tetracycline effects a cure.

Dogs usually contract it from urine of other dogs. They may drink from a puddle with urine in it. Or they may jump into water where a sick dog has previously been. A dog sick with Cavicola fever may become jaundiced and some die but most recover and may be left with damaged kidneys and hearts which materially shorten their lives.

This is seldom a disease of puppies but puppies may be vaccinated successfully against it. Every dog should be, in the opinion of most veterinarians and physicians.

Sick dogs can be helped greatly by tetracyclines your veterinarian can supply, after he has made a diagnosis.

Champion Yung Tony of Dah-Lyn, owned by Mrs. Evelyn Ortega.

Champion Chik's Ku Ku of Tien Hia, owned and bred by Mrs. Murray Brooks.

Champion Ifield Tong-Loo of Portmore, owned by Mrs. R. Chandler. Photo by C. M. Cooke.

DEFICIENCY DISEASES

These are all due to inadequate diets. While puppies are nursing, if they have no parasites, they will come through to the age of weaning with no apparent deficiencies. It is after weaning that trouble develops. True, the iron and some other salts will have become dangerously low if no foods rich in them have been fed, but even then most puppies will seem to be in excellent health at weaning.

It is difficult to devise a formula that will be deficient in any single vitamin or mineral, especially when natural foods are fed. Consequently deficiency diseases are not common.

A deficiency of several of the vitamins results in a loss of appetite, in weakness, or in death. Making a diagnosis of vitamin deficiency requires a very careful consideration of what has been fed the pup for several weeks. Vitamin deficiencies do not manifest themselves in a day. Some vitamins are stored and some are not, but most of them have to be deficient in a diet for several weeks before their absence is apparent.

Champion Pedmore Christopher, owned by Mrs. Shaw. Photo by C. M. Cooke.

It is impossible for either a layman or a veterinarian to look at a puppy that is very sick, won't eat and is getting ready to die and realize immediately that he hasn't been getting enough pantothenic acid. No veterinarian could, on the basis of one examination definitely ascribe a puppy's paralysis to a deficiency of biotin.

Vitamin A Deficiency. You have perhaps read that an eye disease, *xerophthalmia* is caused in puppies by a scarcity of Vitamin A. This is true, but don't jump to the conclusion that sore eyes in your puppy means that he needs cod-liver oil. Sore eyes can also be caused by infections and injuries. The kind that Vitamin A deficiency causes requires many days to show. It is an extreme symptom.

One result of a mild deficiency of Vitamin A is an upset in the cellular picture in the blood. The detection of this is a matter for specialists.

Vitamin A deficiency causes a loss of thrift; and, when the deficiency is serious, the affected puppy is rendered more liable to disease infection because the cells lining the nasal passages and other parts of the body fail to develop. Infertility, night blindness, deafness, loss of weight, stunted growth, incoordinated movements, unthrifty coat, and scaling skin may be seen in a dog deprived of the vitamin long enough.

Various estimates of the amount of Vitamin A needed by growing puppies show that the largest puppy needs about 7,500 units a day and smaller puppies much smaller amounts. We shall consider means of supplying it in the section on Vitamin D deficiency because the two so often go hand in hand. However, it cannot be repeated too often that if you are feeding a complete diet, you need not worry about any of the supplements mentioned here. They are needed only for puppies who have a demonstrated deficiency or are receiving an unnatural inadequate diet.

Vitamin D Deficiency. Vitamin D is a marrying agent which unites calcium and phosphorus into bone. The deficiency of it causes rickets (faulty bone development). The amount of Vitamin D which dogs need has been estimated at anywhere from five and a half units per pound for large dogs, up to 123 units. The reason for the differences is that some investigators used minimum amounts of calcium and phosphorus in the experimental diets, seeking to supply just the amount they thought the puppies needed. Other

Champion Wei Bella-Twee of Kyratown, owned by Mr. W. Hindley Taylor. Photo by C. M. Cooke.

investigators furnished more. When far too much of these two elements are provided, the picture changes. In the summer time, when enough calcium and phosphorus are provided in the diet, the puppy makes enough Vitamin D in his skin to provide for his needs. Some investigators feel however, that the very largest dogs need more than they can make, while others say it is doubtful. The studies were made in the dark.

Many of the best dog foods contain so much calcium and phosphorus that there is but little need for much Vitamin D to be added. Ground bone is one of the least expensive ingredients of dog food, so a considerable amount is generally used, providing abundant calcium and phosphorus. Besides, it supplies 24% protein. One of the leading brands of dog foods was found, upon analysis, to contain 6% calcium and 5% phosphorus, whereas some other foods used in studies contained only a fraction of each.

To insure enough Vitamin D in the diet you need to know the best sources of it. The sources of Vitamin D are generally rich in Vitamin A also, so let us consider them together.

Champion Punchinello of Ingford, owned by Mrs. L. Dubbin. Photo by C. M. Cooke.

Champion Ku Chik Ku of Loofoo, owned by Mrs. R. Jones. Photo by C. M. Cooke.

Fish liver oils are very rich in both Vitamins A and D. However, the oil part is toxic if fed in large amounts, and the concentrated oils such as percomorph oil are much better buys anyway. Percomorph oil sells today in small amounts for about 75c per 10 cc. which furnishes 750,000 units of A and 8,000 units of D. In larger amounts it is considerably cheaper. Compare this with the best cod liver oil costing about $1.25 per pint. The pint furnishes about 400,000 units of A and 40,000 units of D, making the unit cost much greater than that of the A and D in percomorph oil. In fact, percomorph oil is probably the best and cheapest form in which to buy these vitamins.

Vitamin D alone may be bought least expensively in the form of irradiated yeast. The best commercial grade furnishes 900 units per gram. There are four grams in a level teaspoonful. In a level teaspoonful of cod liver oil, which meets U.S. standards, there are 400 units of D. If your dog required, say, 100 units of D per pound and weighed seventy-five pounds, one gram of irradiated yeast would furnish him all he could use. For the average dog, a small pinch is enough. Irradiated ergosterol and other products in which Vitamin D is found generally are not as good buys as the above.

Champion Toydom Nanette of Glenjan, owned by Mrs. A. C. Williams.
Photo by C. M. Cooke.

Carotene is a favorite with some to supply Vitamin A. Each of its units splits into two units of the true vitamin in the animal's body, but even it is more expensive to use than percomorph oil.

When milk is supplied a puppy, especially in the summer time when cows are on grass, there is little need to worry about the Vitamin A supply.

Vitamin B Complex Deficiency. Lack of Vitamin B_1 (thiamin), B_2 (riboflavin) nicotinic acid, pantothenic acid, biotin, the filtrate factor W, and some others about which less is known, has been shown to be responsible for some symptoms of disease in puppies. There are three reasons for considering these vitamins as a group instead of separately:—they are usually found combined in nature; lack of only one of them is a rarity, and they are most effective in treatment when given as a group.

If your puppy, in the absence of any demonstrated disease, shows any of the following symptoms, his trouble may be ascribed to the lack of one or several of the B-complex vitamins. These symptoms are rather typical: digestive disorders, nervousness, irritability, redness and inflammation of the skin on the abdomen, insides of the legs, and the chest, loss of weight, ease of fatigue, staggering gait, paralysis and black tongue.

Some of these symptoms require a little amplification. The redness observed on the belly may come from many other things, especially external infection. Paralysis may also be due to other causes, but a lack of biotin is one of the causes when nutritional deficiency is to blame. Black tongue is a disease which does not turn the tongue black at all. Rather the tongue becomes inflamed and the mouth has a particularly obnoxious odor. After death the tongue may be so purple that it appears black.

Meat, organs, fish, egg yolk, yeast, whole grains and wheat germ are all rich in this group of essential vitamins. In the case of Vitamin B_1, fat in the diet exerts a very sparing effect. More B_1 should be fed when diets are low in fat, and less when they are richer.

Whether or not your puppies should be fed the complex depends upon the diet. If you are feeding a diet containing 5% wheat germ meal, 7% alfalfa, some yeast and some meat, there is no need for supplementation.

Heat destroys B_1 easily, and long exposure to heat is devastating to most of it. The canning process destroys a large percentage of vitamins; canners add much more vitamins than they expect the finished product to show, and

Champion Goofus Ravenswood Pixie Ku, owned by Mrs. R. Ogle. Photo by C. M. Cooke.

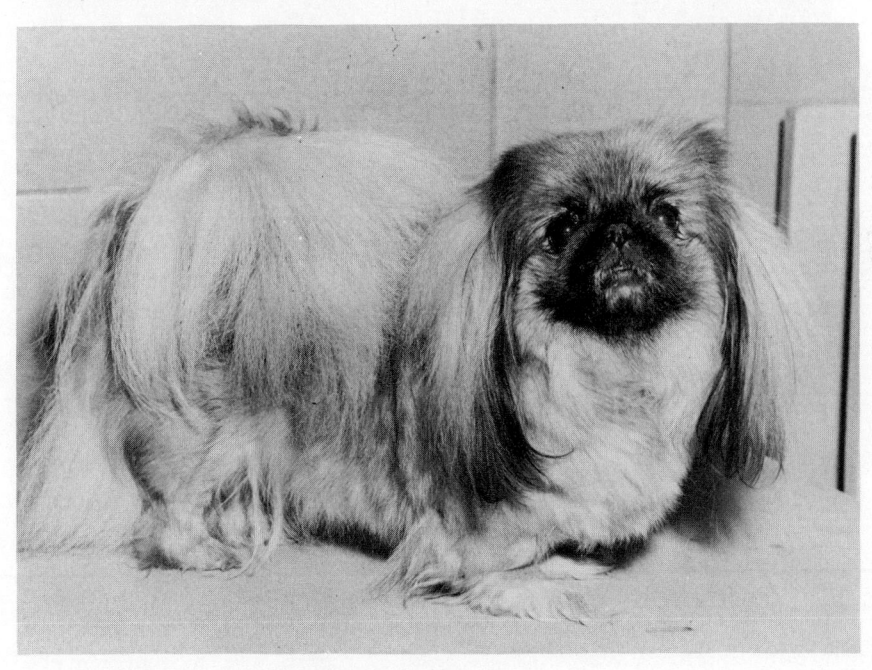

the conscientious ones see that the final unitage is sufficient. Baking biscuits at great heat and long exposure destroys most of several of the B-complex vitamins. For this reason you must add B-complex supplements if you feed the baked products as certain biscuits or kibbled biscuits.

The Animal Growth Factor. For many years scientists suspected that there was something in animal protein which produced growth. The factor, when discovered, was called by many names. Finally it was learned that the element, *Cobalt*, was the key to this growth factor. Today nutritional scientists have a chemical name for it while laymen call it the animal protein factor, vitamin B_{12} or the animal growth factor.

It is essential to growth. If cobalt is present in the diet even in minute amounts mature dogs seem to make their own by the work of bacteria. Dogs fed meat, fish and byproducts of them, even in dry form obtains plenty of B_{12}.

Other Vitamin Deficiencies. Although mature dogs manufacture their own Vitamin C, cases have been reported in which puppies seemed unable to do so and developed some of the symptoms of scurvy. Anemia, swelling of the jaw, and partial paralysis were reported by one investigator. Another found that his puppies were sensitive to pressure near the joints and wanted to lie

Champion Twee Too of Caversham, owned by Mrs. A. C. Williams. Photo by C. M. Cooke.

Champion Silverdjinn Splash, owned by Mrs. N. McFarlane. Photo by C. M. Cooke.

down most of the time, as if standing pained them. Supplying a little orange or lemon juice cured them.

We have already mentioned the need of puppies for Vitamins E and K, and how both may be supplied in alfalfa leaf meal or in the form of wheat germ meal of Kayquinone, giving very small amounts a day. However, there is no evidence that the puppies require either vitamin as they get older. Both may be omitted when the diets given dogs contain wheat germ and alfalfa.

Mineral Deficiencies (Calcium and Phosphorus). We have discussed Vitamin D as a marrying agent of the calcium and phosphorus in the diet. Investigators have come to the conclusion that, when these minerals are present in only the minimum amounts necessary the ratio of calcium to phosphorus should be 6:5 for best assimilation; that is, one fifth more calcium than phosphorus. However, we do not hear much about the efficiency ration when the diet contains far more of both than is needed. Consider the dogs that you know that lived to old age on diets consisting mostly of bones. Aside from the constipation they experience, they are not harmed by the superfluity of these minerals.

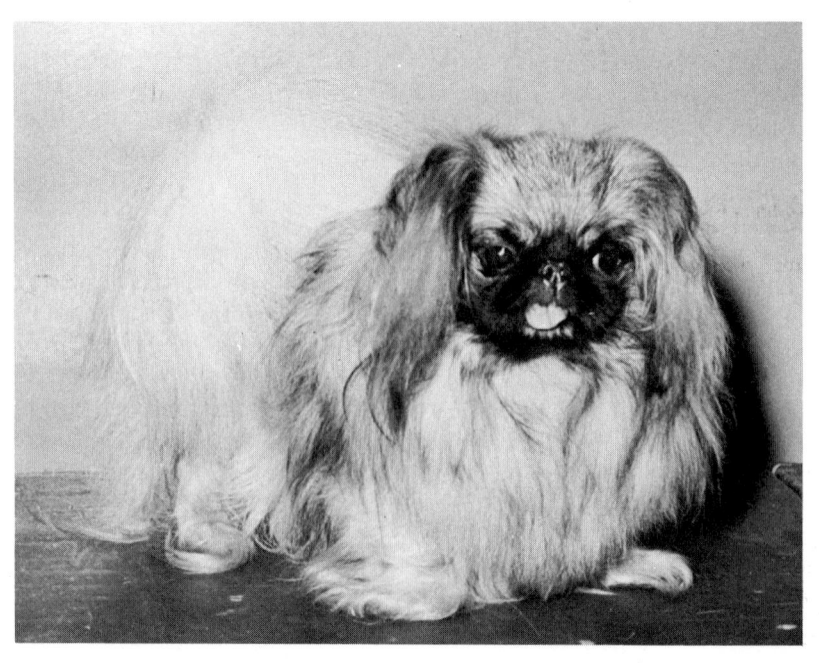

Champion Char-Ming Ku of Chantoi, owned by Miss E. A. Page. Photo by C. M. Cooke.

When manufacturers add bone meal to their formulas to help supply protein, they add more calcium and phosphorus than dogs can possibly use. Under such feeding regimes, rickets is almost unknown, even when small amounts of Vitamin D are added. On this basis, I suggest feeding more of these two minerals to your pups than they require. Apparently there is no harm and your worries about rickets are banished completely.

Iron. Iron is sometimes short in diets. When puppies are bled white by hookworms or are anemic from other causes, the addition of small amounts of ferrous iron does wonders in bringing them up to par. You may obtain it in the form that humans take and give it in proportion. Meat, either fresh or in the form of scraps, contains so much iron that if a diet is 10% meat scraps the puppies will have enough iron.

Other Minerals. Copper is necessary, but most foods have enough so that more need not be added in chemical form. Occasionally one sees a puppy respond to tiny amounts of magnesium, given as Epsom salts. On the whole, deficiencies of calcium, phosphorus and iron are far more prevalent than those of other metals.

Salt (Sodium and Chlorine). Manufacturers of dog and puppy foods usually see that their products contain 1% of salt. It is taken for granted that anyone preparing a diet for pups will flavor it by using a little salt. Milk contains very little, and you should provide salt in the food of the pup. Wild animals get much salt from the blood of their prey. If you do not feed blood to your puppies, you must see that they are fed sodium and chlorine in the form in which you eat it.

Iodine. Iodine is an essential mineral, but most diets have enough. If bitches are starved of iodine, their puppies may be born deformed (cretins); and no puppy can thrive if all iodine is withheld from his diet. However, providing iodine is a simple proposition when natural foods are fed. They will have more or less iodine depending on where they are grown. If you add iodized salt to the food your puppies will get all the iodine they need.

Perhaps some of you may consider this advice about salt and iodine superfluous, but it is amazing how many dog breeders act surprised when their veterinarians ask them if they ever put any salt in their dogs' diet. They just never think of it.

Intussusceptions. A condition not infrequently in puppies, but rarely in grown dogs is *intussusception*, a telescoping of the bowel.

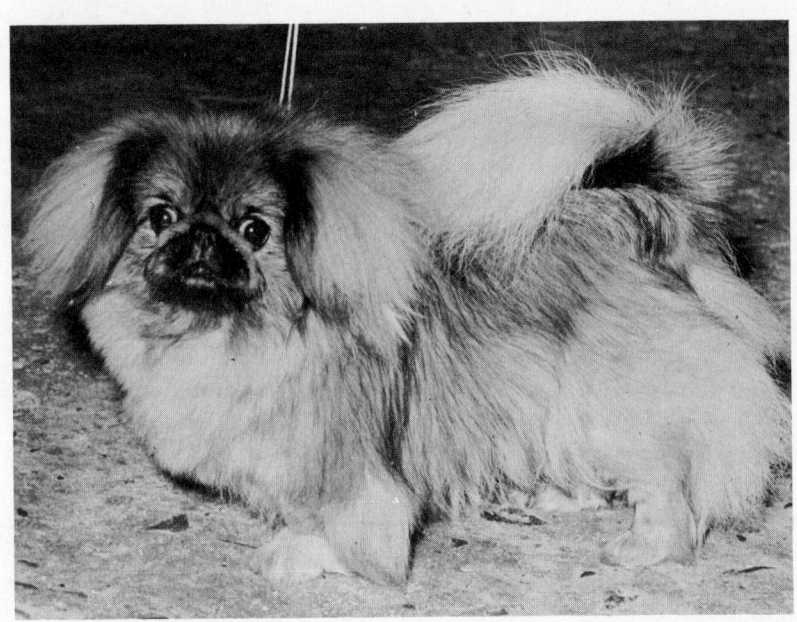

Champion Do Do of Shangte, owned by Mrs. E. P. Bull. Photo by C. M. Cooke.

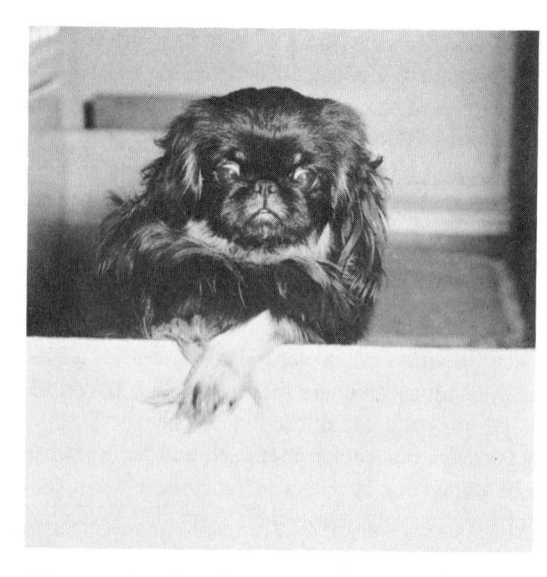

This Peke pup is being confined to the kitchen behind a small board. Photo by Louise Van der Meid.

Frequently, after deworming, when too drastic physics are administered, a portion of the intestine folds inward and is pushed downward by the movements of the intestines. Gradually the fold moves along until congestion becomes so intense that it can move no further. The inside fold becomes dead and decomposes in some degree. The blood supply becomes pinched off because of the swelling. The puppy invariably dies unless surgery is resorted to.

Diagnosis is quite a simple matter. The first symptoms are vomiting, scant passages of feces and loss of appetite. Puppies have been known to live for three weeks after intussusception but they become thinner and thinner. It is generally possible and easy to palpate the abdomen. The sausage-shaped lump may be felt clearly. There is often some pain, and occasionally puppies hold the abdominal walls so tense that the thumb and fingers cannot feel through the stomach walls. Persistence will reward the examiner. Gradually the abdomen will become relaxed until the lump may be felt.

FITS

As in the case of diarrhea, fits are more often than not a symptom of some disease. They are actually convulsions, no matter how mild or how severe they may be. The convulsions may be caused by toxins or brain inflammation. Some of them resemble epilepsy in human beings and have apparently no ordinary cause. The following principal causes which I have noted in my work with dogs are listed in the order of their importance.

Encephalitis. Encephalitis easily ranks first. There probably is no real disease called encephalitis; rather it is the result of brain damage, generally by a virus of some other disease. The encephalitis which on rare occasions

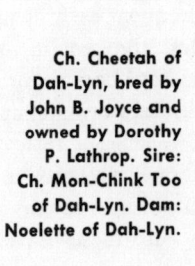

Ch. Cheetah of Dah-Lyn, bred by John B. Joyce and owned by Dorothy P. Lathrop. Sire: Ch. Mon-Chink Too of Dah-Lyn. Dam: Noelette of Dah-Lyn.

follows whooping cough or measles in children is caused by the virus of these diseases getting into the brain and inflaming it. You say that the child has the condition of encephalitis rather than the disease. When this condition follows P-L-T, the dog has it as a result of the P-L-T virus.

When a puppy develops encephalitis from any cause, it may have fits, although some never have fits. When a dog or puppy is brought to the Whitney Veterinarian Clinic, with a temperature in the vicinity of 102.6F we naturally suspect encephalitis, due to the common P-L-T virus, and make tests to show if this disease is present or not.

Kibbled Dog Food used to rank second as a cause of fits. The agene bleach used in some batches of kibbled dog foods produced fits in a positive manner. We have often tested such foods. I have seen young dogs have fits after being fed kibbled biscuits for no more than three days. Bakers are now leaving the agene out of foods and bleaching flour with other chemicals.

Deficiencies in kibbled dog food may be another cause of fits. Baking foods at the high temperature to which biscuits are subjected for long periods of time cannot help but result in some losses of essential nutriments.

The texture of kibbled biscuits and whole biscuits, which fill stomachs of puppies, often produces fits. Many a time we have had little puppies in violent fits rushed to us. Their stomachs have been emptied of loads of kibbles and their fits stopped at once. Many people who feed dog biscuits often do not soak them long enough.

Combinations of causes sometimes produce fits when kibbles are fed. The positive cause coupled with deficiencies is just too much for many puppies.

Parasitic infestation may cause convulsions in puppies. Hookworms, roundworms and tapeworms are the offenders in younger puppies, but whipworms come into the picture as the dogs grow older. Occasionally a puppy affected with coccidiosis has fits. Four instances of fits after a severe case of coccidiosis have come to this author's attention. The felis form of coccidia was not involved in any. Each of the puppies acted as though the seizures were virus fits, but examinations of their brains by a competent pathologist revealed the presence of coccidia.

Temperature fits are quite common. They are a frequent early symptom of Carre distemper among certain breeds, though less frequent in others. High temperatures due to influenza and to pneumonia have been reported as causes, and high temperatures accompanying other diseases bring about the conditions propitious for fits.

Autointoxication due to intestinal impactions (stoppages) which in turn may be accounted for by food masses or foreign bodies, ranks as one of the positive causes of convulsions. Simple enemas often cure these impactions and subsequent regulation of elimination works wonders.

Foreign bodies in the stomach produce such pains that they lead any casual observer to believe the puppy has a fit, and often they do actually produce the real thing. Among the objects positively known to have been the direct cause of the upset which I have removed from puppy stomachs are four iron jacks, the porcelain part of a spark plug, a 10-inch knitting needle, many lumps of coal, small stones (in one case a puppy had four ounces of pebbles in his stomach), wads of grass, wads of hay, bones, sausage casings, half a rag doll, and a lump of tissue paper. Generally the worst fits are caused by hard objects.

Teething can cause fits. It must have done so much more frequently in the past than it does now, because most of the old books on dog diseases have paragraphs on teething fits and talk about them as if they were among the commonest of all puppy ills.

SKIN DISEASES

Puppies are subject quite early in life to many forms of skin disease, the majority of which are of fungous origin. A whole book could be written on this single subject. Some of the early treatises tell us that most of the puppy skin diseases are either moist or dry eczema, but recent research shows that this is untrue. The old idea of eczema was that the blood was of improper composition and the skin disease "boiled out." We used to read that certain foods were "too heatening to the blood," as if such a thing were possible. It may make you smile now, but our forefathers were very much interested in the "blood heatening" idea. Then, too, we were told that the puppies were exhibiting allergies or idiosyncrasies to the first solid foods, or even to the mother's milk.

It is obvious that if a skin disease can be cured externally with no change in the diet, the food is not responsible. If curing skin disease were as simple a matter as changing the diet, there would be very little to it. But recall, if you can, any case in which a skin disease was cured by changing the diet, and without the application of some local medicinal agent. If it was ever done, it

Ch. Rosy Ridge Kai Chu, owned by Merritt Olds. Sire: Ch. Sunt Yung Wong Sing Lee. Dam: Ch. Rosy Ridge Ah Chu.

was such a rarity that it may be explainable by causes other than change of food. For instance, cold weather will often cure skin diseases which thrive in summer. In all my experience in the handling of many thousands of dogs, I have yet to see the first dog that was affected with skin trouble which was caused by any positive ingredient in the diet. In our hospital during 1946 we treated over 2,000 cases of skin diseases. Not one was caused by any food.

There are some kinds of skin disease which are caused by vitamin deficiencies, but they are not the kind that you are likely to see if you are feeding

Ch. Jalna's Firefly of Melana, owned by Zara Smith and Anne L. Samek.

an ordinary diet. Very severe infestations of intestinal parasites can cause coat effects, which disappear when nothing else is done than to deworm the dogs.

The common puppy skin diseases are generally infections, and can be cured by external applications of remedies which your veterinarian will recommend. Often they get their start from flea and louse bites. I have done considerable research using mixtures of flea-destroying drugs and fungicides and find that it is possible to keep dogs freer from skin disease when combinations of the two are used than when one is used alone.

All through his life every dog is subject to skin disease, especially when the weather is moist and hot. Fungous disorders spread best under these

Ch. Roh Kai Tassie, a Sleeve Pekingese of unusual soundness and substance.

conditions and bathing is one of the best ways to spread such afflictions. Puppies with small spots, easily controllable if treated early will become infected all over their bodies if given baths. They must be cured first, even though they do give off offensive odors during the curative stages. There are few effective fungicides which work well in water bases unless they are applied several times a day. Oil bases or soap are best; therefore the diseases should be cured before the dog is washed.

The earliest skin disease is generally a rash on the belly, which soon spreads all over the body. But as the puppy grows, the more prevalent types are those which first start on the back in front of the tail.

Many, if not most of the diseases affecting older dogs also cause sicknesses

Could we fool you with this one? The pup at right is stuffed. Jean Waring puppies.

in puppies, but abnormal growths like cancer are seldom found and kidney disease is rare, as are diseases of the urinary tract, paralysis, and certain eye disorders.

Rabies is common in puppies but not as much so as among older dogs, especially those which roam. Puppies haven't learned or felt the urge to roam. In states where rabies is prevalent all puppies should be vaccinated against it. Once-a-year vaccinations will usually prevent rabies effectively throughout the life of the dog.

Left: Rokes White Wing of Wanstrow; right: Tiny White Wings of Roke. Father and son, both belong to Jean Waring.

X
Parasites

Internal and external parasites must be diligently eliminated if puppies are to thrive. In order to know how to take care of these pests, one has to know at least a little about their life histories.

ROUNDWORMS

While not so severe a tax as some parasites which puppies harbor, roundworms do untold damage in the aggregate. They account for the deaths of thousands of puppies annually. The puppies die not only because the worms are in the stomach and intestines, but because of lung infestation which leads to pneumonia. How does this situation come to be?

A puppy gets a roundworm egg in its mouth. The egg may be ingested from the mother's teats, fur or feet. Or it may be picked up from a bone which the mother has dragged around in her run and brought into the puppy box. Or, if the puppies are old enough, the worm egg may have been picked up directly by the mouth from the ground or possibly have been blown in dust onto food which the pup then eats. However, after the egg reaches his mouth, here is what happens: It is swallowed. It has a tough coat or shell, so resistant that it will live in the soil for years and stand soaking in some disinfectants, but when the acids of the stomach attack it, the shell is dissolved and the little worm within the shell is liberated. In this form it is the *larva*. The tiny, microscopic thing is moved into the intestine and at once it bores through the intestinal lining until it gets into the blood or lymph, by which route it enters the general circulation.

It floats about in the blood stream until, after further development, it ends up in the lungs, and there it bores through from the blood side of the lungs to the air side. It causes irritation and, as it moves and is moved upward from the lungs to the throat, produces the cough characteristic of heavy infestation. One lonesome larva probably would have little effect, but large numbers of them cause great irritation and often pneumonia, as they damage the lungs.

The larva is finally gagged up into the throat and is promptly swallowed. Now it grows to adulthood and lives in the stomach or intestine the rest of its life, migrating up and down so as not to be too close to other roundworms, except at mating time. When mating time arrives, male and female copulate, and the fertilized female lays great numbers of eggs which are passed out of the puppy with the feces, and if not cleaned up, may become scattered and infest the premises. Rain is especially helpful in scattering feces and washing the eggs which are passed out of the puppy with the feces and washing the eggs into the ground. Here they incubate for considerable time, the period depending upon the temperature and amount of humidity.

A roundworm egg is not infestive until incubation has occurred. For this reason bitches can keep their puppies clean, sometimes consuming thousands of eggs daily along with feces ingested in the process of cleaning the puppies, and yet not become infested themselves. The eggs pass through her and are left in her stool. The incubation period is nearly a week whereas the eggs are in the bitch's body not more than 24 hours.

There, in a nutshell is the life history of the roundworm. There are two general kinds which may infest your puppies, but both have more or less similar life histories. Both are characteristically parasites of puppies and young dogs. As dogs get older, they seem to develop an immunity to this type of worm so that one finds very few roundworm eggs in the feces of adult dogs.

HOOKWORMS

In some respects the life cycle of the hookworm and that of the roundworm are similar. This is principally due to the fact that both spend part of their embryonic stage in the blood.

Hookworms are not harmful as eggs because the eggs are not infestive. After the egg appears in the puppy's stool, it hatches, if the temperature and moisture are both correct for their development, and the larval form goes through five pupations before it finally is infestive. Then it is usually ingested, although it is believed to be able to bore through the skin and the toes. When it reaches the intestine, it works itself through the intestinal lining and becomes a blood parasite.

By whatever way it gains admission to the blood, it finally arrives at the lungs, is coughed up and swallowed, and attaches itself to the intestinal lining by the hooks at its mouth (these hooks are responsible for its name). It lives by sucking blood. One hookworm can draw about a thimbleful of blood from a puppy in a week, so you can see why very early recognition is imperative if you are to save your litter or infested puppies.

While in the blood of a bitch, the larvae can and do bore through the uterine wall into the placenta and are carried to the puppy's body where they lie dormant until birth. But at birth they immediately start developing; the larvae do not have to go through the entire cycle as they do in older dogs which pick up the larvae themselves. This is the reason your puppies may show hookworm eggs in their stools as early as at two weeks of age. If they were to pick them up in their mouths, it would be three weeks before they exhibited eggs in their stools.

WHIPWORMS

These little parasites are about half an inch long in their body parts but have a long protrusion or flagella from their front ends which gives them the appearance of a whip. The flagella is about $1\frac{1}{2}$ inches long and is sewed into the intestinal lining to act as the means of holding on. A favorite place for whipworms is the cecum, a blind gut arrangement located at the upper end of the large intestine. There was a time when whipworms presented a problem in elimination, and operations were performed to remove the infested dog's cecum, but this is never necessary any more.

The whipworm egg is believed to require 20 days for incubation at optimum heat and moisture conditions. Like the roundworm egg, it is resistant. Once it is ingested and its shell removed, the little larvae are believed to become attached to the intestine without spending any time in the blood of the dog.

You will rarely find puppies with whipworms in the first few weeks of life.

TAPEWORMS

The tapeworm most commonly found in young puppies is the type whose intermediate host is the dog flea. The second most common one is that which has the rabbit as its intermediate host.

The flea type's life history is as follows: The puppy eats a flea in whose body is a tapeworm head enclosed in a cyst. When the flea is partially digested, the tapeworm head is liberated. It adheres to the intestinal lining by suckers which hold it there throughout its life. This microscopic head section grows and from it an extension develops. On the tail of this extension, another is added. To this another is added, and so on, the worm becoming longer and longer. Each addition, known as a segment or proglottid, puts a strain on the segments above it. When the worm is finally developed, the segments closest to the head have been pulled out by the strain upon them until they look like a long thread. Naturally, the closer the segments are to the tail end, the fatter they are.

These last segments become filled with eggs after the tapeworm has mated. It is interesting to note that one segment on the same worm may be male and another female so that the worm can often mate with itself, by twisting around and letting the lower segments touch those higher up.

The segments at the end with their ripened eggs, which when seen with a microscope, appear like bunches of grapes surrounded by a thin envelope, drop off. They may be found crawling out of the puppy's anus, on his bed, or sometimes clinging to the hair under his tail, dried and looking like small grains of brown rice.

The larval form of the flea, a worm, feeds on these segments and finds much nourishment in them. In consuming the meat of the segment, the larvae ingest the eggs which, as we have seen, become cysts in their bodies. Then the flea larvae spin cocoons where they pupate, and from each one of them a little flea emerges, containing within its body the head of a tapeworm. The fleas crawl into the mouths of puppies or grown dogs, and the cycle starts all over again.

In less than three weeks after an infested flea is swallowed by your puppy, you can find tapeworm segments on or in the stools of that puppy. These segments hold the eggs quite well, and it is exceptional to find eggs from the flea tapeworm in a dog's stool unless one of the segments happens to be mashed. Diagnosis can be easily made by seeing the segments on the stool or around the anus.

The rabbit-host tapeworm has a different life history. A dog with the worms in his intestine defecates where there is grass. Some of the eggs from the tapeworm (this type lays eggs) sticks to the grass and the blades grow up, carrying the eggs with it. An unsuspecting rabbit eats the blade of grass and the egg. The egg contains the larval worm which, unlike the flea-host worm larva, gets into the blood and eventually ends up in the liver as a favorite spot. Here the rabbit's body forms a cyst about it, and it lives within the cyst until the rabbit is shot, skinned and its liver fed by an unsuspecting hunter to his dog. The liver is digested, but not the worm, and it promptly attaches itself to the intestine and grows many segments, each somewhat fatter and larger than those of the flea-host tapeworm.

Then the eggs are laid and pass out in the feces, and segments of the worm also drop off where they are pushed around in the intestine and eggs mashed out of them. The presence of these worms may be determined both by the segments on the stool and eggs in the stool, which may be found with a microscope.

HOW THE PRESENCE OF WORMS IS DETERMINED

So many people appear to think that all they have to do to see if a puppy has worms is to look at the stool. Once in a while you may see roundworms which have died of old age and been expelled, or eliminated in some other way. They are about four inches long in adult form and easily seen, but because you do not see them, don't think that your puppies are free of them. Most puppies have worms. The only safe and sure way of determining their presence is by finding their eggs in the stool with the aid of a microscope. They must be magnified by over 100 times their real size to do a very good job of diagnosis.

Hookworms are so small very few people would know one if they saw it. Many think that tapeworm segments are hookworms or "pinworms." Most people seem to think that because worms are curled up at both ends they are hookworms. Most roundworms are curled up in this fashion. Very young roundworms often pass for hookworms in the eyes of many amateurs. Whipworms are very seldom seen even after a thorough worming because dog owners don't take the trouble to wash the stool apart over a fine screen to find them.

Tapeworm segments take so many forms that it is no wonder they are confusing to the amateur. Some will have shortened up to about an eighth inch square, others will elongate until they seem to have little heads, some will be pink, some yellow and some white, with all shapes and sizes in between. And when they are dry, as I have said, they shrink and harden so they look like little rice grains. So do not expect to see all forms of worms, and don't expect your veterinarian to find eggs of the flea-host tapeworm if he makes a fecal examination. He may see the segments in the stool and yet not be able to find a single egg. You can tell that they are there and help him.

THE LOUSE

Large numbers of puppies die every year because of louse infestation. If a bitch is infested as soon as she whelps most of the lice will leave her and attach themselves to the pups. The pups soon take on an untidy appearance and gradually develop a boardy feeling. It is amazing how many people have puppies infested this way and never think of looking closely enough to find the cause of the loss of puppy condition. I have seen experienced kennel men have a litter infested with lice and not know what was wrong. In fact, it is such a common experience for veterinarians to find well-kept dogs heavily infested that one wonders why.

A louse lays its eggs and sticks them to the hair of the dog. The eggs hatch and the little lice go to the skin, and, depending on whether they are the sucking or biting variety, stay put or move around sluggishly. They will be found nearly anywhere on the young puppy but on older dogs they tend to like the ears best, especially in long haired dogs. One should inspect every pregnant bitch for nits (the eggs) well before time of whelping, and see that they are removed by dipping her, or powdering her with a harmless potent louse powder. It is well, too, to remove the nits with any one of the solutions sold for the purpose.

It is the opinion of many that dogs pick up lice from their premises, and that they can live for long periods off the dog, but it is more likely that they pick up the lice from other dogs, and that lice live no more than three days off their host.

A large number of lice will make a puppy exceedingly anemic and cause death early in life. I have had to resort to transfusions to save several such puppies and transfusions in such young pups are difficult indeed.

FLEAS

Fleas, unlike lice, do not develop on the dog, and for this reason your puppy is not very likely to pick up fleas from another dog. The adult fleas ride around on the dog, mating and the females laying eggs, while they eat to their heart's content. The female fleas, when full of eggs, can be recognized by the huge yellowish or brownish abdomens, which make them look very different from the lithe and graceful high jumping males. The female fleas lay their eggs and rely on the travels of the dog to scatter them. That's why, although you keep your dog as free of fleas as you are yourself, a neighbor's flea-covered dog may stay around your house and yard, leaving thousands of flea eggs behind him.

If your puppy or dog has fleas and you keep him in the house, you can be sure he will leave eggs all over your house. There they will stay as long as it is dry and cold, but let a nice damp warm day come in early summer and all those eggs hatch out. Each occupant emerges as a tiny worm, eats organic matter, and grows until it is quite visible. Just before it pupates, it may be seen as a little brown and black worm, slightly more than an eighth inch long, moving about in cracks in the floor or maybe even in the tufts of the best overstuffed chair.

Worms spin cocoons and stay in them for several days, then they emerge as fleas, just as butterflies come from cocoons spun by caterpillars. At this stage the male and female fleas look alike, and both can jump prodigious distances. They climb on anything upright and jump for the first thing that goes past. My lady's calf, or the mother of the pups. If enough get on the bitch and she lies down with her pups, they will crawl off onto the pups and chew on them, producing little spots where skin disease can find a place of access.

You can easily control fleas by using good flea powders or by dipping your puppy in rotenone dips. D.D.T., properly used, is also effective and safe.

TICKS

In some sections of the world, ticks are a very serious problem, but they are rare in young puppies, unless the house in which the puppies are kept is infested. For this reason we shall not take the time to discuss their life history. Most dogs become infested by running outside in brushy country; seldom do the ticks let go their holds on the mothers and attach to the puppies. They can be eliminated by dips containing rotenone, or by being pulled out of the dog's skin with tweezers. Be sure to pull the head out if possible.

MANGE

Three forms of mange caused by tiny mites often affect dogs. They are as follows:

Sarcoptic. This is the form of mange that is caused by a roundish parasite, too small to be seen without magnification, which bores or tunnels through the skin. The disease spreads to human skin and back to animals.

Sarcoptic mange may appear anywhere on the puppy's body. Small points of infection appear as red spots somewhat raised, like little mounds. These spread and become continuous with the next until the skin shows large areas of reddish, thickened skin. Constant scratching inflames the areas so that the combination of internal and external irritation leaves the skin in a pitiful condition. There is often some moisture if the inflammation is very severe. Your veterinarian can give you medicine which will quickly eradicate mange from your puppies, but be sure that you yourself are not infested and spreading the parasite to the dogs. There is no disgrace in getting any kind of parasite; the disgrace is in keeping it. If you have a skin condition resembling mange, and you know your puppies have sarcoptic mange, tell your doctor about it. The information will help both him and you, as it may make it unnecessary to do painful skin scraping from one of your own affected areas.

Demodectic. Often called *red mange*, this is the skin affliction that used to be considered incurable. With the discovery of the effectiveness of rotenone, it now is among the simplest skin diseases to cure, but it is an insidious disease because the incubation period of the causative mites is so prolonged.

The cigar-shaped mite gets into the hair follicles and reproduces there, and young mites spread to other follicles. They are so small and require so much time to reproduce and grow that many weeks pass before they show on the dog's skin. When they do show, the first indication is a spot of thinned hair, not entirely bald. This more often than not occurs on the face, somewhere around the eyes, or on the front legs. There are, of course, exceptions, but certainly 75% of all cases show up first in these areas. There is no serious escape of fluid, but just a harmless looking baldish spot. This spot may be soon cured with medicine which you can obtain from your veterinarian, but meanwhile, in many other spots on the puppy, incubation is proceeding. The next thing you know, there are a dozen or so larger areas where the hair is coarser.

Dogs are often brought to our clinic with nine-tenths of their bodies nude, but they are curable even in such a condition. It takes some time to do it, and usually a month elapses before the hair returns. If your puppy has suffered from demodectic mange, your must keep everlastingly on the watch for the reappearance of new spots and treat them early.

Ear Mange. The mite which causes this painful and irritating condition is roundish in shape like the sarcoptic mange mite. It, too, is very small. It generally creates a greyish, dry type of wax in dog's ears, which is quite different from the sticky black wax of canker; also the odor from the ears is different from that produced by canker disease. Microscopic examination of the wax reveals eggs and mites of all sizes and conditions.

Since it takes several weeks for a few mites in the ear to reproduce enough to be irritating, this disease is a slow starter. Your veterinarian can show you what the mites look like when he examines the ear scraping. Very weak solutions of rotenone cause their death and prove effective, but the solution must be put around the outside, as well as inside the ear. I have found them close to the outside of the ear. Your veterinarian will show you how to apply the solution he gives you.

MISINFORMATION CONCERNING WORMS

It would hardly seem necessary, but in view of the fact that so many people have such fantastic notions of where worms come from, something must be said regarding the places worms do *not* come from.

Somehow the notion has become widespread that milk causes worms. It isn't quite as prevalent as it was, but it still is believed by thousands. If milk caused worms, why would doctors recommend that children be fed it? I often ask that question, and some of my clients say that they have heard that it is not milk itself which causes worms, but that milk helps them to develop. This is like saying that milk is such a good food that worms also thrive in it as an environment. That might be so. But no puppy should be allowed to harbor worms. There is no known parasite of dogs that comes from milk, because *milk does not contain worm eggs.*

Some people believe that meat causes worms. As we have seen, feeding raw rabbit livers to dogs may cause the rabbit-host tapeworm. Occasionally feeding raw beef or raw pork will cause the beef-host or hog-host tapeworms, but I can assure you that these are great rarities in dogs. Feeding raw pork or undercooked pork to dogs or puppies can produce trichinosis in them just as it can in us, if the pork was obtained from hogs harboring the trichina worm.

From a practical point of view, it can be said that it is safe for you to feed raw beef because the chances of your dogs catching tapeworms from it are very slight; it is better not to feed raw pork. Pork loses very little food value in the cooking process and any trichina worms present are thereby destroyed. Even though beef and horsemeat also lose little food value when cooked, you have little reason to cook them for your dogs in the hope of preventing parasites.

Perhaps you have heard, too, that meat tends to help keep some parasites in check. It has been found that hookworms seem to do more harm to puppies when they have inadequate amounts of proper proteins than when they have enough. The meat can be raw, cooked, or dehydrated. Meat provides proteins and to that extent reduces parasitic damage.

Another superstition regarding worms is that garlic will act to remove them. This idea is given constant bolstering by the people who sell it. We do not see it advertised for the purpose because no substantial research has shown that it has value. But somebody at one time fed garlic and his puppy passed some worms. That person never bothered to ask whether the pup might not have passed the worms had he not been fed the garlic, nor did he bother to have a fecal examination made to determine whether there were still worms in the puppies. Dogs and puppies are brought to us which sometimes smell almost like a garlic bulb. We see many attempts at deworming with garlic. The very puppies that smell so strongly of it often will be among the worst infested animals. This is usually because the owners haven't bothered to try efficient worm-expelling drugs but depend on garlic, which is not very useful.

DEWORMING

A debatable question which interests both the veterinarian and the layman is: "Shall the dogbreeder deworm his puppies himself?" Some veterinarians will say "NO, NEVER!" Others will say, "Of course they should. I give my clients the medicine to take home and deworm their puppies every time I can."

Some dog owners will say, "NO, NEVER." They will go on to tell you of disastrous experiences they have had in doing it at home themselves. Others will tell you how they have been deworming their puppies for years and have never had one single bad experience.

The United States Department of Agriculture, largest employer of veterinarians in the world (the Bureau of Animal Industry employs thousands) believes that the dog breeder is capable of deworming his own puppies and dogs. It publishes a folder telling anyone how to do it. The department also believes that the layman is interested in understanding the diseases of his pets, and to encourage and assist him in this interest, it circulates a folder on the diseases of the dog. In the 1942 *Yearbook of Agriculture*, it published a fine chapter on "The Diseases of Dogs."

And to cap the climax, the U.S.D.A. developed and tested an anthelmintic (worm killer), normal butyl chloride, which was shown to be safe and useful. Today, in every corner drugstore across America, you can buy this drug, put up under different trade names by concerns which sell remedies for dogs. That the drug is safe has been attested by the Pure Food and Drug Administration of our government. It is effective against round-, hook-, and whipworms, but must be given in very large doses for whipworms.

From what I have said so far, you might conclude that I believe that there is no place for the veterinarian in the deworming of puppies, but this is not the case. We see the advantages and disadvantages of home treatments.

Approaching the problem strictly from the dog breeders' point of view, my opinion is that it is more than worth the price of a visit to, or from, your veterinarian to have the job done properly.

Without his assistance, you don't know what kinds of parasites your puppies have. Therefore, you don't know what kinds of medicine to use. You may decide on the basis of finding a few tapeworm segments, that your puppies have roundworms or hookworms. You give them medicine to eliminate these pests, but for some reason they get no better and continue to pass segments. Wouldn't it have been better if your veterinarian had made an examination and prescribed for them?

Again, you may assume that your unthrifty, anemic puppies have worms when actually they may be suffering from some disease. Many clients bring puppies to us who are ailing not from worms but from a severe case of coccidiosis. On the other hand, you may think that your puppies have a disease when they really have a severe worm infestation. Only your veterinarian can tell you definitely what the trouble is.

You may occasionally see your puppies sliding on their tails, and a helpful neighbor or a statement in a "dog book" will assure you that this is a positive sign of worms. On the contrary, it is usually a sign that the two glands located just under the anus are filled and irritating the puppies. Your veterinarian can probably tell you many amusing stories of how his clients have been mistaken as to the cause of this symptom. He squeezes the glands properly and expresses the acrid-smelling fluid out onto a piece of cotton, with which he covers his hand, showing that it was not worms that caused the irritation at all. He explains that severe roundworms infestations sometimes will produce sufficient toxin possibly to be the cause of this dragging or "playing sleighride" but that in many cases the accumulation of substance in the glands is what caused you to think the puppies have worms.

We have had hundreds of puppy raisers bring us feces and we soon learn the facts about their worms, give them the medicine and explain explicitly how to administer it. And even then one will occasionally phone to say one of the puppies was sick, but the owner found later that it had gotten to the cat's milk, or that the mother had jumped into the pen and one of the puppies nursed. So we advise leaving the puppies with us, if there is any chance that instructions cannot be properly carried out.

It is easy to see how the veterinarian comes to regard some clients with suspicion until he knows he can trust them to follow instructions. Looking at it from his point of view, can you blame him when some clients will bring back capsules and say, "The medicine was no good. You said on the directions, give both capsules, etc., etc., but the puppies refused to take them." That often happens.

Or take the case where the medicine did not work, and possibly made the puppy "drunk." The veterinarian makes inquiry and finds that the puppies were given all the milk they wanted, even though the instructions say to *starve*, underlined, for 24 hours. The client says, "But milk isn't food; milk is like water."

Some veterinarians maintain a mail diagnosis service. For trusted clients too far away to conveniently visit them, small receptacles are provided which may be filled and mailed. Careful studies are made, diagnosis is reported and the proper medicine sent for puppies whose weights are known. One southern veterinarian told the author that most of his fecal examinations are made on this basis. It is well worth the money for any dog breeder to know what kinds of worms his dogs harbor and know that the correct medicine is being given, in the correct amounts.

DEWORMING LITTLE PUPPIES

How young may a puppy be dewormed? This depends on the drug that is used. Wormseed oil and normal butyl chloride are somewhat more toxic to little puppies than tetrachlorethylene. Research indicates that even a week-old puppy may be safely treated but puppies that young do not have worms. At three weeks, there is little danger in deworming reasonably healthy infested puppies with tetrachlorethylene, provided they are starved for at least 20 hours. The drug may safely be given at the rate of 0.1 cc. for each 12 ounces of the puppy's weight.

One of the worst pieces of advice that can be given to the owner of a litter of heavily infested puppies is, "Don't deworm them until you have built

Medicines and vitamins may be administered by eyedropper, but you must be careful to see to it that no harm is done to the mouth. Photo by Louise Van der Meid.

them up." I have seen one fancier advise another in this way time after time, and then had the breeder consult us after the puppies were too far gone for help. You can't deworm them too soon; you usually don't have time to build them up because it is the worms that are debilitating them. Don't wait another minute to start starving them for the process.

It is often said to be advisable to give a little glucose before deworming. I find this unnecessary and have found no better results with it than without it, because I have never seen any harm come to a litter if they are thoroughly starved. Remember that tetrachlorethylene is soluble in fat. It is by the absorption of fat carrying the drug that the dog gets it from his intestines. If there is no fat, he gets very little of it.

But he does get some with or without glucose. Here is a nice little thing to know: After a litter of puppies has been wormed, in about half an hour you can smell the ether-like odor of the drug on the puppies' breath. Suppose you deworm 10 puppies which are all badly in need of it, and later on you find a capsule in the pen and realize that one of the puppies has spat it out or regurgitated it. How are you going to tell which one lost it? Just hold the nose of each one close to your nose and gently inhale. If you find one without an ether odor on his breath, you have located the pup you want and can see that he gets his medicine.

Puppies won't lose a capsule if it is pushed down the throat far enough. Drop the capsule on the back of the tongue and follow it down the throat with your finger as far as you can push. If it gets over the pharynx, and you see the puppy make a swallowing motion, it won't come up.

Another method of deworming dogs and puppies for roundworms is to give piperazine with the food. This quite benign drug was first used for human infants to rid them of pin worms. In dogs it is used in several forms such as piperazine citrate. The animals do not object to the taste. Your veterinarian can supply you.

But do not depend on any form of piperazine to dislodge all kinds of intestinal parasites; it is effective only against roundworms, removes about half of the hookworms and none of the whips.

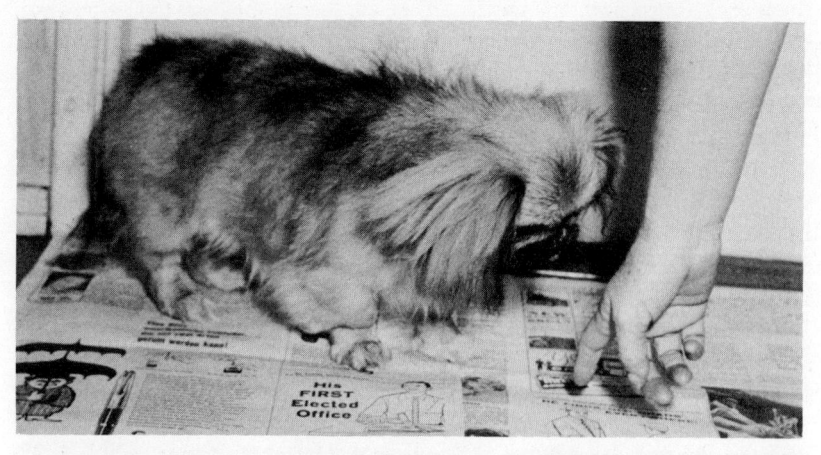

You can help your puppy to become housebroken by showing him newspaper, gradually moving it to the place to which you want him to become accustomed.

XI
Early Training

"As the twig is bent, so is the tree inclined" is only partly true in dog training. A tree, once it inclines, remains that way, but an animal's mind, once it gets untrained by a long period of non-use, can be re-educated nicely. It is amazing how quickly and well little puppies can be trained in useful ways in the first place.

The principles of early training are so vital that I have thought it worthwhile to call your attention to the most basic of them before proceeding any further.

Housebreaking is one of the main concerns. A puppy eliminates in response to the feel of what he stands on. If he first does so on the wire of a wire-bottomed pen, he will more than likely do so subsequently on the grating of a one-pipe furnace if he can fine ond. If he learns first on newspaper, he will try to find that, and if he learns on a clipped lawn, he will sense that your rug with the deepest nap is the proper place to relieve himself.

Breeders often raise pups in a pen the bottom of which is covered with straw. Is it any wonder, therefore, that a pup whose only strawy environment is his new dog house with its straw bottom will soil only that. To make the buyer realize that he is getting an easily housebroken dog, start your pups on newspaper, and explain to the prospective buyer how to housebreak. When the puppy, in his new home, has become accustomed to using the paper spread on the kitchen floor, explain how it must be moved by stages out on to the back lawn or wherever it is desired to have the dog eliminate, how the

189

pup should be taken out after meals when it normally feels the urge, and how the whole thing is a matter of habit formation, that the exceptions are serious, and how, if a puppy be given the opportunity he needs, there will be few failures.

Prospective buyers admire the response of young puppies to commands. You can teach them what *go in the house* means, and to come to a whistle, the word *come*, or the clapping of your hands. Use words distinctly as you shoo them into their house, or when you call them out to feed them. It does not require very many repetitions of words to establish a conditioned reflex, and the word will have a meaning.

Only a minutely small percentage of dogs are ever field trained, but I feel sure that if more owners knew the fun they are missing by never giving their dogs a chance at their work, many dogs would be field trained. Even ten-week-old puppies will show interest. It pays well to be able to demonstrate these early aptitudes to prospective buyers. Only a few minutes a day need be spent in rolling a ball for puppies to chase and catch. Once they start this, it is easy to train them, one at a time, to drop the ball in your hand or at your feet.

Shirley Stone preparing to put her Champion Livingston's Kai-Lung Do-Ton's (CDX) through his paces. Photo by Louise Van der Meid.

Step 1 in the single broad jump: coax him over the bar. Photo by Louise Van der Meid.

At the tender age of four weeks every puppy in a litter can be standing like a rock in show position. Indeed this is the best age to start them. A connoisseur can make a fairly accurate appraisal of the best of any litter by this early posing and training and the pups enjoy it.

A small tidbit given at the conclusion of the posing session will help you establish the pattern. With one of your fingers under the puppy's jaw and another under his tail, the puppy will stand as if hypnotized for some minutes. Examine his mouth, and don't let him win should he resist your efforts. End each training period by showing him that you and your hands are much stronger than he is, and that you are boss.

I am often amazed at how ineffectual many people are. Almost unable, apparently to use their hands enough to force a puppy to their will, these persons will complain, "If I discipline him, he comes right at me and bites." Some dogs are thus trained to be ugly. Why, the weakest woman could easily kill a half-grown pup with her bare hands. Poor training cannot be excused by saying, "I can't." What it really means is, "I won't try."

The "Up!" command in teaching the single broad jump. Photo by Louise Van der Meid.

A puppy which is made to submit to human beings, and which acknowledges early in his life that they are his superiors, will usually remain tractable throughout his existence, unless he possesses inherited meanness—an unreliable temperament. Even such puppies can be trained to be more reliable, but they should not be used for breeding.

TRAINING YOUR DOG

Now I realize, of course, that there are thousands of dog owners who have rationalized the dog up into the realm of the human being. You even read such statements by authors on dog training as, "The dog is not a seal, so don't feed him when you train." Many dog owners, especially those who have helped give dogs an evil reputation by spoiling their dogs until they have nasty dispositions, will tell you it is cruel to discipline a dog in any way except scolding.

Well, it is true that dogs can be trained without rewards by the system presently in vogue—the force system—and it is true that they can be trained without physical discipline. But just compare the efficiency of the methods and the effect on your dog of those outworn fifteenth-century methods with

"And Over", and another trick has been performed. Photo by Louise Van der Meid.

the new ones based on modern psychology. A dog isn't a seal; he may not be quite so bright as a seal, and he is definitely not of human mental caliber. So treat him and train him for what he is, and your rewards and pleasure from what you will learn yourself will be immeasurably increased.

With the new methods you can train your pet in a tenth of the time most persons spend.

BASIC PRINCIPLES FOR TRAINING

We start out with the established fact that *a dog's behavior is never uncaused*. The brain receives impressions from the senses and reacts to them. The pattern of reaction depends in part on the dog's inheritance. As we have observed in Chapter I all dogs have inherited, through many generations of selection, certain patterns of behavior. In training, our best results may be obtained by building on this fact.

Every dog has reflexes. He hears a sound, and cocks his ears; he smells food, his mouth waters; he tastes disagreeable food, and spits it out; he touches a hot coal, and jerks his foot away, and so on *ad infinitum*. We can let him be a child of nature and do whatever his reflexes cause him to do, or we

Here Shirley Stone's champion Peke is in for a little advanced training: the double broad jump. Photo by Louise Van der Meid.

can condition his reflexes so that he does what we want him to do. Most dogs are practically untrained because the owners are too ignorant, too indolent—or both—to train them.

This is the way a reflex is conditioned: simultaneously with the stimulus which evokes the action we add another stimulus—a sound, a flash of light, or a sensation. If the two occur enough times together, either part of the combination may be dispensed with and the dog will react in the same uniform way. Salivation was the original reaction on which conditioning was studied, and it makes as good a one as any to use as an illustration. Show a dog food and his mouth waters. Ring a bell at the same time you show him food, and his mouth waters. Repeat many times. Now ring the bell without the food being present, and his mouth will water just the same.

How does this differ from such an action as the following? You are walking around the rough in a golf course. Your dog has been taught to retrieve golf balls—an uncommonly easy feat for him. You throw a golf ball into the rough and he retrieves it by sight and by its odor. He learns by the direction you swing your arm where to run. So now you swing your arm but do not throw a ball. Away he tears into the rough and sniffs around for the rubbery odor.

All alone, Ch. Livingston's Kai-Lung Do-Ton's makes it over the double bar.
Photo by Louise Van der Meid.

He finds a faint odor and gets a golf ball, bringing it to you. With a dog equipped with such a conditioned reflex you can earn spending money and get exercise most enjoyably.

Or another—your puppy scratches at the lower corner of the door to get outside. You see him doing it and open the door for him. He repeats this a few times and has thereby become conditioned to "know how to get out." And by the same token, to get in.

Or how does the saliva illustration differ from the case where your dog jumps up against you. This you have inadvertently conditioned him to do previously. But now you decide that it must stop, so you seem to pet him as you have always done, but as you cover his eyes with a hand you also step on a hind foot, hard enough to hurt him. You and every other member of the family step on his foot every time he jumps up, but you try not to let your dog know you do it. What have you accomplished? You have simply made him realize that jumping up gives him a pain in a hind foot. So he doesn't jump up.

If you have never thought about it, remember that you must give a meaning to a sound. Words are sounds of no meaning to your dog until you have impressed on him what the meaning of each word is. A toot on a whistle, the ringing of a bell, the sound of a hunter's horn, and even the hum of the motor in a certain car are all sounds which can be given meanings. Giving meaning to sounds is a principal part of training.

Ideal training conditions as many reflexes at one time as possible. Actually much more of a dog's brain is involved in the conditioning of most reflexes than was formerly thought. When a dog feels a hot coal, not only does his foot snap away from it, his whole body recoils, and he trots a considerable distance from the pain-producing spot.

Conditioning over and over amounts to habit formation. That you must keep in mind. Results may be achieved by punishments and by rewards. Punishments may be the sort of thing which the dog realizes he brings on himself, such as an electric shock when he barks, or he may have an out-and-out realization that his misdeed causes you to punish him.

Rewards may be accomplishments—the realization that an action brought the desired result—or they may simply be some food you give the dog when he is hungry. Rewards supply your dog with fulfillment of a strong desire. As an example, you take his kennel mates for a walk and leave him behind. He jumps frantically at the gate and strikes the latch. The door opens: he dashes after you. Two or three repetitions of this behavior, and the dog has learned how to open the door. Or he is hungry, and he learns that doing a certain act a certain way brings a reward—food.

To train, we need to establish in our dog a great want—a drive, a stimulus—which we can fulfill with a reward, and to keep on supplying the reward until we have carried our conditioning forward to such an extent that it becomes the established pattern of behavior.

These rewards psychologists call reinforcements. Now what are some of the drives and the rewards which you can use in training?

Food. Small tidbits to be given only when the dog is *hungry*.

Companionship. Used negatively—making a dog think you are leaving home when he wants to go can have excellent results.

Love of work. Giving your dog an opportunity to do what his inherited behavior patterns urge him to do can be an excellent reward. Suppose he loves to hunt rabbits, and at every opportunity will go out into a brush lot and drive rabbits by the hour; simply giving him this privilege can be used as a reward. Letting him retrieve is an excellent illustration. He naturally, by inheritance, loves to carry small objects. He also naturally loves to run after one, but he doesn't know you will throw it until you have shown him. So in a few minutes he will learn that to drop the object at your feet means that you will throw it and that is all the reward he needs. You need not give him food for returning the object, but if you do, you will reinforce the lesson even more strongly.

Brushing with a stiff brush can act as a reward once a dog has been taught to stand. You can show him the brush and point to a chair or table, and he will bounce on to it. Or you can say a word—chair, table—and he will act the same way after a few lessons.

On the negative side, what means of punishment are available for training? First, the old, simple methods:

The open hand. A sharp slap beside the face is generally an excellent punishment. Don't let anyone convince you that the hand must be used only to reward the dog. The hand, he soon learns is just, rewarding for right acts, and disciplining for wrong.

The feet. Many experienced dog trainers believe that a dog watches their feet first, so they use them as indicators and as means of punishment. Big-game hunters often ride down miscreant hounds who have run on deer tracks and let the horse trample them. Some dog trainers kick and stamp on their dogs or, as some Midwestern backwoodsmen say, tromp on 'em, and whether we approve or not, they have dogs that work for them like demons, and behave ideally.

The rolled newspaper. This makes a crackling noise when the dog is struck with it. The trouble is that most amateur dog trainers do not strike hard enough.

Shaking. There are few more satisfactory means of punishing than picking the misbehaving dog up by the neck and shaking him until you think his teeth will drop out. A mild shake at first, of course, but violent if the mild one has proved ineffective.

The switch. A proper switching must really hurt the dog. Don't "cut the tail off an inch at a time" by a lot of annoying little taps, but pick the miscreant up by the back of the neck and wallop him along the side.

The broom. There is no more natural means of punishment in the hands of a woman than a broom. A good swish is excellent punishment for a puppy, and for a really obstreperous dog, a well-worn broom makes a wonderful tool. But it must never be used to chase a dog with. The dog must be tied where he can't crawl into a doghouse or under a bed. A barking dog can be chained to a radiator, for instance, and when he barks, the words *be quiet* can be said accompanied by a wallop with the broom. After a while you can discontinue using the broom and *be quiet* is all you need say.

The dark closet. Most dogs dread being alone and confined in the dark. For punishment, simply bundling the dog ignominiously into a dark closet for an hour can be used to excellent effect.

Water. Squirting water on an outdoor dog, throwing a half bucket of cold water over him, and filling the bucket and leaving it where he can see it ready for the next lesson works well. So does placing a half barrel of water next to his kennel and, when he barks, rushing out, making him realize he is calling you, and picking him up and pushing him under the water. But water is a warm weather punishment of course.

The electric shocker. For many years now—more than thirty—I have occasionally used a device I made which beats every other method of negative training. This is based on a dog's dislike of an electric shock. An amount of electricity which to us is almost pleasant will make a dog recoil with a jolt. And if such punishment is properly used there is no better method. I like it because it makes the dog realize that his action gives him a shock. Anyone can make such a device, but only a serious trainer or breeder is likely to do so. It consists of a dry cell, a small induction coil, a dog collar with pointed studs (two on each side, with two insulated), and a pair of wires running from the studs to the coil. There is a switch, of course. The collar is placed on the dog and the double wire acts as a leash. To give you one example of its use if the dog chews on his leash a touch of the switch gives him a shock and one or two shocks will stop such an action.

There are a few specifications of punishments which must be kept in mind:

It should hurt or frighten him. This is nature's way. Watch dogs discipline one another, or a bitch teaching her pups, and you realize that anything you or I are likely to do will be mild by comparison.

It must make your dog know that you are his boss and master, and no fooling.

You must not undertake any training on even a small problem unless you are prepared to follow through to final conditioning.

In positive conditioning there should be no punishment until your dog is performing the act correctly at least 75 per cent of the time. That is the punishment must be for the dog failing to do something he has learned and knows how to do.

Punishment must be immediate, if possible as part of the wrong act of the dog, like the burn from the hot coal, or the electric shock or mouth burn when a puppy chews an electric cord. A dog's attention may be on something entirely different, if punishment is postponed, and you will give him the feeling he is being punished for that instead of the act for which you are really chastising him. A good illustration of such stupid training is when a dog owner returns home and finds a dog has evacuated indoors and he sticks the dog's nose in the stool and scolds. I doubt that any dog who ever lived was housebroken by that method.

TRAINING THE HOUSE DOG

Behavior training classes have become exceedingly popular, but not nearly so popular as they should be. Behavior training is basically the training of a dog to be a good companion. But it goes much further than that, because those who are bitten by this benign bug become filled with enthusiasm and the spirit of competition, and show no desire to quit. Soon they are exhibiting

Here the Peke is being trained to drop on recall. Photo by Louise Van der Meid.

their dogs for prizes, and many people go on from one class to another, often aiding the newcomers to learn the lessons they have already learned themselves.

Almost all of the trainers were taught in the old or force system: that is, you push your dog's rear end down and say *sit* until he has learned to do it to order. Contrast this system's result with those of the reward system of getting the dog to sit of his own volition and then rewarding him! Surely the latter is ten times as efficient.

POSITIVE TRAINING

Let us take a few simple positive acts we wish our dog to perform. What shall our incentive or drive be? Hunger. That is painless and, apparently, magic. So we shall see our pet has only water to drink for 36 hours. He will then be hungry enough really to *try*. (He will not be harmed—a dog has lived for 117 days on water without food.)

We are going to teach him:

1. To get on the *table*. This is a useful command for him to execute, because an old table makes an excellent place on which to comb and brush him;
2. *Down* from the table;
3. *Shake hands;*
4. *Other paw;*
5. *Lie down;*
6. *Stand;*
7. *Sit.*

How long would it take by the force method to train him to execute these seven commands? Try it on your dogs if you have untrained ones, and compare. By the reward method you will certainly have your dog executing the orders within two evenings if you keep him hungry. Starve him first for 36 hours, after which your reward will be his food. Then give him nothing but water again for 24 hours. Then let him rest a day, and thereafter feed him only what he barely needs to live on. He should be hungry enough to eat eagerly a dry crust of bread, and you will choose something more tempting than that. I suggest half-inch lumps of frankfurter or pieces of hamburger as large as a thimble.

You have probably read enough about training, or seen enough of it, to know that nearly all trainers want you to pronounce your dog's name before any command. But this I know is entirely unnecessary unless you are training a lot of dogs performing together and want to call one out from the pack to perform individually. "George—sit" and "George—lie down" and "George—jump" get tiresome and are needless. Your dog knows you are talking to him.

Get on the *table*. Your key word is *table*. So use only that. Set a chair beside your training table; neither of them must shake or tremble. With Nero—that's your dog's name in this chapter—having sniffed the reward in your hand, you say *table* and let him follow your hand first up on the chair and thence on to the table. He gets his reward and wants more.

Down from the table. Say *down*, and let him follow your hand down. When he is down, he gets his reward.

Pause a minute, get his attention, and say *table*, going through the same routine as many times as it takes for him to get on the table without a movement of your hand. All this will probably take you 30 minutes at most.

Shake hands. Put a harness or collar on Nero. Put a ring—an eye bolt—in the wall behind the table, which will be tight against the wall. The ring should be about ten inches from the table top. Run a light chain with a swivel in it from the ring in the harness or collar back to the ring in the wall. This chain should be just long enough for Nero's chest to come even with the front edge of the table.

Did you ever see what a hungry dog does when he can't reach food with his mouth? He reaches for it with his paw, doesn't he? Take advantage of that fact. Let Nero smell the meat, and the moment his foot comes forward to reach it, say *shake*, and give him his reward. In a few minutes you'll have him batting at you when you say *shake*. Then it is your time to teach him *other*.

Other paw. When he finds pawing with one foot doesn't get him the food, he will try to reach it with the other foot which will be accompanied by your word *other*. Feed him only for the correct foot coming forward on the word *other*. He will soon learn that *shake* means the right foot and *other* the left,

In teaching your Peke to return thrown objects, praise him when he returns them. Photo by Louise Van der Meid.

or, if you prefer, *shake* may mean whichever he presents first and *other* the alternate foot.

After he is proficient at this job on the table, let him get down and try his reactions on the floor.

The second evening can well start with repetition of the previous evening's training before beginning new commands.

Lie down. Tie Nero with a short chain running from his harness or collar to the ring in the wall behind him. Let him shake a few times and then say *lie down*, and hold your reward just below the table top so he must lie down to reach it. When he is down, give it to him.

Stand. At once teach him what *stand* means. I like the word *up* but, as you will see, the word *hup* is used as a field trial command meaning to sit, and the two words sound too much alike for contradictory uses.

You teach *stand* by holding the reward high so that Nero has to stand up to get it.

Sit is taught by holding the reward in your closed hand close to his face and making him back up. He will soon sit, and you say the word as he does so. Repeat until he knows the meaning of the word.

Having taught him this simple execution of your words, or, to put it another way, having conditioned Nero to associate word sounds with actions, you can go on applying the principle to actions off the table.

Repetition over and over again finally evokes immediate response to the words. If he does not respond, he needs more table training. Here are a few useful actions you can elicit by the use of words:

Come. Train your hungry Nero in an enclosure. Let him wander away and say *come* or just whistle. Feed him his little reward and wait for him to wander again. When you and he have repeated the action so many times that he seems to understand the word, try him another day in the open with a long training cord. When he seems to respond without a mistake, get a friend to provide something alluring, to see if the dog will fail to mind you. Walking a strange dog on a leash where Nero can see him is one of the best lures. Hold on to the training cord so the dog completely upsets himself when he comes to its end, and when he is thus discommoded call him and reward him when he comes. Or let a cat out of a bag so he can see it run away. Call *come*, and when he fails to do it, he tumbles in a heap at the end of a training cord. A few such lessons teach him that you can reach out and control him. You can then make the cord longer and longer.

Please note that you cannot train Nero vicariously: you do it, not sit in an armchair and think about it.

Fetch or *get* is a useful action to teach, and easier than many know. Since Nero loves to retrieve, just throw anything and he will run to it, pick it up, and carry it. If you start with a hungry Nero, you can use reward to teach him to discriminate between several objects, say a brush, a slipper, and his leash. Under negative training we shall see how to train a dog to realize what *no* means. In this case you can throw two objects and tell Nero to *get slipper*. If he starts to pick up the brush which you have tossed with the slipper you say *no*, and then when he picks up the slipper and brings it to you, he gets his reward. Later you can teach him what *brush* means, and *leash*, so you can throw out all three objects and he will retrieve the one you tell him to bring you.

From his differentiating in this way it is only a step to teach him to get your slippers, his brush, or his leash whenever you request them, or to take the evening paper from the paper boy and bring it to you.

I hope that by now you see how easy it is to train. Of course it takes hours of patient repetition as you give word and other sound meanings to Nero, but what could be more worth-while?

Teaching him to walk at your side, which obedience class trainers call *heeling* is only a matter of walking with Nero, keeping him on a leash at your left side, and commanding him to *sit* every time you stop. I prefer the words *at side* for this, and to train him that *heel* means what it used to; namely, to

This is a little more difficult. The Peke has to jump the bar in order to retrieve. Photo by Louise Van der Meid.

walk behind me just as the heel-driving Shepherd dogs "dog the footsteps" of cattle, sheep or their owners, or Dalmatians heel behind horses. All one needs is a leash and a switch and some reward to accomplish both objectives.

NEGATIVE TRAINING

This general kind of training in what not to do is simpler and requires much less thought than positive training, and here is where punishments are used intelligently.

When a dog misbehaves, he is not doing it because he is necessarily innately bad or trying to annoy you: he was inadvertently trained that way by you or someone previously. The barking dog furnishes an excellent example. It is a natural reaction for any dog to bark. He begins very young, and usually nothing is done to stop him Why wouldn't he bark?

But he does it, and here he comes back with the dumb-bell. Photo by Louise Van der Meid.

As he grows older he may bark when he is hungry. What does his owner, who is annoyed by the barking do? Unfortunately he feeds him, and thus reinforces the barking reaction to hunger.

Once a reflex has become conditioned in this way, to uncondition it is to see either that it is not used for several months, or to shock the dog severely with punishment, so that the one reaction overcomes the other. We know this not only from animal psychology, but from human. Most of us have been conditioned in certain ways: to stand when "The Star Spangled Banner" is played, for example, and if we were to sit when it was played before a ball game we should have a guilty feeling. For months after Hitler died, if someone said "Heil, Hitler" to a German, it was difficult for the hearer not to salute.

The less-complicated dog acts simply, positively, and negatively. So, brainwashing for him—washing out the previously conditioned reflexes—can best be achieved by punishment. We have seen what some of those methods can be. And now, knowing roughly what the conditions are, one

This Peke loves his bone. Photo by Louise Van der Meid.

The dumb-bell is returned. Photo by Louise Van der Meid.

realizes how much sternness, persistence, and patience may be necessary to brain-wash, to decondition, and to recondition Nero. Here are a few useful negative commands and how to apply them:

No. I start every dog I ever train by teaching this simply taught expletive. It is easy to say, and the dog learns it as easily as a puppy learns to keep away from his mother's food when she growls—her way of saying *no*. And your punishment need not be so severe as the bitch's, either, to accomplish similar understanding by the puppy or dog.

If you are using your hand to discipline, drop a bone with meat on it before your hungry dog. Be sure the food is too large for him to swallow. Say *no* sharply as he goes to take it, and slap his face. Train him in an empty room where he can't hide away. I would not use an electric shocker here, because it will be ever so much more difficult to get him to take the food when you come to teach that.

As you slap him, he drops the meat. Leave it there, and every time he starts to take it say *no* and slap. In a few minutes he will know the meaning of *no* as it applies to that one object. So now you must train him to know the meaning of the sound *take it*, or *take*. You may actually have to put the meat in his mouth and let him chew on it. Keep dropping rewards and say *take it* over and over, and suddenly intersperse the *take it* with *no*. If he takes the meat, reach right into his mouth and pull it out, and slap.

When he has learned these commands, try throwing the enticing food a distance of, say, five feet from you and saying *no*. and, once the dog has obeyed, *take it*. Next, stand in the doorway of the room and repeat this. The whole thing should not take you more than an hour to teach Nero. Now you are ready to apply the word *no* to other activities, and if you are firm, never letting an exception occur, you will have done your dog and yourself a great service. You can use the word for anything he should not do—chase cars, bark, hook his chin on to the food or water dish and tip it, and so forth.

Stay. Staying in one spot while you, the dog's master, walk away is a negative response. Nero's natural response will be to follow you. Have him lie down, and say *stay* while you back away. If he moves say *no*. After a few minutes' delay, tell him to come, and reward him. Repeat, lengthening the delay until he will stay as long as you wish. You can accompany your command with a motion if you wish, such as a Hitler salute (this is the usual obedience-class gesture), and when you drop your hand, call *come*. Soon the dog will watch your hand, and you can dispense with the word. Practice him often, and he will become adept.

Getting set for a trip, this Peke is being put into his carrying case. Photo by Louise Van der Meid.

XII
Pens and Bedding

We have already discussed bedding material for little puppies as well as whelping and nest boxes. Here we take up the matter of pens and bedding for older pups. It is one of the more important questions in cynidiatrics.

If we are not fortunate enough to be able to use wire bottom pens, which will be discussed later, then we must keep puppies on something solid, and inside some house where they will be protected from the rain, the sun's direct rays, heat and cold. Until I invented the wire bottom pen for puppies, mine were regularly raised on the ground, in winter and in summer. This brings us to a consideration of how much cold a little puppy can stand, provided of course, he is with his mother. The answer seems to be that he can stand very low temperatures so long as he is dry and has his mother to cuddle against, and something under him which he can heat. I never can recall losing one from cold. Over the front of the doors of their houses was hung a few thicknesses of burlap. Under them was six inches of packed straw. Usually they were whelped in these houses. Each house had a porch. If a bitch whelped on a very cold night, she was taken inside so that the puppies would not be frozen when they were wet. The bitches were always taken inside to whelp so someone could sit with them, when there was some reason for wanting to save as many puppies as possible. The puppies were generally put outside again the day after they were born. No harm resulted.

Think of these puppies raised in the cold of the north. Yes, they can stand a lot of cold so long as they have their mother with them. But let her desert them and they soon freeze. Indeed they seem to stand cold much better than heat. They can reduce their temperatures to some extent by panting, but to no such extent as they can when grown. I have seen fewer puppies recover from overheating than from chilling.

So, houses for puppies should be sufficiently solid to keep out winds in the winter and sufficiently ventilated to allow for cooling in the summer. If the box is large enough for the mother to stand in after the bedding is packed down, and six inches longer and wider than she is long, it will be large enough.

Bedding can be almost any absorbent material which has good insulating qualities. Some breeders have done well with bare boards in the summertime when puppies were housebroken, but in winter time and summer too, when there is mud present, bedding is generally advisable. Straw, hay, sugar cane and shavings all are good. Change the bedding every 7 days at the outside so that worm eggs will not have a chance to incubate and no worm damage can result.

These Pekes are going to the dog show, and some of their grooming equipment is going with them. Photo by Louise Van der Meid.

Ch. Coronation Lee Sing (female). Sire: Ch. Mi Go Sing Lee. Dam: Dawn of Dah-Lyn II.

MATERIAL FOR RUNS

One of the first things that occurs to puppy raisers is that they should obtain the cleanliness of concrete runs. Now, actually there are probably few worse media on which to raise dogs than concrete. If the surface is made glass smooth as, it must be to be sanitary, it becomes very slippery in wet weather. When it is coarse, the surface sometimes will harbor millions of worm eggs. To keep it clean requires constant scrubbing with a stiff brush and much water. The wormiest puppies that are brought to our hospital are those raised on concrete.

The hoe or shovel used to take up the stools just scrapes over the surface, usually painting it with stool, filling up the roughness and affording the most admirable environment for the worm eggs to incubate in. Admirable, that is, from the point of view of the parasite, but filthy from the point of view of the dog. Many people have had their concrete runs chopped out because of their difficulty in raising clean puppies on them.

Another material not to use is gravel. It sounds very fine to say "My puppies have fine feet; no wonder, they are raised in packed gravel runs." But that gravel offers a very coarse surface and cleaning stools from it is next to impossible.

The same may be said for cinders.

The best material that we have ever found is washed sand. It is inexpensive and clean, easy to renew, easy to remove stools from, without rough surfaces in which part of each stool can hide. As each stool is removed a little sand may be scraped up with it. As the pens are cleaned the sand is gradually removed and soon needs replenishing. Several times a year the whole surface for two inches may be dug off and renewed at small cost. The runs seldom have any odor. The sand soon packs solidly and its appearance is good.

It, like all others except concrete runs, offers the objection of affording a wonderful place for the dogs to dig in. The surface is sometimes irregular due to the propensity to dig, especially in summertime. Some breeders have gotten around this by pouring concrete runs four inches lower than the final surface of the runs and covering them with sand. This does away with the digging, but prevents drainage, with the result that the sand stays wet too long after a rain.

Grass runs look very nice. Portable pens are often advertised which may be moved all over a lawn. How excellent this seems to the amateur! But the appeal is quickly lost after trial. The spot becomes covered with stool—and puppies' stools are often soft—and nobody wants to lie on the spot where the pen was placed for many a day. If there are fleas on the puppies, the eggs develop in the lawn, and all in all, the whole practice has so little to recommend it that only one who had never tried it would succumb to the enticements of the beautiful advertisements we see to sell such pens. Even if we could be sure that the puppies' stools were extra firm, and we took them up as fast as they were deposited, the lawn is still no fit place to raise a pup.

WIRE BOTTOM PENS

The first public suggestion on the value of wire bottomed pens for rearing little puppies came from the author in an article in Popular Science, entitled "Wire Walking Puppies". The second was a popular article in the American Kennel Gazette. Both of these articles told of the value of such pens in the raising of puppies, not only in their early life but up until they were grown.

Since that time, thousands of these cages have been built and found to keep dogs as well as puppies in excellent condition. Wire bottoms are being used in pet shops, under sick dogs in hospitals, and in many and sundry ways where it is desirable to keep dogs out of their own or other dogs' filfth.

Today we can give the experiences of nineteen years in raising puppies on wire. Literally thousands of puppies have been raised in this manner. Every puppy attests to the fact that the method is not harmful, but very beneficial. It is good for the professional and is even better for the individual who has no kennel and who is planning to raise a single litter of puppies in his home or apartment.

The whole progress of the wire bottom pen has been one of great caution. For many years people raised pet squirrels on it. Then the mink breeders and raccoon breeders began using it. The fox men tried it also. We dog breeders were the last, and many who tried it, often in the first experiments with them,

These puppies are only four days old. They are offspring of Jean Waring's Snowman of Roke.

did so in such a gingerly fashion that sometimes it was almost comical.

What held nearly everyone back was the wonder whether the wire was going to harm the puppies' feet. I was no exception. But after just one try I plunged and wouldn't exchange the system for any other, at least none that I have seen. Thousands of these wire bottom pens have been built and are being used all over America.

My work calls me to homes where many litters of puppies have been raised. Usually the pups are in the cellar. Sometimes, one doesn't need to be told that there are puppies in the cellar, because on being admitted through the front door, one's nose tells all. Anyone who has tried to raise puppies in the cellar knows what they do to the floor. It is almost impossible to keep such a cellar clean. Spread newspapers around all you will, take them up as often as you want, but there is still plenty of odor left in the floor. Very few people realize how rough is the surface of a concrete floor. A hoe can be scraped over it and there is still much stool left in the pores or valleys, speaking microscopically. And because of this it is very difficult to eliminate the worms from infected puppies. They may be cleaned out of the intestines, but if there are worm eggs in the bottoms of the concrete pores, the puppies will continue to pick them up. If you looked at a worm egg with a microscope and saw it at the bottom of a tiny depression in the concrete, it might be, relatively speaking, about as large as a tennis ball on the floor of the room,

Jean Waring with some Pekingese puppies in a London department store.

if the ceiling of the room represented the surface of the concrete. No amount of scrubbing or sweeping will disinfect the cellar; it may help to deodorize it. Remember, too that a heated cellar is an excellent environment to incubate worm eggs, or for hookworm larvae and fleas to develop.

So, if you are going to raise puppies in your cellar or any other part of your house, put them on wire so that the feces will have to drop on newspaper which won't move, because the puppies' feet never touch it. That paper may be rolled up and burned and fresh paper put down, and a much cleaner litter result. A much sweeter smelling home will also result.

Probably no better way has yet been devised for inside rearing of puppies in winter than raising them on wire, at least until the puppies are half grown. Allowing them to have daily runs is worthwhile to develop muscles. But this is not necessary. We have never seen poor muscular development result from raising puppies to maturity in this fashion. Repeatedly I have raised litters of small sized dogs from birth to maturity in food tests, and in other studies, with only good results. The lack of exercise does not cause muscular shrinking. If greater muscles are desired, exercise at maturity is sufficient.

I realize that there will be those who will say it is cruel to keep puppies in this way. But that is not so. If they never know any other existence, they will not miss what they don't know. Sometimes the very people who have told me it was cruel were those who sat in a rocking chair more than half their lives and actually took perhaps a tenth as much exercise as a litter of puppies get in a wire bottom pen. They play and frisk and have a fine time. No, it is not cruel.

CONSTRUCTION OF WIRE BOTTOM PENS

The wire part of the pen illustrated is 3 ft. by 6 ft. This will accommodate six small puppies of any breed or four grown cocker spaniels. The pen is 2 ft. high and stands 1 ft. off the ground, bringing the tops of the cages to about the same height as an ordinary table.

The top of the hutch folds back over the wire top, permitting puppies to be stood there and displayed or groomed.

In the cage part is a door, 1 ft. by 3 ft. which opens back, as may be seen in the drawing.

The hutch is 2 ft. by 3 ft. This is plenty large enough to be used as whelping quarters for dogs weighing up to 30 lbs. Larger pens are naturally required for the larger breeds. The illustration shows a battery of wire bottom pens used in one of the veterinary colleges. These have been constructed somewhat differently. The extra leg is located at the back of the hutch, which is a good idea. If it is placed at the front of the hutch, when a lot of heavy puppies fill the hutch, there is a possibility of the cage's tipping backward unless another leg is also placed under the back.

A battery of wire-bottomed cages. Dogs raised in such cages have excellent feet, and the parasite problem is kept to a minimum. They are of more interest to the kennel owner than to the owner of one dog.

Jean Waring's Tiny White Swan of Roke and Nobby, his stuffed friend.

In constructing the pens, it is advisable to staple the wire onto the inside of the 2 × 3 in. framework so as to allow no rim on which feces can collect. Then the heavy 1 in. mesh wire on the bottom can be stapled on last. This wire must be strong, and the staples should be longer than ordinary poultry wire staples.

Wire for the top and sides is 1 × 2 in. turkey, heavy gauge, such as is sold for fox ranches, and should be tightly stretched. It is almost essential to run a brace across the middle of the bottom stringers to which the square mesh wire can be stapled. You can have a blacksmith bend a light piece of angle iron the ends at right angles and bore holes through the ends so that the brace may be attached to the inside of the stringers, thus preventing the wire from sagging. If this brace is not used, sags develop that in time lead to breaks, which necessitate attaching new wire.

Remember, it does not pay to skimp by buying lightweight wire. The heavier grades have proven themselves to be much more economical over a period of time.

The suggestions above are given as a starting basis. They have been found to be practical and economical, but you may have ideas of your own that will work out much better in your particular circumstances. You can exercise your ingenuity in developing variations which answer your individual requirements.

XIII
Exercising and Grooming

The plain truth is that no puppy needs more exercise than he gets in a pen six by ten feet in dimension. It is nice to give him more—his leg muscles will be better developed—but it is not essential to exercise him. The best part of it is that taking him for a walk exercises you.

Many people when they say "exercise a dog" mean taking him for a walk where he can evacuate and urinate. If you had seen as many thousands of happy puppies of all sizes—even Saint Bernards—grow to full size in runs eight by twenty feet, you would realize how little exercise puppies need. Hundreds of beagles and cocker spaniels have been raised in wire-bottom

Ch. Charlesbank Kim, owned by Mrs. Fred De Senso. Sire: Ch. Caversham Lin Yuan of Hayreed. Dam: Charlesbank's Chloe.

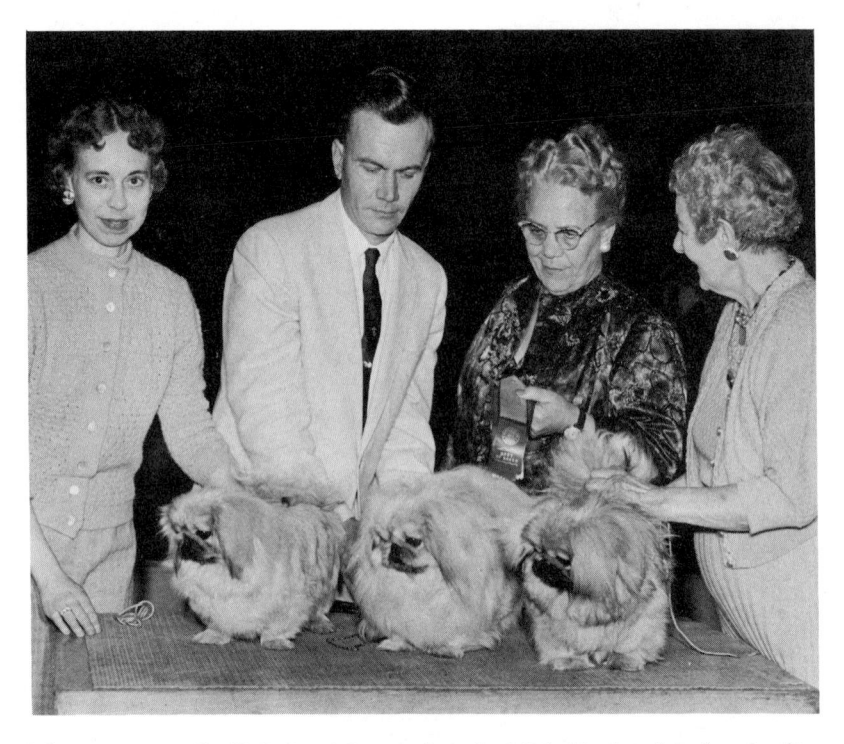

Peke at center is Ch. Hi-Oasis of Brown's Den. At left is his first champion daughter, Champion Lindys Desert Sand of Loring. At right is his first champion son, Ch. Lindys Mr. Frosty of Loring.

runs three by six feet, and because they never know anything else, they have been supremely happy.

But we said *need*, not *how much puppies can stand*. Five-month old puppies, which were raised in eight-by-twenty foot pens have been taken for six-mile walks the first time they ever left their pens and one is amazed at their endurance. But then, few persons realize how much a mature dog can stand. Sled dogs, six to a team pull sleds with ton loads miles and miles a day. Foxhounds have been known to run forty-eight hours pursuing foxes, and during that time may run well over three hundred miles.

So exercise, while not necessary, is most pleasant. And there are simple, useful ways to exercise your puppy. If he is a hunter, get him into the woods and fields to accustom him to the environment he will come to love. If he is a retriever, teach him to fetch. Go to an open place and throw a ball. Fifty yards is a short retrieve. While you stand in one place, the pup runs one hundred yards for each throw. Seventeen retrieves and he has run a mile.

Here Ch. Roh Kai Tor Chi is awarded Best of Breed and group 3rd. This Peke is owned by Mrs. Florence Gwynne and was bred by Rose Marie Katz.

If you live near a golf links, teach your pup to retrieve a golf ball.

Puppies of larger breeds can be taught to pull wagons or sleds by the time they are six months old. Some puppies love to swim and will bring out sticks the owner throws into the water. If you have no natural way to exercise your pup, don't worry; he'll probably be just about as healthy with none.

Probably rough playing gives puppies all the exercise they need. Some puppies will play with you, some with toys which they will toss into the air, wrestle with, then chew on. Give your pup plenty of playtime and encourage playing up to the point where he bites too sharply. Old rag dolls make excellent playthings. Even a well-knotted towel amuses some pups for hours. If you give him a rubber toy, be sure he doesn't chew it apart and swallow the pieces. During teething, pups love to chew, and chewing becomes almost play with them. Encourage it throughout teething—from three and half to six months of age—but stop it if the puppy uses his second teeth where he shouldn't.

217

Ch. Fei-Lee of El-Acre, bred and owned by Vivian H. Longacre. Sire: Ch. Jalna's Ching-Lee. Dam: Ch. Fei-Ying of El-Acre.

XIV
Grooming the Pekingese Coat

For the pet Pekingese, grooming is important to his comfort and good health, to help avoid scratching and skin conditions, to minimize hair in the house. It is the equivalent of cleanliness to a human being.

To the show Pekingese, grooming is the equivalent of make-up to the movie star. It adds to his glamour and attraction. He should never be seen or photographed without it.

COAT CARE OF THE AVERAGE PEKINGESE

Every Pekingese should be brushed vigorously at least twice weekly (more often if possible) with a natural bristle ladies' type hairbrush; nylon brushes tend to tear out the coat. The coat should be aired and brushed against the grain to make the hairs stand on end. Any tangles or snarls behind the ears or under the legs should be separated first with the fingers from the skin outward, brushed, then combed through with a wide-toothed metal comb

Brushing the coat of a young Pekingese. Photo by Louise Van der Meid.

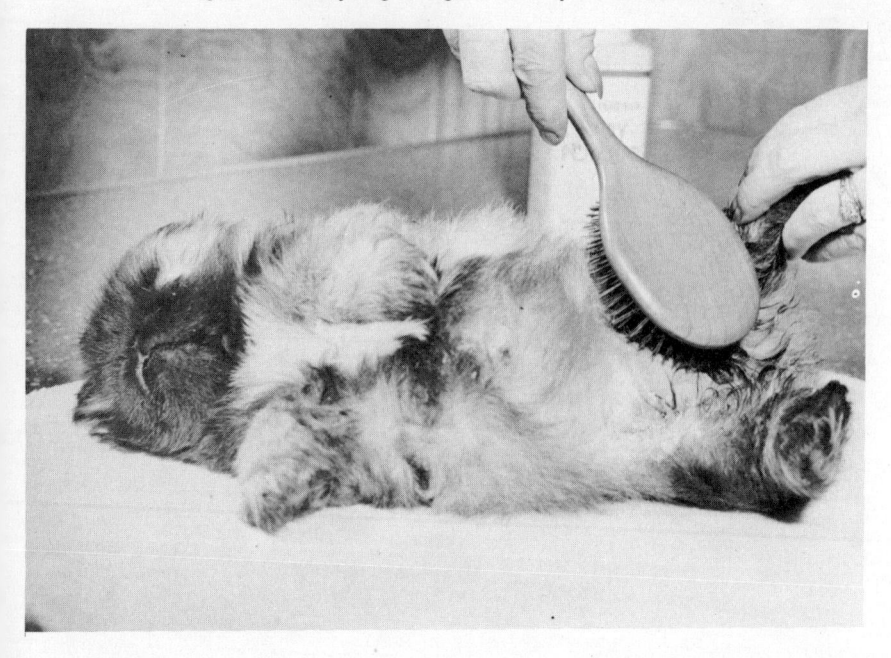

and brushed again. A bit of baby oil or talcum massaged into a stubborn mat may avoid some loss of coat. Talcum sprinkled behind ears and in skirts close to the skin will discourage such snarls in the coat as well as keep your Peke smelling sweet. If mats are so bad that they need cutting, use blunt tipped scissors and make only a few slanting slashes in order to keep the loss of the coat to a minimum. Then separate the mats with your fingers before combing.

No baths. Pekes should never receive a bath unless they are very, very soiled. In the Roh Kai kennel of fifty show dogs, an average of not more than six baths a year is given.

If the skin is dry, it is sometimes desirable to massage baby oil into the skin several hours before a needed bath. Before bathing, give your dog a *careful thorough brushing* to remove any tangles or loose hair. Select a good shampoo suitable for human hair. Stuff cotton into your Peke's ears to keep out the water. First wet your dog thoroughly and then make a ring around his neck with the shampoo and work downward on his back to the tail, then wash his tail and underneath him, and finish with his paws. A damp washcloth is next used on the face with great care being exercised to avoid water getting in the ears. After the main soil is washed away by a rinse, a second soaping,

Giving the Peke a bath; don't let water get into his ears. Photo by Louise Van der Meid.

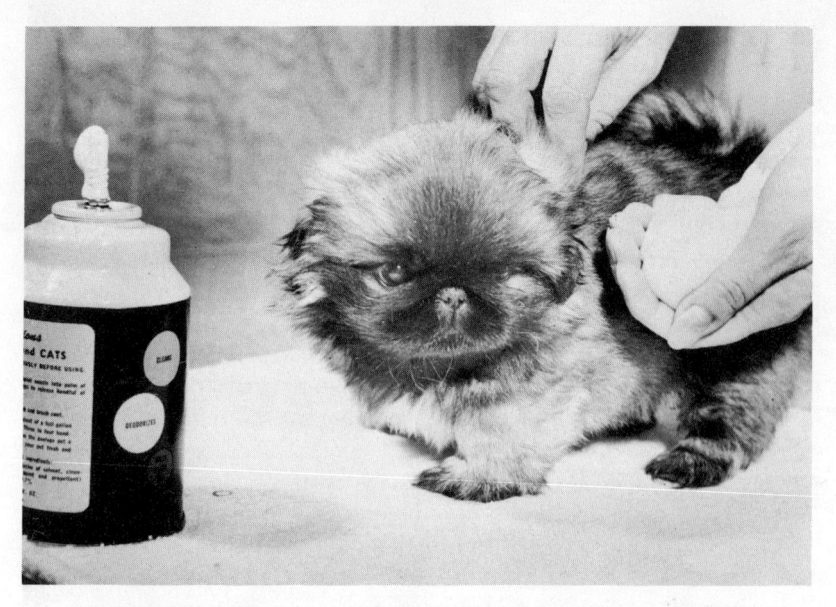

A dry bath for a Peke who has soiled himself. Photo by Louise Van der Meid.

followed by a *thorough* rinsing, is given. Soap left in will cause snarls in the coat later. Care must be taken to *dry* the dog down *completely* to his skin before exposure to the outdoors. Such drying takes a good deal of time with a heavily coated Peke. When nearly dry, a little talcum sprinkled into the coat and then brushed out will hasten the final process.

Never use a comb on your Peke when he is wet; it breaks off the hairs. Combing should always be done gently, with more of a teasing through the coat than a combing straight through the fur.

Under no circumstances give a bath less than one week before a show; the washing out of the natural oils seems to flatten the coat for several days.

Instead of a bath. If a Peke is soiled, first remove surface dirt with a vigorous brushing. Next wipe over the coat with a washcloth wrung out of hot water and follow with brisk toweling. When nearly dry, sprinkle talcum close to the skin and massage well into the coat. Then brush thoroughly again to leave the Peke clean and sweet smelling. This procedure can be followed at any time, even the morning of a show, and as often as required, without loss of natural oils in the coat.

Care should be used in handling ear fringes and tail. A softer brush is recommended for use on them than for body coat. Such softening can be accomplished by boiling the *bristles only* of the brush. This can be done in a shallow pan with water covering the bristles only. When ear fringes are

Ch. Sorena of Mathena. Photo by C. M. Cooke.

Ch. St. Aubrey Kimono of Tzumiao and Roh Kai.

Ch. Jalna's Me Go Tu, owned by Vivian H. Longacre.

broken or torn off, they seem to take an interminable period to grow back, if they ever do so. If any food particles should happen to coat these hairs, gently separate them with the fingers before brushing. Under no circumstances use a comb on them when they are wet.

Such brushing care for the pet Pekingese is necessary to maintain cleanliness, comfort, and good health. It will also reduce the quantity of hair on furniture and rugs.

GROOMING FOR THE SHOW

Grooming a show Peke is perhaps the most intricate and important single item advantageous to winning that is controllable by you or your handler. Sometimes grooming and handling alone spell the difference between failure and success at dog shows. For this reason, constant and continuous practice is necessary to *experiment in advance* on your individual dog. Each dog requires a little different care and treatment, because coat textures differ and respond differently to different coat dressings and the handling of them.

There are a number of good coat dressings on the market, and each one may be superb for occasional use on some types of coats. Some coat dressings may have a drying or other unfavorable effect on some coats if used often over a period of time. However, for *constant* and *frequent* use on practically every type of coat, rain water does a very adequate job at a greatly reduced cost. Observe for yourself, that your Peke will never look better than when he

Closeup of a show Peke with good head and ears. Photo by Van der Meid.

Am. Ch. Livingston's Kai-Lung Do-Ton's C.D.X.

Ch. Pedmore Cream Puff, imported from England, owned by Mrs. L. Shallenberger.

is drying out after a soaking in the rain—nature's own coat dressing. Such rain water is best collected in glass, plastic, or crockery containers (not metal), and should not be allowed to drip off roofs or gutters. Lacking rain water, a softened water or distilled water is a satisfactory substitute. It is best sprayed on with an atomizer.

First turn the dog on his back. Then starting underneath at the neck, brush to separate the hairs, clean and eliminate tangles, and then spray with rain water or coat dressing to dampen. Then brush again. When brushing, all strokes should be aimed *toward the nose*, brushing the fur upward, outward, and forward. Make each hair stand on end by brushing just a little hair at a time. Strokes should be short, made by a flick of the wrist, and should cover a small area at a time. Next brush the cuffs on the front legs and take the wide-toothed metal comb to separate the hairs so that they stand out. Be very careful not to pull or break off the feathering underneath. Work down underneath toward the rear legs and, here again, brush, spray, then brush again the skirt.

Ch Lin Yutang of Fourwinds, owned by Mrs. Robert M. Jackson.

Turn the dog on its legs and start the same procedure at the head. Always remember the head of the Peke should be flat, so brush the hairs flat on top of the head away from the nose for the first time. Brush, spray, and dampen to the skin behind the ears and leave to dry to a dampness before sifting in just a bit of talcum. Never use talcum on wet fur—it cakes, but if used when hair is just slightly damp, it cleans and adds a bit of body to the coat as well as imparts a pleasant fragrance. Brush, spray, and brush again the hairs along the body on the back trying to lift each hair and make it stand on end. Brush, spray, and brush again the tail. By this time your dog will have dried underneath to a proper dampness. Now you can turn him on his back again and sift a bit of talcum powder close to the skin under neck, around the cuffs, skirts, and feathering. Massage with the fingers, then brush vigorously to get every bit out. When ears and tail have dried to a proper dampness, sift a little talcum close to the skin behind the ears, massage well into the fur of the ears with your fingers, and *brush out completely*. There must be no powder evident on the dog when he enters the show ring. It must not fly; there must not be any white specks; and it must not be used to change the natural color of the dog. Keeping in mind that the Peke should have a tapered body, start at the waist (particularly if coat parts as it sometimes does in a very long haired Peke) and give one brush stroke toward the tail to cover the part and to flatten the fur near the tail. Treat the tail much the same as you did the ear fringes; use just a bit of talcum and again be sure to brush it all out. Part the tail down the center especially on young dogs. Do not powder the body coat on the back the day of the show, for it dulls the lovely gloss and sheen of a healthy coat.

Japanese Champion Chun-Chu-Fu's Chuck-A-Luck, bred by Shirley Stone. Sire: Langridge Sno Tong. Dam: Tsoo II.

Ch. Rosy Ridge Mr. Digby, owned by Merritt Olds. Sire: DeRoy of the Dell. Dam: Ch. Rosy Ridge Ah Chu.

As a last minute touch-up, comb the ear fringes forward and upward, gently separating each hair; use the comb gently to separate all the tail hairs; brush the back of the skirts down and forward to shorten the appearance of the dog; brush the cuffs of the front legs close to the body so the dog won't look out at the shoulders. As the dog is standing, use a brush just under the rear legs at the sides to pull featherings down and forward. Keep the Standard in mind. Make your Peke look as much like the dream dog as possible with flat topskull, wide front, short back, etc. Brush skirts down and forward to give the appearance of a short back.

Wash the face and eyes and wrinkle. *Dry the wrinkle very carefully.* If your dog has a light face and his eyes have teared, a little boric acid powder worked underneath the eyes will dry these unattractive moist spots. Be careful not to get it into the eyes—any powder can be very irritating. If the hairs under the eyes are darkened by constant tearing, bleach them with a mild hydrogen peroxide solution used daily, starting a few weeks before exhibition.

Ch. Ku-Ting of Loofoo, owned by Mrs. R. Jones. Cooke photo.

Ch. Sing Hi's Sun Tu of Dah-Lyn.

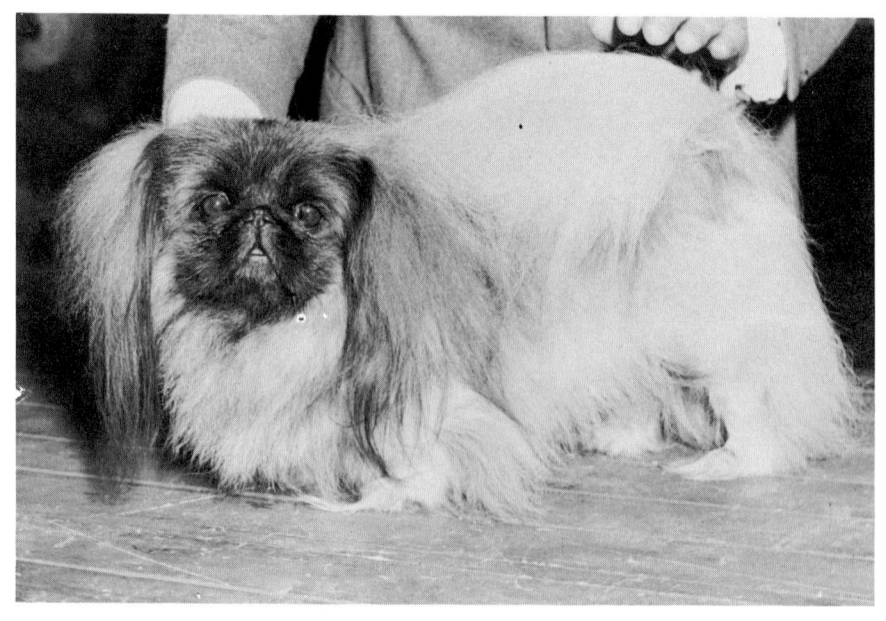

Ch. Kyratown Yung Mr. Twee of Kanghe, owned by Mr. W. Hindley Taylor. Cooke photo.

Ch. Ku Jin of Caversham, owned by Miss I. de Pledge. Cooke photo.

Ch. Roh Kai Tom-Mi, owned by Rose Marie Katz. No American-bred Peke has ever approached his show record.

Comb the hairs of the face forward with a small pocket comb. Use this same comb to comb the wrinkle to make it look neat. Some owners trim whiskers well in advance of the show, but experience has proved that such trimming makes some dogs very nervous. Furthermore, it isn't really necessary to trim the whiskers on a Pekingese, especially if he has a black mask or muzzle. In addition, some persons contend that the whiskers add to the desired grotesque appearance of a Pekingese, therefore, the best advice is not to trim them. Nails or fur in the footpads should never be trimmed less than a week before the show. Then if they are accidentally cut too short, they will have time to grow out and become comfortable to walk on by show time.

Grooming for the show means making your dog's coat appear immaculate and as beautiful, glamorous, and luxuriant as possible and doing everything you can to enhance him so that he appears as near the Standard, or dream dog as is possible.

Ch. Wei Tiko of Pekeboro and Roh Kai, owned by Rose Marie Katz.

Canadian Ch. Sanell Hai Puff of Acol, owned by Mrs. C. de P. Doniphan.

Ch. Caversham Ki Ku of Pendarris, owned by Mrs. M. Brooks.

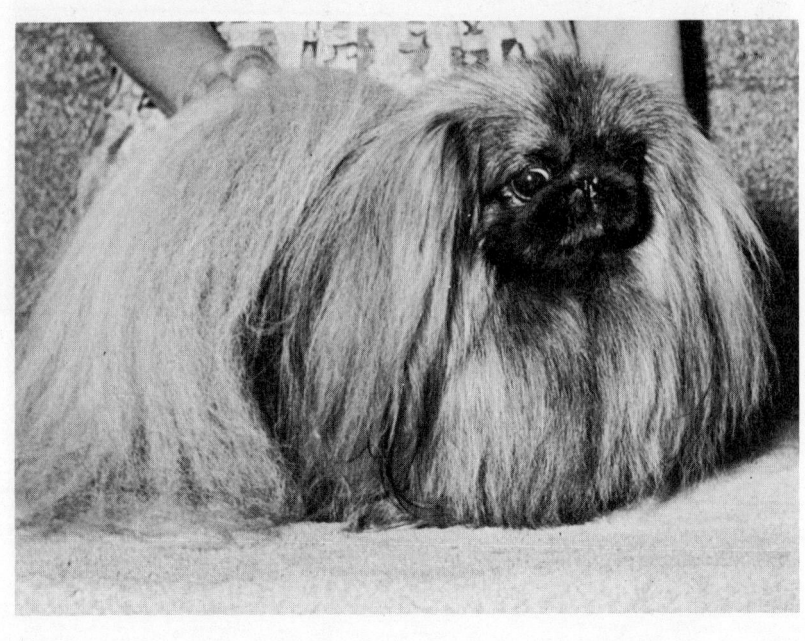

Ch. Muh Yin's Boi of Po Yen, bred and owned by Wanda M. Brown.

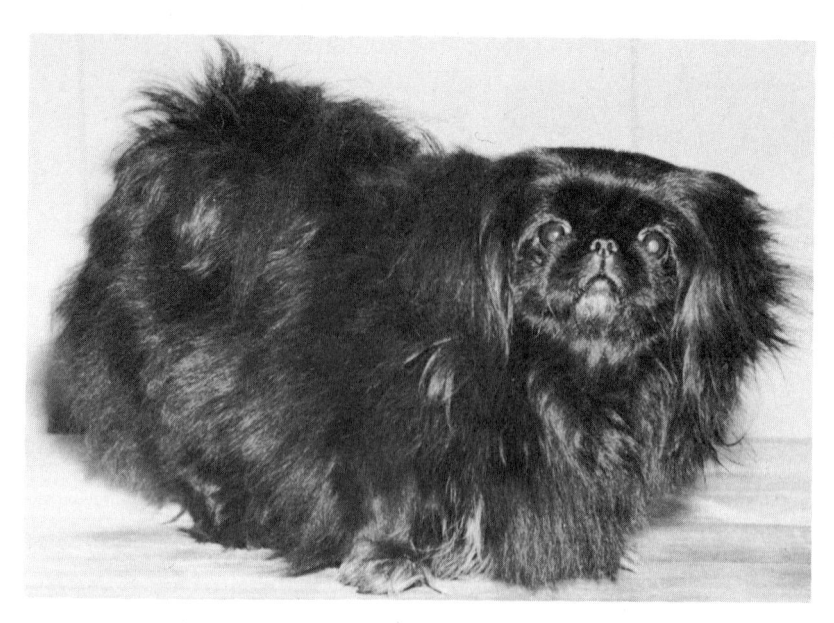

Ch. Ku-Coon of Caversham, owned by Mrs. I. de Pledge. Cooke photo.

Ch. Ku Chik-Ku of Loofoo, owned by Mrs. Richard Jones.

Ch. Sheena of Norimor, owned by Mrs. E. Stewart. Cooke photo.

Ch. Calartha Yen-Lo of Sualane, owned by Mrs. S. North. Cooke photo.

Jean Waring's tiny pup is able to fit comfortably into a teacup.

Ch. Tim-Tam of Wi-Ja, bred and owned by Mrs. Al James.

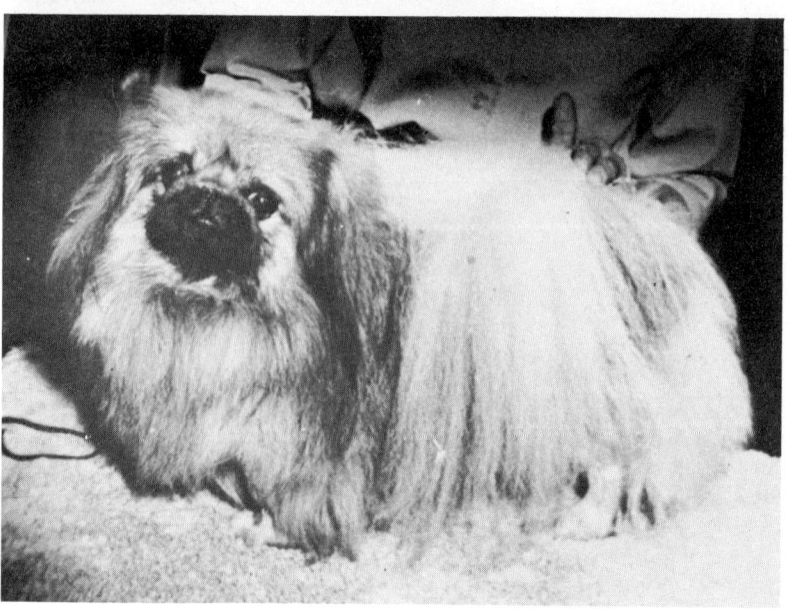

236

Jean Waring's Pom Pom of Roke with Folly the Great Dane.

Mirabile Vivu, owned by Mrs. W. A. Bailey.

Ch. Don Wong-Ti of the Dell, owned by Mr. S. Lowe. Photo by C. M. Cooke.

Ch. Charterway Yung T'Sun, owned by Mrs. E. B. Partridge. Cooke photo.

Ch. Antoinette of Loofoo, owned by Mrs. R. Jones. Photo by C. M. Cooke.

Bey Li Fu Chik, at age of five months, owned by Mrs. W. A. Bailey.

Ch. Caversham Ku-Ku of Yam, owned by Mrs. I. de Pledge and Mrs. H. Lunham.
Photo by C. M. Cooke.

XV
Eye Diseases of Pekingese
BY I. HERBERT KATZ, M.D.

In keeping with the practical aspects of this book, this chapter will be devoted mainly to considerations of the common eye diseases.

MEDICATIONS

Medications used are called *ophthalmic;* they must be labeled as such and must be sterile. Some of these medications will be sold at your drug store without prescription; others require prescription from either a veterinarian or physician. The principal drugs are as follows:

For dilating the pupil (as in ulcers and inflammation of the cornea):
1. Atropine Sulphate 1% (lasts 7 to 10 days)
2. Hyoscine Ophthalmic Solution $\frac{1}{4}$ of 1% (for milder cases) (lasts 3 to 5 days)

The above two drugs are most easily available in the brands made by Alcon, Ophthalmos or Iso-Sol.

This Peke is suffering from pigmentary degeneration of the cornea. There is no known successful treatment.

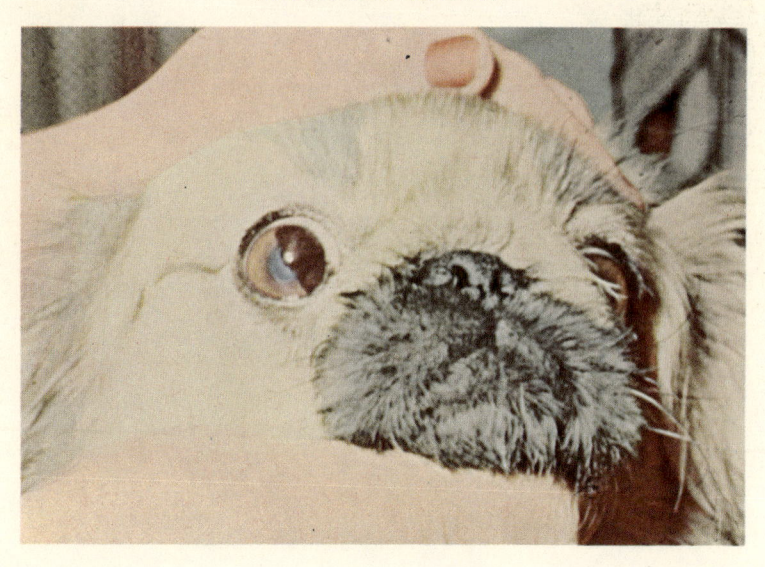

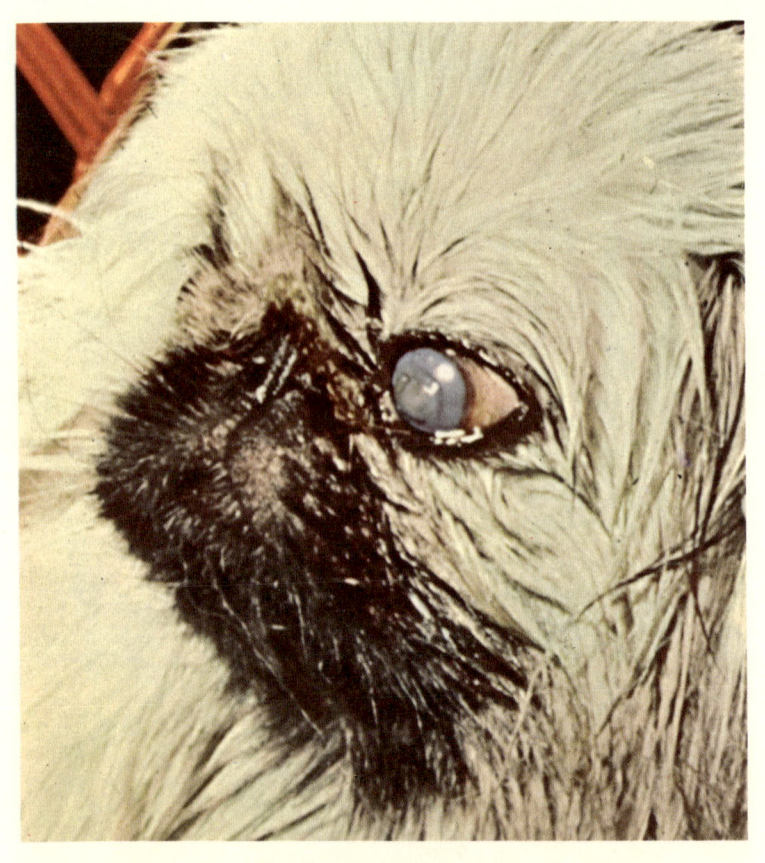

Severe corneal ulcer in the central location. Note the clouding of the entire cornea. This eye is in danger of perforation and needs active, vigorous treatment immediately.

For constricting the pupil, Pilocarpine 1%, or 2% by any manufacturer. Antibiotic drops are the following:
1. Gantrisin
2. Thio-sulfil
3. Cetamide
4. Neosporin
5. Chloromycetin diluted to 10 cc.
6. Biomydrin

The preferred drops are Neosporin and Chloromycetin.

Antibiotic Ointments are:
1. Myciguent
2. Mycitracin
3. Bacitracin
4. Sulamyd
5. Gantrisin
6. Terramycin
7. Achromycin
8. Neosporin
9. Polysporin

The preferred ointments are myciguent, mycitracin and neosporin. Steroid antibiotic mixtures, drops and ointments are:
1. Neo-Decadron
2. Neo Delta Cortef
3. Metimyd

This is a small corneal ulcer. It also shows pigmentary degeneration of the cornea.

ESSENTIAL ANATOMY
1. Cornea—Clear Transparent portion of eye behind which is iris and pupil.
2. Sclera—White of eyeball.
3. Conjunctiva—Transparent membrane covering the sclera and lining the lids.

EYE DISEASES
1. **Conjunctivitis**—Conjunctiva is red and may be swollen: tearing and watering; purulent (pus) discharge especially on awakening.

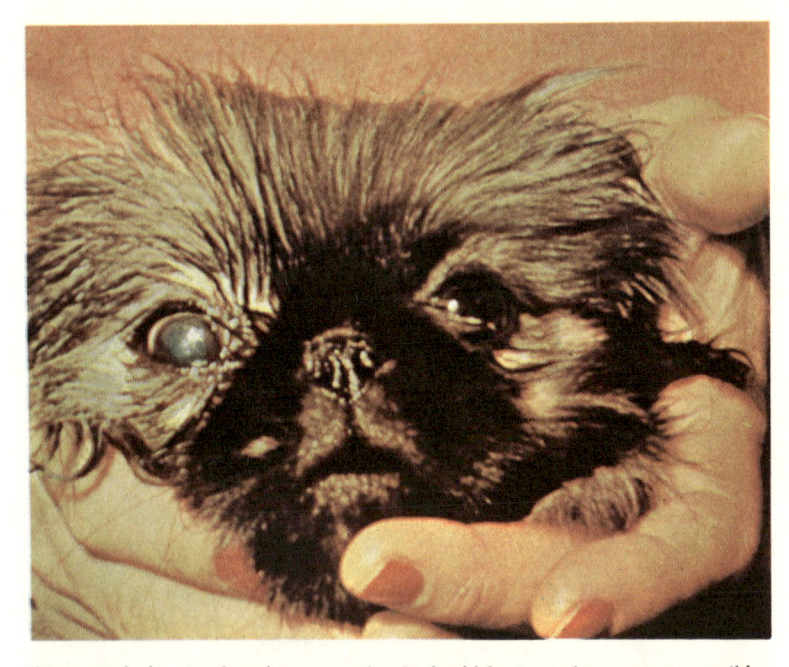

This corneal ulcer is of moderate severity. It should be treated as soon as possible.

Treatment: (*a*) Cleanliness by wiping away matter and mucus. (*b*) Remove any eyelashes or hairs rubbing on eyeball with fine tweezers, or cut with scissors dipped in vaseline to catch loose hairs. (*c*) Antibiotic drops in the eyes every two or three hours. (*d*) Antibiotic ointment at bedtime for two or three nights.

Treatment is gradually reduced.

2. **Diseases of Lids.** (*A*) STYES, like small boils. *Treatment:* Best treated by hot compresses of plain water for ten minutes or longer followed by application of an antibiotic ointment, 2 to 3 times per day.

(*B*) INFECTIONS OF LIDS AND EYELASHES. *Treatment:* Antibiotic ointments two or three times daily gently rubbed into affected areas.

3. **Diseases of Cornea.** CORNEAL ULCERS. The most important and the most common eye disease of Pekes. This is due to their large bulging, prominent eyeballs, and with the Peke's head being so low to the ground, they are prone to abrasions and subsequent infection. Because of the lessened sen-

This is a severe corneal ulcer in the central location. There is imminent danger of perforation and sloughing off of the outer corneal layers.

sitivity of the cornea in this breed it is possible for a dog to have a severe ulcer and still keep his eye wide open. Ulcer is characterized by roughened surface that loses its lustre, sometimes best seen by viewing obliquely in a good bright light; gray discoloration of the cornea under the ulcer area extending sometimes over the entire cornea; and sometimes white pus in the anterior chamber (space behind cornea and in front of iris).

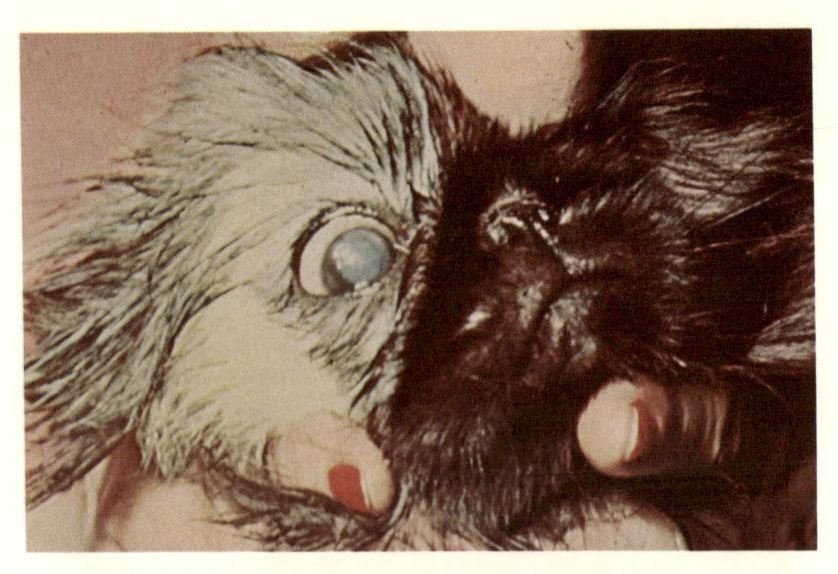

This is a small corneal ulcer, but most of the cornea is cloudy. This type of ulcer requires an active, but not vigorous, treatment.

Treatment: (*a*) Small ulcer, one to two mm. in size. Use antibiotic drops every three hours or antibiotic ointment three times per day.

(*b*) Larger ulcer, more than 2 mm., accompanied by small pupil. Use Hyoscine or Atropine drops once daily. *Guard against medicine running into the mouth as it is toxic.* In addition, antibiotic drops every two hours and salve at bedtime.

(*c*) Severe ulcer, covering one-third or more of cornea; with small pupil, pus in anterior chamber and possible bulging of ulcer. Use Atropine drops three times a day; hot compresses applied with towels to closed lids for 15 minutes every two to three hours followed by antibiotic drops which in turn are followed in five minutes by antibiotic ointment. In addition, antibiotic eye drops should be instilled in the eye every one to two hours. At this stage, if improvement does not occur, professional help is necessary as this treatment should be supplemented by Chloromycetin by mouth or injection. Also, if ulcer appears to be in danger of rupturing the lids should be partially sutured over it allowing room for instillation of eye medication. Treatment is gradually reduced as improvement occurs. Older treatment of cauterization of ulcer is not advised.

(*d*) Chronic ulcer, the type that drags on and on without evident infection and without pus in the anterior chamber. This is best treated with drops or ointment of steroid-antibiotic mixtures. Drops in the daytime and salve at bedtime.

Caution: It is very important that steroid and steroid eye drops and ointments with or without antibiotics should *not* be used in corneal ulcers that are definitely or presumably infected. This medication encourages growth of bacteria by hampering the body defenses against them and will permit dangerous progression of an ulcer.

By following the above rules the vision of an eye should be saved in the vast majority of instances. It should seldom, indeed, be necessary to remove an eye following corneal ulceration. The type due to distemper from neglect of vaccination can be the severest of all. Frequently, these dogs do not survive.

4. **Pigmentary Degeneration of the Cornea.** This consists of infiltration of all the layers of the cornea with brown or black pigment which may cover part or all of the cornea. It appears to come from the deeper tissues within the eyeball. There is no known successful treatment to date.

This is the most severe type of corneal ulcer and there is danger of perforation and sloughing off of the outer corneal layers.

This is a cloudy cornea in a Peke pup only four weeks old. Since there is no ulceration and the hazy areas are irregular there is every chance that the situation will clear itself up in a few weeks.

5. **Glaucoma.** Characterized by large pupil, hazy cornea and hard eyeballs. This disease responds poorly to treatment. Pupil constricter drugs and special mouth medication can be tried. Surgery gives only temporary relief in most instances.

6. **Cataract.** The pupil, instead of being black, becomes white or gray. Fortunately uncommon in Pekes. When vision gets down to only light perception surgery can be considered. It consists of removing the opaque lens of the eye and is successful in many instances.

7. **Proptosis of the eyeball.** This is an emergency! The eyeball is bulged forward with the lids in back of it. The dog is in pain. This is caused by violent shaking of the dog; holding it too tightly by the neck and head as in giving medication; excitement; or fighting with another dog. *Treatment:* should be very quick. If more than a few minutes goes by this eye can be lost. Apply any ointment or vaseline to cornea and gently but forcibly push the eye back into the socket at the same time pulling the lids over it. Hold the lids firmly for a few minutes, then let go. If the eye stays in position well and good.

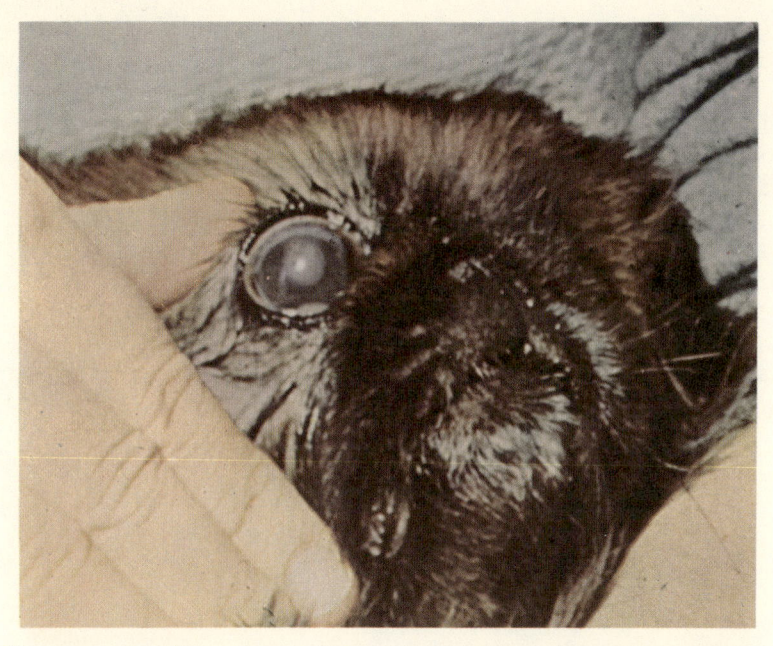

This is a moderately severe corneal ulcer. Note the layer of pus at the bottom of the anterior chamber. This type of ulcer can be healed in a very short time with proper treatment.

The eyelids have been sutured over the cornea to prevent perforation. Sutures are silk tied over pieces of rubber tubing. This treatment is used for treating prolapse of the eyeball also. Note the scarring of the other cornea from an ulcer.

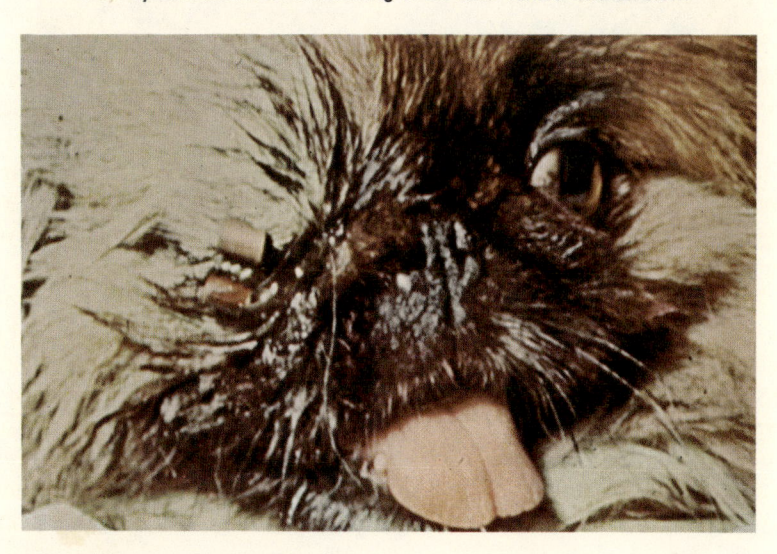

If it pops out again, pull the lids over it and rush the dog to a veterinarian for suturing the lids over this eyeball, allowing a little room for instillation of medication.

In treating eye diseases of dogs the veterinarian may call in an Ophthalmologist (Eye Specialist) for assistance. The important differences from conditions found in humans are:

1. Pneumococcus infections in dogs are uncommon.
2. Bowman's Membrane is so thin in dogs that it is almost non-existent and offers no barrier to organisms.
3. Herpes of the cornea does not occur in dogs.
4. Corneal perforation in dogs is quicker than in humans.
5. The Lens Zonule is very resistant to rupture in extracting a cataract.
6. The tarsal plate is very thin.

The end result following prolapse of the eyeball. The eye is in a good position but the dog has lost his sight because of a complete clouding of the cornea. This is a permanent blindness.

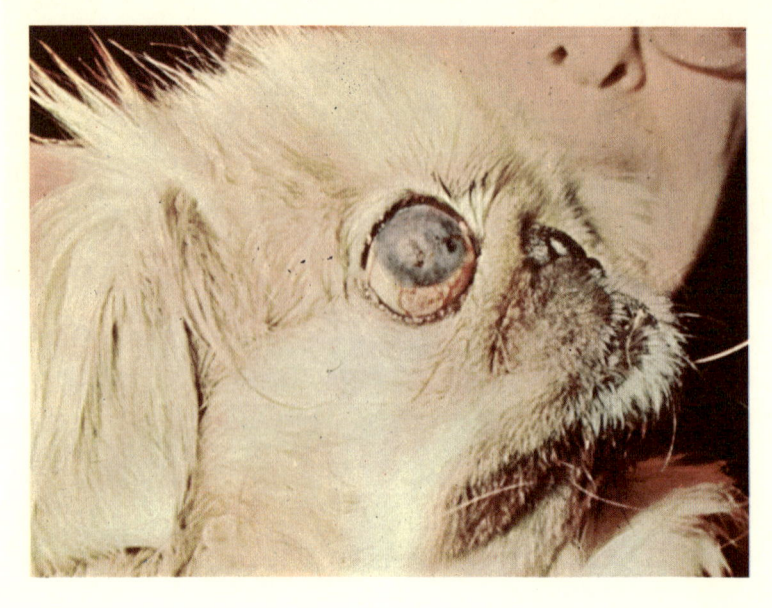

A puppy sired by Wei Tiko and bred by the author.

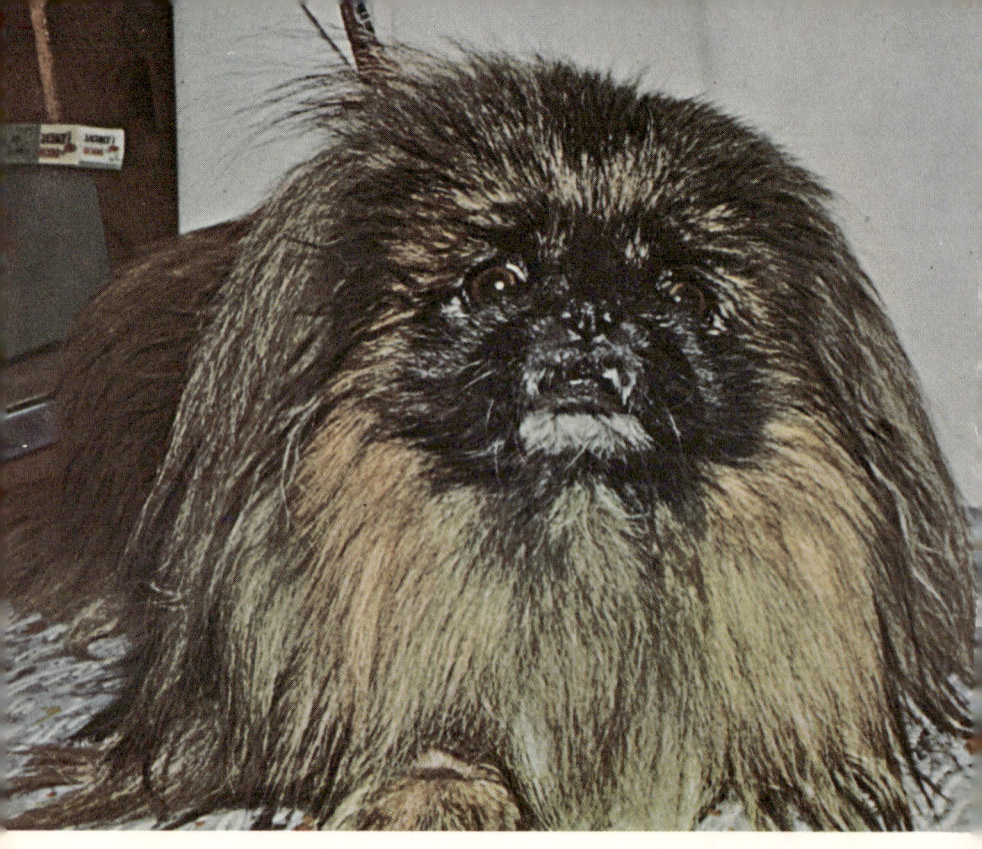

Champion Wei Tiko of Pekeboro and Roh Kai. The most famous Pekingese sire in America. He sired 23 champions and won, himself, 11 best-in-shows.

Roh Kai Tarka at 10 months of age. This puppy, bred by the author, is of the highest calibre. It has a classic face, black mask, small flat nose, dark lustrous eyes, complete overnose wrinkle, flat head, short legs, perfect spring of rib and an enormous coat with a large tail and long ear fringes.

Various Pekingese kennels have adopted Oriental names . . . it doesn't mean that their dogs were bred in China.

This young lady is carrying the Oriental motif through from dogs to garb. It sure helps selling puppies!!!

Your Peke's coat requires daily brushing if you want him in the peak of Peke perfection.

A Pekingese is small enough to be bathed in your kitchen sink! The new tear-less dog shampoo is a boon since soap is so irritating to the delicate eyes of the Pekingese.

"Why did you wake me up so early?"

Just by looking at a Peke, it is fairly difficult to evaluate its potential worth as a show specimen. It takes the experience and ability of a top judge to be able to pick out the qualities and faults of a good dog. These specimens all have good and bad features, but they are still valuable specimens.